SELECTED
TAKES

SELECTED TAKES

Film Editors On Editing

VINCENT LoBRUTTO

Foreword by Robert Wise

PRAEGER

New York
Westport, Connecticut
London

Library of Congress Cataloging-in-Publication Data

LoBrutto, Vincent.
    Selected takes : film editors on editing / Vincent LoBrutto ;
foreword by Robert Wise.
        p.   cm.
    Includes bibliographical references (p.   ) and index.
    ISBN 0–275–93378–4 (alk. paper). — ISBN 0–275–93395–4 (pbk. :
alk. paper)
    1. Motion pictures—Editing.   I. Title.
TR899.L63   1991
778.5'35—dc20   90–24262

British Library Cataloguing in Publication Data is available.

Library of Congress Catalog Card Number: 90–24262
ISBN: 0–275–93378–4 (hb.)
        0–275–93395–4 (pb.)

First published in 1991

Praeger Publishers, One Madison Avenue, New York, NY 10010
An imprint of Greenwood Publishing Group, Inc.

Printed in the United States of America

∞™

The paper used in this book complies with the
Permanent Paper Standard issued by the National
Information Standards Organization (Z39.48–1984).

10 9 8 7 6 5 4 3 2 1

To

Arthur Ginsberg,

who taught me the true meaning of sync

Contents

Foreword

As a movie director for over 40 years and a film editor before that, I found *Selected Takes: Film Editors on Editing* most fascinating and, for me, nostalgic reading. Not only is it a revealing and comprehensive instruction manual on the art of film making, it is also fascinating in all that it covers about the whole process of making a film. It is a must read for all who want to find out about what goes on in the editing room and how and why some film is left on the cutting room floor.

Robert Wise

Acknowledgments

I want to thank my mother, Rose LoBrutto, for her constant encouragement and for reading to me long before I could actually read, and my father, Anthony LoBrutto, who helped me to see my talents in the arts. My son, Alex Morrison, has been an invaluable source of inspiration by sharing hours of conversation about movies and listening to many of the ideas that went into this book. My daughter, Rebecca Morrison, has given me unconditional support on this venture. The spirit and dedication with which she pursues her own passions have held me in good stead. To my wife, Harriet Morrison, mere thanks fall short of acknowledging her contributions to this book. Not only has she kept our lives in order, she has listened and counseled with neverending patience for the five years during which this project developed. Her input to the final result is invaluable and has made me love and respect her even more.

This project would never have gotten off the ground were it not for William Bender, former business agent for the Motion Picture and Video Tape Editors, Local 771. He immediately embraced the idea of this book and was instrumental in securing the first interviews I conducted. His constant support of me and the book is much appreciated.

My thanks to James Blakeley, former president of American Cinema Editors (ACE), who introduced me to many ACE members who appear in this book and made it possible for me to interview them. Harriet and I thank him for his hospitality and warm company on several of our sojourns to Los Angeles to conduct the West Coast interviews. Georgie Marcher, who ran the ACE office in the early days of this project, facilitated much of my paperwork. Former ACE President John Martinelli also was instrumental in securing several interviews and invited me to his home in Los Angeles for a warm and encouraging conversation. I want to thank the ACE board of directors for its support of this project.

My most sincere thanks to the 21 film editors in this book who took many hours and days out of their incredibly hectic work schedules to talk to me about their editing lives. They invited me into their homes and cutting rooms to share their knowledge and love of film editing. My respect and appreciation to all.

At Praeger I want to thank Alison Bricken for the enthusiasm she showed from the outset and for acknowledging the importance of giving film editors a forum. The manuscript was given expert care by my editor, Anne Davidson, production editor John Roberts, and copy editor Frances Rudner.

This book started out on a typewriter and very quickly made the transition to computer. My thanks to Saal Lesser for helping me get started by setting up my trusty Kaypro and allowing me use of his office facilities.

Thanks also to my wife's aunt, Martha Strongwater, for her hospitality during our stay in California. My gratitude goes to Theresa Bach, John Howard, and Joe Rosner; my appreciation to Lynzee Klingman, Robert K. Lambert, Thelma Schoonmaker, Fredric Steinkamp, and Neil Travis.

To the many friends and colleagues I have met along the way who helped me to see the significance of this book, I thank you for listening and for the encouraging words—they meant a lot.

As in making a film, this book has been a collaboration and would not be the same without those mentioned above. You have all made this dream come true for me.

Introduction

The purpose of this book is to let film editors speak in their own voices about the art and craft of feature film editing.

No one would dispute the importance of the film director in the movie-making process, but we have progressed from the auteur era to a recognition of the collaborative nature of filmmaking. The movie-going public can envision the writer, producer, director, production designer, cinematographer, and other members of the crew working together to create a film, but it still does not understand what happens in the editing room.

The role of the film editor in the making of a feature film has long been shrouded in mystery. If the nature of film editing is to be invisible, then its importance as a major part of the filmmaking process has been misunderstood because few realize when the editor is working. Generally, it is believed that editors only cut things out and take their instruction exclusively from the script and the director. The viewer can easily attribute a contribution by the editor to the work of the writer, actor, director, or cinematographer. In reality, the editor interacts with the work of all these craftspeople. By structuring the myriad elements at their disposal, editors are an integral part of the making of a film.

The discussions in this book open the door to the cutting room. The editors talk about their relationships with directors, the technical procedures, and techniques they use, the structure and development of scenes, the organization of the cutting room, their interrelationships with the production staff and the postproduction team, the films they have worked on, and the far-reaching involvement of the editor.

The 21 interviews that follow are presented in an order that attempts

to give a historical scope and to help the reader to see the many con-
nections among these diverse individuals and their craft.

The filmographies that precede each interview list the subject's work
as an editor of feature films. Many of the editors interviewed here have
extensive credits in television, documentaries, and other media. They
have worked as producers, directors, and in other aspects of filmmaking.
The listings have been compiled from many sources and ultimately were
confirmed by each editor. No filmography can reflect fully all editorial
contributions to a film. Editors have worked uncredited and films may
have additional editing after the credited editor has completed work. In
situations in which more than one editor has worked on a film, one
cannot be sure if two editors worked in concert or even met. Consequently, the word "with" in the filmography is used to help present
information but should not be taken as proof that a direct collaboration
took place.

Film editors speak eloquently using their splicers. They make order
out of chaos and help make the contributions of all who toil in the film
business the best they can be. Here their words speak eloquently about
their work and passion for the art and craft of film editing.

Harold Kress

The career of Harold Kress spans the golden age of Hollywood studio filmmaking. Raised in Hollywood and surrounded by stars and industry insiders who frequented his father's drugstore, Kress began his long career in the film business with the encouragement of the legendary Irving Thalberg.

Kress worked with many of the most important directors and producers of his time, including George Stevens, Louis B. Mayer, King Vidor, William Wyler, Vincente Minnelli, Mervyn LeRoy, and Rouben Mamoulian.

Harold Kress always believed that an editor's contribution to a film had no bounds. On his own he devised a solution to the complex problem of turning Spencer Tracy from Dr. Jekyll to Mr. Hyde and directed the transformation scenes himself.

Always willing to tackle a challenge, he undertook the tremendous responsibility of editing *How the West was Won* in the Cinerama format, solving aesthetic and technical problems that the Cinerama Company itself thought impossible.

Harold Kress garnered six Academy Award nominations for best achievement in film editing, and won his first Oscar for *How the West was Won*. He received his second Oscar along with his son Carl for *The Towering Inferno*. This was the first father and son team in the history of the Academy to share the Oscar for film editing.

1939	*Broadway Serenade*
	Remember?
	These Glamour Girls
	The Adventures of Huckleberry Finn (supervising editor)
1940	*Andy Hardy Meets Debutante*
	Bitter Sweet
	Comrade X
	New Moon
1941	*Dr. Jekyll and Mr. Hyde**
	H. M. Pulham, Esq.
	Rage in Heaven
	Unholy Partners
1942	*Mrs. Miniver**
	Random Harvest
1943	*Cabin in the Sky*
	Madame Curie
1944	*Dragon Seed*
1946	*The Yearling**
1948	*A Date with Judy*
1949	*Command Decision*
	East Side, West Side
	The Great Sinner
1950	*The Miniver Story*
1953	*Ride Vaquero*
1954	*Green Fire*
	Saadia
	Valley of the Kings
1955	*The Cobweb*
	I'll Cry Tomorrow
	The Prodigal
1956	*The Rack* (with Marshall Neilan, Jr.)
	The Teahouse of the August Moon (with Harry H. Komer)
1957	*Silk Stockings*
	Until They Sail
1958	*Imitation General*
	Merry Andrew

1959	*Count Your Blessings*
	The World, the Flesh, and the Devil
1960	*Home from the Hill*
1961	*King of Kings*
1963	*How the West was Won***
	It Happened at the World's Fair (supervising editor)
1965	*The Greatest Story Ever Told* (supervising editor)
1966	*Alvarez Kelly*
	Walk Don't Run (supervising editor)
1967	*The Ambushers*
	Luv
1970	*I Walk the Line* (supervising editor)
1971	*The Horsemen*
1972	*The Poseidon Adventure**
	Stand Up and Be Counted
1973	*The Iceman Cometh*
1974	*99 44/100% Dead*
	The Towering Inferno (with Carl Kress)**
1976	*Gator*
1977	*The Other Side of Midnight* (with Donn Cambern)
	Viva Knievel

*Academy Award nomination for best achievement in film editing.

**Academy Award for best achievement in film editing.

How did you land your first job in the movies?

I've been around Hollywood since I was a kid. My father bought the northeast corner of Hollywood and Vine. We ended up with seven drugstores on Hollywood Boulevard. Mervyn LeRoy discovered Lana Turner at the soda fountain at the Sunset store. Every Saturday we'd put a teller's cage in the middle of the store and people would come over from Universal City and the other studios to cash their checks. When I was eight years old, Wallace Reid used to pick me up every Saturday at our corner drugstore in his big Duesenberg and let me off at a movie theater. I never thought I would go into the motion picture business, because I definitely thought I was going to UCLA to be a lawyer. Then the Crash came, my father lost more than three million dollars overnight, and we all had to go to work. My father opened up a little restaurant on Hollywood Boulevard. I was a maitre d' at night and going to school during the day. One night, Bernie Hyman, Irving Thalberg's right-hand man at MGM, walked in. He was an old family friend. He asked, "How are you doing?" I said, "Working at night and going to school is a lot tougher than I thought." He said, "I'd like you to meet Irving Thalberg, come out to the studio tomorrow morning at 9:30." I went in and Irving Thalberg, the god of Hollywood, talked to me for an hour. I got a job in the test room.

What were the tests and did they involve editing?

When a producer or director was casting the second leads for a picture they would make tests. The test reels were in a little room with a rewind bench where you could run picture. The room got full of film. I said, "Why do they keep the film piled up like this when we could just have one can of film?" I asked the director, "If you're through looking at this, can I put it together?" Nobody had ever done that before; they just ran it in dailies form. There might have been six reels of dailies, but when it was boiled down, it was just a four- or five-minute scene from the script. If the director wanted to run it for the producer, it was cut together.

With no editing experience, how did you proceed to cut the tests?

I asked the director if I could run the dailies with him and he'd say, "I like this or that take better." We didn't have the tape recorder. I was one of the first editors to use tape recorders in the projection room when they did come out, but I'd make some scribbles on the pink lab report. He'd say, "Use your own judgment, I want to feature the person I'm testing, don't worry about the stock actors." I just had an intuitive feeling for it. They liked it and said, "We'll keep doing it."

How did you get on the editorial staff at MGM?

They were short an assistant for Huey, a cutter on *Ice Follies of 1939*. Joan Crawford sprained her ankle, and the picture was delayed so long that Huey had another picture coming up, *Broadway Serenade*, with Jeanette MacDonald—Robert Z. Leonard was directing. Pop Leonard was a sweetheart of a man, he always played Santa Claus at Christmas. I told Huey that the dailies were coming in on Pop Leonard's picture and he said, "Put them in the corner, I'm up to my neck with this picture." I said, "Do you want me to go in and run dailies with the director?" I started running the dailies every evening with Pop Leonard. Pop said, "Are you the editor, Harold?" I said, "No, I'm the assistant editor, the editor is still cutting the *Ice Follies* picture." By the end of the first week all these reels of dailies were ready to be broken down. I said to Huey, "Would you mind when I'm through with you if I stay here at night and start putting this together?" I started doing that.

I hardly had any home life. I'd come home for a bit of dinner, maybe a shower. I wanted to see my son. Sometimes I would go down to the projection room and use a seat cushion as a pillow to get some sleep. During the last few days of shooting Pop Leonard said, "Can I see it a week after I finish shooting?" I said, "Fine, we will be ready for you." I always said "we," I didn't say "I." I had knots in my stomach that Saturday morning, I was pacing and pacing. I had a yellow legal pad ready to take notes as fast as I could. We sat down and ran the picture; he didn't stop, he didn't say anything. I'm waiting to write. He kept saying, "That's good, I like that!" So the picture's over, the lights go up and he says, "Where's Huey?" I said, "He's still busy on the *Ice Follies* picture." Pop said, "Who put this together, this is the best first cut I've ever seen!" I just floated out on the air. I said, "Pop, I did this on my own time at night and on Saturdays, sometimes Sundays." He said, "Didn't you ever cut a picture before?" I said, "No." Pop said, "It is an excellent cut. You can make your dupes and we can get the musicians and the sound effects." I said, "You don't want to make any changes?" and he said, "No, I wouldn't know what to tell you to do."

Monday when I told Huey, he said, "That's great, but you better go tell the head of the department." I'm in the head of the department's office, he picks up the phone and calls Eddie Mannix. Boy, when they throw that name you know you're fired. Mannix said, "Pop told me you did a good job." Pop said, "I want Harold to get back salary from the day I started shooting, and I want him to have his name on the picture as film editor. Call Mr. Mayer, I want to take him up and introduce him." Mr. Mayer said, "I'm very proud, you've done it on your own, congratulations." So I got a check. I went back and told Irving Thalberg what had happened and he said, "I knew you'd do it."

The last word he had told me was tact, T-A-C-T. You have to have tact, because you are going to be stuck in the middle between the producer and the director. You can't come to the head of the studio and cry because nobody will listen. You're only a film editor, but if you're tactful you can become more, you can become an asset to the studio, you can go on to production and directing—which I did. I became talent test director besides film editor, then I went into second unit directing. MGM had 15 to 20 top editors, we made 52 features a year. After *Ice Follies* I went on to picture after picture, until I became one of the top three editors at MGM. It was the golden era, all the big stars were there. If you proved yourself it was like joining the club. It's not like that anymore. Now if you do a picture, bang, you have to start looking for another, but I worked year after year for 30 years.

What responsibilities did you have on the set in your early days as editor at MGM?

When they brought stage directors out from New York to become film directors, they had no knowledge of camera, of breaking down a script;

that was one of my jobs. *Pat and Mike* with Tracy and Hepburn had golf and tennis matches. The director, George Cukor, had never been to a golf match and never played tennis. So Hepburn said, "We're going to have to get a second director." George said, "Why don't you let Harold do it?" I directed the tennis matches with a double and the golf stuff with Hepburn's double, Babe Didrikson. Cukor was on the set and if he saw something he didn't like, he'd let me know.

What were the technical challenges in editing the 1941 version of Dr. Jekyll and Mr. Hyde?

The shooting hadn't started yet. I went to see Spencer Tracy and asked him if he knew how they were going to do the transitions from Jekyll to Hyde and Hyde to Jekyll. He said a still cameraman had taken several head shots of him. They hired 65 animators and were going to do it the way they did the old flip cards. They put this animation stuff on his face and told me to take it over to Walt Disney to see if they had any ideas. Disney said, "This is terrible, it's a bunch of crap, you've got to find a better way." I ran the two other Jekyll and Hyde pictures. Every time they showed Jekyll and Hyde, Fredric March dropped his hands down, they cut to the hand, hair started growing, cutaway, cutaway, all cutaways. I said to Spencer, "I've got an idea. The motion picture camera will be locked off, steel riveted to the stage floor so nobody can move it. Next to you we'll have one of those old-fashioned cameras with the big plate behind it and an artist who will sketch you. I'm only going to shoot your face, it will be so effective if we can see your face changing. There will be a long make-up table, all the pieces for your changes will be laid out and you'll be in a barber chair with wheels." Spencer was getting so excited. We went to see the director, Victor Fleming, and he said, "Harold, Spencer and I have faith in you, go ahead and do it. You have to go up and see Victor Saville, he's the producer." Saville said, "Young man, you're just the film editor on this picture, this is none of your goddamn business and I'm going to have you fired!" So I left the lot and went home. My wife Zelda said, "What are you doing home?" I said, "I've been fired." Now the phone rings and it's the assistant director and he says, "We hear you're not on the lot, stick by the phone." Fleming canceled the day's shooting, he had Ingrid Bergman, Lana Turner, and Spencer Tracy on the set—that's an expensive day. He and Spencer Tracy went up to see Louis B. Mayer and they said, "We want Harold to do it, it's the only way, or else we have to do it the old way with the cutaways." Louis B. Mayer picked up the phone, called Ben Goetz at the London Studio and said, "Call Victor Saville and tell him you have a picture that's in bad trouble over there and that he's got to go to London tomorrow morning."

Tracy was a dream to work with. There were over 40 make-up changes. To keep the registration perfect we had to put him back and realign him. An artist sketched him and we lined up his nostrils. You couldn't touch the camera, I was ten feet away with a remote control switch. The camera was never changed and overnight a guard was on the stage. I would say, "Okay Spence, get ready, we're rolling, now just a little grimace, a little more, you fight it, fight it, cut." That went on for 46 changes of make-up. There were just a few times when the eyes blurred, but I couldn't help it, I had to make a continuous series of dissolves. The result was that you would stay on his face. For the scene when he was dying, Spencer wanted to say something. I said, "We'll do it just like a music number with playback. We'll make the sound track first." I had a disk cut. When we shot it to playback he mouthed the words. I got a nomination just because of my work. The picture didn't get a nomination. The editors all knew that I had directed Tracy. If the movie is not good, it's not going to be good for the stars or for the studio. It's not going to be good for your reputation, so what the hell, you do the best you can to come up with ideas.

Throughout your career you have always seen the editor's job as more than just cutting film.

Yes. In *I Walk the Line* there's a scene with Gregory Peck and a girl that I felt needed a close-up of the girl's eyes beginning to well up with tears. In another scene there was a close-up where her eyes well up and the tears start to come down, but she had a different dress on. I took it to the optical department and asked them to enlarge it so the dress was not noticeable. I put it in the picture, it's only a short cut, nobody ever knew about it, but I personally think it made the scene better. Those are the little things you do on your own. The picture's been shot, you can't go back, but there are ways.

How did you cut the animal sequences in The Yearling?

I had all this film coming up from Florida of the boy running through the woods with the little fawn and the larger deer. I put it all together and it ran a bit over eight minutes. I never ran anything silent. I'm home having dinner, I put on seven records and along comes Mendelssohn's scherzo for "A Midsummer Night's Dream." I stopped eating my dinner. My wife said, "What's wrong?" I said, "That's it!" I took the record, cleaned it off and put in the sleeve. The next morning I took it to the studio and had them transfer it. It had a few scratches. I laid the track in. I tell you I didn't touch it. I put the 12-foot leader at the front and lined up the first note of music with the first frame of picture. I just let the whole music run. I went into the projection room and I've never heard or seen anything so beautiful in my life. The deer just jumped on every glissando, I didn't change it. I couldn't believe it. I called Margaret Booth and said, "I've got something here that you and Sidney Franklin should run." I asked Margaret if I could run the fader, because I had tested it and wanted to hit those glissandos each time they jumped over logs. I told the projectionist, "Don't run it like you do dailies. I want

you to dim the lights first, count to three, then turn on the machine."
So he dimmed the lights and Margaret said, "What's going on?" I faded
the music up. All of a sudden she leaned forward; when she ran dailies
she would lean back in the chair, but now she kept at the edge of her
seat. Sidney Franklin, the producer, who wasn't feeling too well, got a
second breath of life. I faded the music out at the end as the boy ran
over the hill and the sun was off in the distance. Well, he had tears in
his eyes, she had tears in her eyes. Sidney put his arms around me,
hugged me and said, "My God, Harold, I've never seen anything as
beautiful." Margaret was on the other side, she kissed me and said,
"Harold, that is a beautiful piece of work."

Now we come to score the picture. Herb Stothard, the head of the
music department at MGM, had written other music for the scene. The
studio orchestra had to play it because you couldn't use canned music
in those days. He had done a nice job but not like this. The studio
orchestra could never match the tempo, it just didn't have the spirit.
We had a new record sent out from San Francisco. A new transfer was
made and we left the record in the picture.

Was there a lot more of Gregory Peck's narration than was used?

Most of the narration was cut out. I don't like narration in pictures.
When I hear narration it makes me feel that it's a weak picture and they
had story problems.

Did you do any of the sound editing yourself?

No, we had a big sound effects department. I would go over there
and borrow things if I needed individual sounds like a good door slam
or gun shots. I would put them into the dialogue track. For a chase
scene I would do a rush temp dub job. I'd have my assistant put in a
few sound effects along with the music tracks. I had two racks of music
that I saved from all of the pictures I'd done; love themes, good music
for a chase, happy music, sad music. I would just stick them in. I would
take it over to the mixer and ask if he could put it together. If you give
a picture a little bit of extra life as you're showing it to the producer or
director, they won't be looking for mistakes.

Were the animal sequences storyboarded?

No.

What did it say in the script?

Bear chased by two dogs. Dogs fight bear.

Did you overarticulate the animal sequences in the first cut?

You have to use all the best film that you've got. I used to hang it up
in the film basket in cuts. I would put a piece of paper saying good dog,
good bear, fair bear, good leaps. You use everything that's good. You
want to try to assemble it that way right away.

How the West was Won *was the first film shot in Cinerama to tell a story.
What technical challenges did it present?*

How the West was Won was the toughest job I ever had. Sol Siegel, the head of the studio, wanted me to shoot some tests in Cinerama because the only thing they had done were travelogues; they had never done a dramatic story. He said, "I want you to meet the Cinerama people, learn as much as you can." I said to Cinerama's Tom Conroy and their editor, "If we're going to do a story and have James Stewart throw a knife at somebody, we want to see him throw the knife, and in the very next instance see that knife hit the guy—we're going to have short cuts." They said, "You can't make that kind of a motion picture in Cinerama." I go back and report to Sol Siegel that I think it can be done but we definitely have to prove it to them. So he said, "You've got the script, pick out a couple of scenes and do a western."

I took George Hamilton and other people from our stock company. I had a group of horsemen and did about five different sequences in the western motif. It took me ten days to shoot it because this Cinerama crew worked very slowly. There's one big camera with three magazines and a big plexiglass shield. If I wanted to shoot a close-up of a person their nose was practically touching the front of the camera, because it shoots like our peripheral vision. The sets had to be 16 stories high, you had to put a roof over a room. If you panned, you panned very slowly, or the camera would shake all over the place. On one run-through I tilted the camera up and then down. When we saw it at the dailies the guys were running uphill and downhill; so you could not tilt the camera. I didn't want to work over at Cinerama's studio, so I had one of their cutting benches sent over. I had one of the biggest rooms at MGM, it was Irving Thalberg's old projection room turned into a cutting room. I had them tear everything out and put in shelves because we were going to have so much film. The Cinerama bench was huge. I couldn't lift one of their reels up. The synchronizer was bigger because you had three reels plus the sound track, so you had all that running. We had to code number the picture A-B-C to correspond to the three separate reels. We had to wait a week while our engineers at MGM could make a coding machine that would number every foot and a half, because we were running 90 feet a minute. It was running 135 feet a minute because each frame was six sprockets instead of four. Finally the guys licked that. It was a month getting all the bugs ironed out. I had my assistants break down the reels and I started putting it together.

Did the Cinerama people give you a hard time while you were cutting the test?

Tom Conroy and his editor were in my cutting room. I came to a part in the fight where we had a short cut and they said, "Stop, Harold, you can't put that in." I said, "The screen is big, the human eye is going to see it." I excused myself saying I had to go to the bathroom. I went to another cutting room and called Sol Siegel. I said, "Call Tom Conroy in my cutting room and ask him to please come up to your office. Tell them to leave me alone and go back to their studio and we'll call them when necessary, but be polite about it." We did that, I was at peace with myself, and I put it together. I called Siegel and said, "We can't run this, I can't show it to you, and I don't want Cinerama to see it." He said, "Do you think it will work?" I said, "I'm damn sure it's going to work." He said, "Don't worry about it, just dress it up a little bit." With that, I had a main and end title made. I put it all together with music and effects and it ran about 20 minutes.

I ran it with Tom Conroy at 8:00 in the morning. I said to the projectionist, "I've got fanfare music at the head. I want this to play against the closed curtains and on cue I want the curtains to open." The music is still playing, you see a panorama, all of a sudden from way over on the right you hear the thunder of horses' hoofs and you see a lone rider coming through. Before he gets out of frame you see the posse chasing him. It was exciting! Even Tom Conroy said, "My God, these short cuts, you're going back and forth over-the-shoulder, but I don't mind it, I'm just sitting here looking at them." Time is irrelevant, what your eye sees is what it's going to see. We had a ten o'clock screening for the studio executives from New York, together with the studio executives from Cinerama. As they're all getting seated in the back, a man I had never met in my life walked up the aisle and sat up front. I gave them the signal to start and they were so excited they didn't know what hit them, it was really amazing. Sol Siegel said, "Harold, stand up and take a bow." The man from down front walked up and said, "Are you Harold Kress?" I said, "Yes." He said, "I'm George Stevens." He wanted Cinerama for *The Greatest Story Ever Told*.

What was that experience like?

George Stevens said to me, "I want you to supervise. Get me five top editors." I said, "We're going to need five?" So I got four editors and a floating assistant to put material back on reels. I brought in six to eight extra assistants to do nothing but assemble film in continuity order. We had one whole room, like a half-mile long, that had everything stacked in reels in continuity order. The editor had to go into the projection room with his assistant and run about 50 reels for each sequence because he had to know what was on them. Stevens was falling more behind schedule each day. Finally, he brought in David Lean and Jean Negulesco to direct sequences. David Lean came in and watched me one day. We were just getting into butt splicing. He said, "Gee, the butt splicer is great, can I try it?" He was an old-time editor. I said, "Sure, it saves film, we don't lose anything anymore, remember the old black frames you used to paint?" David said, "Oh yes, I was a pretty good painter." He was a charming guy. I bought a butt splicer, charged it to George

Stevens, and put it in a nice box. When he left I said, "Here's a present for you."

It was tough cutting day after day, night after night. Then William Wyler was going to start a picture and he wanted Robert Swink, his editor, back. Stevens said, "Who are you going to put on?" I said, "I'm going to let his assistant, Hal Ashby, take over as editor." Ashby got an okay on one sequence from Stevens, so we could haul out another 50 reels for a sequence. Stevens said, "What's the new sequence you're giving Ashby?" I said, "I'm giving him the Last Supper." Ashby starts cutting. He gets about half way through the Last Supper and comes into the office to see me privately. He says, "I have to leave you. I got an offer to direct a picture at Lorimar." "Hal," I said, "you're going to make the biggest enemy you ever had in the motion picture business." Ashby said, "Will you tell him? He might get mad and haul off." So the next day I said, "George, we're going to lose Ashby. He has a picture to direct for Lorimar." He said, "We just raised him from an assistant to an editor four months ago and now he's going to walk out on us? Can't he delay the picture until he finishes the Last Supper?" I said, "No, the Last Supper will have to wait until we get another editor."

Postproduction just went on and on until he was running out of money. It was getting pitiful with United Artists coming out every day saying, "When are you going to get this picture finished?"

When I finally finished the work with Stevens, I went back to Meryl Chamberlin, the head of my department at MGM, and I said, "I want to take a couple of weeks off, then I'll be ready to go back to work." He said, "You have to come back at what your salary was when you left." I went up to talk to George Sidney's father, L. K. He said, "George Stevens sent us a letter saying what a great job you did, but I don't think I could do anything about it because we have at least four other top editors who aren't getting the money that George Stevens paid you." I said, "Okay, then I have to leave, I've certainly loved it here for 30 years, it's like leaving my home." That night I went to see Sol Siegel who was now at Columbia in a partnership with Cary Grant. He said, "You did the right thing, you'll come to work for Cary Grant and me tomorrow morning; you'll be my associate producer." I didn't lose a day. He gave me the same salary that George Stevens was paying me.

In the years after you left MGM you were responsible for editing two major blockbusters for producer Irwin Allen. In The Poseidon Adventure, *what role did editing play in making the ship turn upside down?*

Turning the ship upside down was a very exciting sequence. Irwin Allen was shooting things falling, and I asked him if I could take a CinemaScope camera and get some flash cuts. I kept the camera level and started shooting people falling off a stepladder onto mats. I said to the actors, "When you've fallen, get back up and jump again." As they did, I slowly kept turning the camera, so I had four or five cuts at this angle, four or five cuts at that angle, until they were falling the long way.

What was your involvement with the composers of the musical scores of the films you edited?

Alfred Newman was one of the finest musicians for scoring pictures, but on *How the West was Won* I said, "Al, I don't like the music you scored for Jimmy Stewart's introduction to the picture when he's paddling his canoe down river. It sounds like a menacing character—look at the freedom, that landscape." The next day we're listening to it in the big dubbing theater at MGM. He said, "Harold, I thought about it last night and you were absolutely right. Stick around tomorrow and you'll hear a completely different piece of music." You have to be honest with these guys, because the first time you're dishonest with somebody in this business, you're going to get stuck. If you don't like something you've got to tell them in a nice way, as a friend, not as an enemy. That's where that old thing of diplomacy comes in. Those were the two best words that Irving Thalberg ever told me—"Be diplomatic."

Do you think editing has changed over the years?

No, I don't think it's changed. All the basic fundamentals are still there; you've got a scene to do and you've got to make yourself a part of that scene to make it play.

How has the stature of the film editor changed over the years?

What they pay editors now is phenomenal compared to what they used to pay them. When I was the president of the union, I wanted to get our names brought up on the credits list. Film editor used to be on the bottom. They brought it up until we got it above the art director; finally we got single billing. You really must have a love of the business. I gave as much for *H. M. Pulham, Esq.* or *Rage in Heaven* as I put into *Mrs. Miniver*. I didn't rate one picture better than the other. You put your whole heart and soul into what you're doing at that moment. I started at the peak when it was really a pleasure to make pictures. Seeing the world at the expense of a motion picture company is the only way to go. My wife and I have lived in Paris, London, and Spain.

You have been an editor, a producer, a director, and many things in between. Do you see yourself as an editor first?

I see myself as a moviemaker. If you're an editor, you're a moviemaker.

2

William Reynolds

William Reynolds has worked as a film editor for over 55 years. In 1935 he became an apprentice editor on *The Farmer Takes a Wife*, directed by Victor Fleming. As an assistant at Paramount, he was part of an innovative program that allowed him to cut scenes during shooting, while the editors were on the set working with the directors.

At 20th Century–Fox, under the watchful eye of Darryl Zanuck, Reynolds learned to keep the editing close behind the shooting so a first cut could be completed soon after production ended. With a strong studio background, William Reynolds moved on to edit many of Hollywood's biggest projects, including *The Sound of Music*, *Hello, Dolly!*, *The Sand Pebbles*, *The Godfather*, and *The Sting*. Among his many accomplishments, he has established a strong reputation cutting music and dance sequences in films such as *Fanny*, *The Turning Point*, and *Dancers*. He has been nominated for seven Academy Awards and has won twice for *The Sound of Music* and *The Sting*.

Reynolds has worked with such stylistically diverse directors as Joshua Logan, Elia Kazan, Henry King, Martin Ritt, Michael Cimino, Francis Ford Coppola, and Alan Alda. He has had especially long collaborative relationships with Robert Wise, George Roy Hill, and Herbert Ross.

1937	*52nd Street*
1938	*Algiers*
1940	*So Ends Our Night*
1942	*Moontide*

1947	*Carnival in Costa Rica*
1948	*Give My Regards to Broadway*
	The Street with No Name
	You Were Meant for Me
1949	*Come to the Stable*
	Mother is a Freshman
1950	*The Big Lift* (with Robert E. Simpson)
	Halls of Montezuma
1951	*The Day the Earth Stood Still*
	The Frogmen
	Take Care of My Little Girl
1952	*The Outcasts of Poker Flat*
	Red Skies of Montana
1953	*Beneath the 12-Mile Reef*
	The Kid from Left Field
	Dangerous Crossing
1954	*Desiree*
	Three Coins in the Fountain
1955	*Daddy Long Legs*
	Good Morning, Miss Dove
	Love is a Many-Splendored Thing
1956	*Bus Stop*
	Carousel
1958	*In Love and War*
	South Pacific (with Robert E. Simpson)
1959	*Beloved Infidel*
	Blue Denim
	Compulsion
1960	*Wild River*
1961	*Fanny**
1962	*Taras Bulba* (with Folmar Blangsted, Gene Milford, and Eda Warren)
	Tender is the Night
1963	*Kings of the Sun*
1964	*Ensign Pulver*
1965	*The Sound of Music***
1966	*Our Man Flint*
	The Sand Pebbles*

1968	*Star!*
1969	*Hello, Dolly!**
1970	*The Great White Hope*
1971	*What's the Matter with Helen?*
1972	*The Godfather* (with Peter Zinner)*
1973	*The Sting***
	Two People
1975	*The Great Waldo Pepper*
	The Master Gunfighter (with Danford Greene)
1976	*The Seven-Per-Cent Solution* (supervising editor)
1977	*The Turning Point**
1979	*A Little Romance*
	Old Boyfriends
1980	*Heaven's Gate* (with Lisa Fruchtman, Jerry Greenberg, and Tom Rolf)
	Nijinsky
1982	*Author! Author!*
	Making Love
1983	*Yellowbeard*
1984	*The Lonely Guy* (with Raja Gosnell)
	The Little Drummer Girl
1987	*Dancers*
	Ishtar (with Richard Cirincione and Stephen A. Rotter)
1988	*A New Life*
1989	*Rooftops*
1990	*Taking Care of Business*

*Academy Award nomination for best achievement in film editing.
**Academy Award for best achievement in film editing.

What is the film editor's job?

I see the job as trying to get the best possible version of the film that the director wants. You always have to keep in the forefront of your mind that it is the director's film.

When you select a project, is the director the most important criterion?

I am primarily interested in who the director is going to be, but even more in the script. I have had too many bad experiences working on films with very talented directors and lousy scripts. You can work your tail off and do some of your best work on films made from lousy scripts and they still don't come off.

So a good script makes your job easier.

All the difference in the world.

What was your first job in the film business?

When I first came out here to Hollywood from the East, I got a job in the labor department at 20th Century–Fox, what we called the "swing gang." I was interested in editing and I managed to get my toe in the door of the editorial department as an apprentice. I was able to advance quickly because that was before the union was formed. There weren't the restrictions there are now, where you have to be an apprentice for so long, then you have to be an assistant for so long, before you can become an editor. I had just become an editor when the union was formed; that was a stroke of luck.

What was it like to cut your first scene?

I asked the editor, Robert Simpson, if I could cut a particular scene we had seen in the dailies. He said, "Are you sure you want to do that scene?" That should have told me that it was more complicated than I thought, but I plunged ahead. I went back at night and did it, and the next morning he looked at it. Obviously, he knew it was more complex than I thought. He very gently explained why what I did was all wrong, and why he had to do it over again. When I saw what he did, it was clear to me why I hadn't done it well. So that was a tough beginning but after that, he had me do other things and I got to be a little better at it.

What was it like being an editor at a studio in those days?

You were on the editorial staff and your assignments were handed to you. You have no choice really except as you became known by the various directors at a studio. A director might ask for you, if you were available. Paramount had a wonderful set-up made to order for would-be film editors. The editor of the film stayed on the set throughout the filming. In addition to the assistant's work, you also put the film into first cut. Once the filming was completed, the editor took over and re-edited or accepted what you did. That was the greatest learning experience in the world. Paramount was the only studio that had that system. The assistant actually got to cut. I worked with Eda Warren, Elma McCrory, and Eddie Dmytryk.

Has the amount of hours that you put in for a day's work changed over the years?

Not with me. It has varied tremendously with different editors, but my experience tends to have been pretty much a nine-to-six day, whether it's in the independent field or not. For many years it was a six-day week. You worked Saturdays. The motion picture business was one of the last to go to a five-day week. There are lots of horror stories around of editors who have worked horrendous hours. I work very hard in the course of a day and by the end of the day I'm tired. If I have to go back in the evening I can usually have a meal, recharge my batteries, and go back and work more, but I don't like to and I don't usually have to. That's part of the background that those of us who worked at 20th Century–Fox got under Darryl Zanuck. Darryl liked editors and he was a very shrewd editor himself. He wanted to see the first cut on a film as quickly as possible after the filming finished, because he wanted to make decisions quickly. We were trained to stay right behind the filming; that stayed with me. On an epic-scale film with a vast amount of material, you do get behind, but if it's basically a dialogue or a very tight action film, you should have a first cut within a week or so after the end of filming. I'm cutting right along behind it, in a pretty standard number of hours per day.

Did Zanuck also know a lot about the technical aspects of editing?

Yes, he did. He had a great technique. When you screened with him, you would sit next to him. Usually the director was there and other studio higher-ups. Every now and then he would reach over and touch you and you would make a note of where you were in the film. He never said anything. You might end up with quite a few notes. When the screening was finished, he would get up and pace up and down with his cigar and make general comments about what he thought needed to be done. Then he would turn to the editor and say, "What are my notes?" and you'd tell him where you were in the picture. Usually, it would be something just ahead of where you made the note. He would always remember what he had in mind, whether it was major or minor. He could always go through and indicate it in very precise detail. He would say, "Could you arrange it thus and so?" instead of the way you had it now. At times, when I would get my hands on the film in the cutting room, I couldn't precisely do what he had asked for, but then I would come up with an alternate solution. I could call him and say, "I can't do what you suggested, but I can do this." Nine times out of ten he would say, "Fine, do that," so he was approachable and knowledgeable. He knew what you were talking about, editors knew what he was talking about and so we had a good relationship. Somebody once asked Zanuck, who had so many good editors, why he never made editors into directors and he said, "Why should I? I've got the best editorial staff in Hollywood."

Does it bother you when directors try to take credit for the editor's work?

In trade papers you see constantly that such and such a director is now cutting his latest film and that always drives me up the wall. I always say, "Isn't there an editor on that film?" In the last picture that I worked on, there was an item quoting Bob Wise, bless his heart, who said, "I am now working with my editor on *Rooftops*."

Do you think directors should direct editors the way they would direct actors, by giving them colors and feelings, as opposed to taking the grease pencil and marking things?

Yes. You can get a general feel from a director as to what he intends to accomplish with a film. If a director expresses likes and dislikes about various takes while screening rushes, that helps, but no editor really likes it if they get too specific and say, "Cut from here to here at such and such a point." That's the sign of an inexperienced director. The director should pick the editor's brain by giving the editor a free hand to do a first cut. You can always change it, but it's very possible that the editor can come up with a better version than the director actually had foreseen in his mind.

You have worked with Robert Wise, George Roy Hill, and Herbert Ross on many of their films. What is that relationship like when you work often with a particular director?

The relationship is very relaxed. I'm very familiar with the way they shoot. You get to have shorthand communication. I know they are going to approve of almost any scene that I put together. That doesn't mean they don't have suggestions from time to time. They may want a line dropped or a pause shortened or lengthened, but basically it's a relationship in which I arrive very quickly at what I know they want. If you have done a number of pictures with them, mutual confidence develops.

Does Robert Wise shoot scenes with more coverage because he's been an editor?

Not more coverage, but he knows what the necessary coverage is. He shoots what he knows we're likely to need to edit a scene properly. He's much more aware of what the editor can do.

Is your experience different when working with a director who doesn't have extensive editing knowledge?

I did a number of films for Josh Logan and his background was primarily from the stage, so he wanted me to be on the set all the time to make sure he got the coverage he needed. An inexperienced director doesn't always need that kind of help from an editor if he's got a knowledgeable cameraman, but not all cameramen are that coverage-conscious; they like to move on to the next scene.

Do you feel that cameramen should know something about editing?

Oh yes, it's a great help if they do. The kind of thing that can go wrong if they don't, is they get on the wrong side of a person, crossing the line, and if they're not clear about that they can get you into all kinds of trouble.

Before you begin a project do you do any research into subjects related to the film?

No. I feel that the film tells me what I need to know.

Do you feel that an editing room is claustrophobic?

I don't feel it's claustrophobic at all. You're in a room with a Moviola or a KEM, that's your world at the moment and that's enough.

In your opinion, what should an editor's first cut look like?

Basically, a first cut looks like a version of the film that contains everything the director shot. It contains every scene, every line of dialogue. If the filming has followed the script, invariably the film is too long and, in many cases, it is very obvious certain things should be eliminated or shortened. It still should have a very professional look about it. A first cut is not a rough assembly; it's much better than that. Scenes should be cut properly for tempo. If it's a comedy and is meant to go fast, it should go fast.

What is your technique for cutting on a Moviola?

I mark the film on the Moviola, then work it through a synchronizer, and cut it that way. I screen it on the KEM and even make changes if they're not too complex. I have cut on the KEM, but I didn't really like it. I had an assistant who could do anything on the KEM. I would simply mark the film with a grease pencil and he would make the cut for me. The mechanics of having him do that became very bothersome for me. I'd do the crossword puzzle in *Variety* while he was doing it. Even though there is a lot of taking film in and out of the Moviola mechanically, you're thinking about what your next step is while you're doing the mechanical things. I just found that wasn't true on the KEM, and after I did a couple of pictures that way I went back to the Moviola.

How many assistants and apprentices do you like to work with?

Ideally, if you have a first and second assistant and an apprentice it is a pretty good set-up.

After screening the dailies, what is your method for cutting a scene?

I usually screen the rushes a second time on a KEM. I may make some notes about things I want to be sure to use, then I go to work and put it together.

Do you see a scene complete in your mind's eye before you begin to cut it?

No, I don't. I know there are editors who do. They get an overall picture of how it's going to go. It's practically a shot-by-shot process with me. When I look at it again, I may make adjustments, shorten pauses, or change a reaction.

Do you begin simply and then start to introduce techniques like overlaps?

I don't do that. I usually combine those steps, I do the overlaps as I go over it the first time.

Does experience give you the courage to just go for it right away?

Yes. People think I'm fast as an editor. I don't try to be fast. Experience makes it possible to make quick decisions. It is a big time-saving element to make quick decisions that, more likely than not, are satisfactory ones.

What are some of the editor's concerns in cutting a dialogue scene between two people?

Your primary decision is who is more interesting to look at. Is it more interesting to look at a person when they are talking or to see how the other person is reacting? Are they reacting in an interesting manner, or aren't they? It depends on what the listener is doing and if the dialogue is having some effect on him. You try to balance it that way, but it depends on the film in hand. Every scene is different. I've been plagued two or three times with writer-producers who simply seem to be obsessed with the idea that you have to be on the person who is speaking; they seem to feel that the words are lost if you are not looking at that person, and that is a real pain in the neck.

Carol Littleton has called editing the final rewrite. How do you feel about that statement?

That's one way of putting it. When a director is filming, he's not making a movie, he's making the material from which a movie is going to be made, and it's going to be made in the editing.

You co-edited The Godfather *with Peter Zinner. How did the two of you work together?*

We went to New York where the filming was going on. If I finished a scene, I would take a new one from the dailies or if I was busy, Peter would take the scene. We parceled things out as we went along. Once the filming was finished, we moved to Zoetrope, Francis Coppola's place in San Francisco. At that point, well before the first cut, Francis said, "Bill, I want you to take the first half of the picture, and Peter, you take the last half." We had a real wealth of material to work with and were not that close behind the filming. There was still lots and lots of editing to do to get a first cut.

The film's opening, Connie Corleone's wedding, is a remarkable scene that sets the tone for the entire film. How did that develop during the editing?

One of the big projects I had to work on was to edit that wedding. Francis simply staged an Italian wedding reception. That was not storyboarded, it was all ad lib. He had the wedding party at a table with all of the other guests floating around and an orchestra playing. I would be working on the wedding and intercutting it with the scenes inside, where Brando was in his office receiving the respects of his Mafioso people. Every now and then Francis would make a shot in which Brando was out among the guests. I would check to see what I had done on the KEM and would say, "Oh, my God, there's Brando back there." I had just left him up in the office, I'd have to get that shot out of there and put it someplace else. It was an interesting problem to keep the wedding and the indoor scenes going at the same time. There was a great deal of detail that isn't in the film, there wasn't room for it all. You simply have to look for what you feel are the telling bits.

How long was the first cut on the picture?

The picture was very long, well over three hours. Francis said to us editors, "I just can't show the picture at this length to Bob Evans, the producer, and Paramount, because they simply won't buy a film that long." So we did some really drastic surgery on it under Francis' direction. He had us take out handfuls of material. At that point we brought it down and showed it to Bob Evans for the first time. When the screening was finished Bob said, "Well, this looks good, but I remember lots of wonderful material that isn't in the film; where is it?" Francis was very upfront about it. He said flat out that he didn't think the studio would buy a picture at an excessive length and Bob, bless his heart, said, "I don't care how long the picture is, put that material back. It's that good, so let's have it that long." It was because of Bob Evans and the clout that he carried at Paramount at the time that they bought the picture at that length.

There are many optical techniques in The Sting *that shape the editorial look of the film. Were those your ideas and how did they develop?*

Yes, those are mine. I thought about it as I was going along in the editing. The idea of chapters was scripted. The detail of making it a page turn was something that I thought of. I thought, here's a chance to play around and do things optically with page turns and irises.

Did your studio background prepare you for this kind of optical work?

Definitely. I was more aware of what could be done. You don't see too much optical work now. You don't even see dissolves and fades as much; that has been an advance as far as film technique is concerned. We finally realized that audiences will make jumps with you, you don't have to dissolve to indicate a lapse of time or a change of location. If you just cut, the audience will follow you. They won't be confused.

How did you get involved in the editing of Heaven's Gate? *It must have been a monumental task cutting that film.*

Oh, it was. Michael Cimino called and explained he had finished filming except for a prologue and epilogue that he was going to shoot in London. He asked if I would do that because his editor, Tom Rolf, was up to his ears in work on the film. I was very reluctant to have anything to do with it, because I had heard stories about Michael being very difficult to work for and that he worked all hours of the day and night. I said, "Look, I work very hard from when I come in to when I leave, and I don't like night work. I don't like somebody looking over my shoulder when I'm cutting. I like to do it, show it to you, and then we work together on it." He was very agreeable, he said, "Fine." When I walked out at six o'clock he never said a word, so he was as good as his word. I went to London and worked there for a while and then we brought the film back. After I had done the prologue and the epilogue, I got sucked into working on some other parts of the film. I have great admiration for Cimino. I never have seen a director work so hard on the editing of a film as he did. He would be in there day and night, experimenting, screening cut film and outtakes over and over again—hardest-working man I'd ever seen.

The use of sound on the film was very controversial.

I was very much in the middle of that, because I disagreed violently with Michael about the balance between the sound effects and the dialogue. He was really in love with the sound effects. At the beginning, when Kris Kristofferson arrives at the train station, there's a lot of important dialogue to set the scene and you just can't understand him. I said, "Michael, nobody is going to know what the people are talking about." He said, "I understand them." I said, "Of course you understand them. You wrote it and you've heard it a hundred times. The audience seeing it for the first time is not going to understand it." So he said, "Why don't you mix it the way you think it ought to be." I did. I changed the balance until the dialogue was intelligible and he undid it, he didn't like it.

What are your feelings about the film?

I just thought it was never really clear what the film was about. It wasn't clear cut about the good guys and the bad guys; it wasn't focused.

Were you knowledgeable about classical dance before cutting any of the Herbert Ross films?

No, that was really a wonderful experience because I got to work with Herb's wife, Nora Kaye, on *The Turning Point* and *Nijinsky*. Nora, in her day, was a very famous ballerina. Herb Ross had been a dancer and a choreographer himself in his early career, but nothing like Nora. Her interest in those films was that the dancers should always look just as good as they could possibly be made to look. I would put a ballet scene together and then Nora and I would look at it on the KEM. She would say, "Stop, back up, you see that? Her foot isn't the way it should be. See if you can find another take where she has her foot right. If not, find a take where you can't see her foot." It was a very close relationship and consequently, I became much more familiar with the vocabulary of ballet. I had enormous admiration for her, I learned a lot from her.

Prior to cutting a dance sequence, how do you see the whole scene? Are there masters of great portions of it, so you can get a feeling of what is going to happen before you go into it and move things around?

Yes, usually there are. It's rather tricky for a director shooting ballet. You can't make a series of long sustained takes because the dancers don't get better, they get tired, so they are liable to be at their best in the first or second take. For that reason they try to shoot multiple cameras so they can get closer shots at the same time, while the dancers are in their best form.

How do you cut sequences that employ multiple cameras?

For the ballet sequences in *The Turning Point*, Herb Ross very often shot with five cameras. I had two eight-plate KEMs, so I could put up all five cameras, and that was an enormous help in editing. I could look at all five at once. I would edit it on paper first, by screening with my assistant, saying, "We'll use this angle to open with, we'll go so far, and let's try going to this camera at such and such a point"—sort of mapping it out that way. Once I put it together, I could screen it again on the KEM and at the same time screen all of the remaining material and make adjustments or additions. You can imagine the difference between having to put on a great big roll and run it on the Moviola, and then put on another great big roll, and do that five different times and try to know what you had. Without the KEM I would still be doing it.

Do you feel that a multiple camera set-up gives you a smoother cut?

Oh sure, it's an editor's dream because the action matches, but on the other hand, that isn't always the best way to film. Cinematographers don't always like it, because the lighting may be fine for one camera, but it's not that good for another. So very often multiple cameras don't work, you do have to go in for separate close-ups and restage them in subsequent set-ups.

Do you think it's important for an editor to understand music editing?

It's a big help. Now and then in my experience at 20th Century–Fox, when I cut musicals, there would be a situation when I knew that a music track had to be shortened. I could usually do it myself rather than call in a music editor. In *The Turning Point* there was a dance scene with Baryshnikov and Leslie Browne. It started out with a dance in a rehearsal hall to the Prokofiev score and then it dissolved to a scene in the bedroom, which eventually culminated in a love scene. In the actual love scene, Herb Ross had shot some unchoreographed shots of their activity. The big trick was there wasn't any way to make any jump cuts in the Prokofiev. I listened to the music very carefully with that in mind; it just wasn't that kind of music. So from the time they started dancing, to the love scene, I had to make a montage out of this material and make it all come out even with the Prokofiev.

How did you develop the montage?

I cut the bedroom scene without any reference to the music at all, just to get the material all together. Then I started making it fit within the limits of the music. I had to condense it a bit. The material in the bed was just a series of different kinds of shots. I was able to make it interesting just by dissolving from one thing to another. That gave me the freedom to expand it or contract it to fit the music. It looks as though it was scored after it was cut, but that wasn't the case.

When a scene is not working, editors constantly are presented with these kinds of problems to solve. Can you give an example of a pictorial problem that you had on a film and how you solved it?

In *The Day the Earth Stood Still*, the spaceship landed in Washington on the Mall. Bob Wise made a shot in which the figure came out of the machine and stood by the door. It didn't look good, it just looked like some actor in an uncomfortable costume. So I thought, why show that? We had a shot of the crowd reacting to the ship. I cut to the people looking and watching and all of a sudden they gasp, and I cut to the figure just standing there. I simply took the entrance out, so that we didn't see any of the awkwardness of it.

Have you used material that was originally intended for one part of the film in an entirely different section?

That's what we did at the very end of *The Turning Point* where we had end credits over shots of the girl dancing. There were a lot of shots scripted to be in the body of the film that didn't fit. When we got to the end of the movie we thought, "What are we going to use for background for the end credits?" We hit on the idea of using the shots of the girl dancing. They were not choreographed in any definite continuity, so I was free to make it fit the requirements to cover the titles. I used the material as far as I thought it would stand, and then we froze the frame for the continuation of the end credits.

Can you think of a specific example where you decided not to cut and to let a piece of material play?

In *The Great Waldo Pepper* there was a scene which required a stunt man to transfer in midair from one plane to another. It was photographed from another plane in the air with a couple of different cameras, but I played it all in one angle. I didn't want to give anybody a moment's suspicion that there was anything fake about it. So I was screening the scene for the director, George Roy Hill, and this transference was taking place. George says, "I think we'll cut right about here to the other angle." I said, "The hell we will!" He nearly fell out of his chair, because he was really testing me. He knew perfectly well that it had to play in one angle and shouldn't be fancied up in any way.

When you work with a writer-director, is the work process different than with a director who has not written the script?

Writers find it very difficult to understand why a certain scene or line of dialogue may not be needed, because they know why they wrote it, they had a reason for it. But things happen on film that they can't foresee. Things in a previous scene may have made a subsequent scene totally unnecessary, but it's very hard for a writer to see why that reason doesn't still exist; that happens a lot.

Alan Alda wrote a very good script for A New Life. *You can feel that the quality of the script resulted in a good film.*

Yes, that's true, and Alan was awfully good when it came to the editorial process. He sensed which jokes played and which jokes didn't, which I admired, because directors aren't always able to stand back and judge their own material. Alan was able to be quite ruthless about taking out things that he felt were not funny when I wasn't so sure. I thought, "How does he know that's not funny?" He seemed to have a very sure sense of it.

Ishtar was a film with an enormous amount of material. What techniques did you use to handle the workload?

Everything was put on videocassettes so that we could run down and look at any or all of the takes on a given scene. Elaine May shot more film than you needed for 20 pictures. I like her a lot, she's a very bright, very amusing lady, totally unable to make editorial decisions. I came in on *Ishtar* late, they had finished cutting. They already had two editors on it, and then Warren Beatty called me and asked if I would help because they had so much film. I got there just before the filming was completed and started in. She would go over individual scenes and get us to work on them in great detail and refine them, but never eliminated any scenes at all. We finally got a version of the picture that was very long, but each individual scene was quite refined. So then she was faced with the problem that the film was too long. She said, "I'm going to take a scene out and I'll screen the film and see if it plays without the scene and if it doesn't, I'll put it back and take another scene out." At that point I called Warren and said, "As this is the procedure she is going to follow, you don't need three editors anymore, can I go?" That's how I got off of it.

Does an epic film like The Sand Pebbles *take a different kind of thinking?*

Yes, it does. You don't feel that you have to race along at an undue pace, you can really take the time to get all of the juice out of a scene. When you have big scenes with multiple cameras and lots of film, you just have a sense of being overwhelmed by it. Rather than let yourself be overwhelmed, I do it a shot at a time. If it isn't obvious what the first shot is, pick your shot. Then I say, "What do I want to see next? What's the important thing to see next that will progress the scene?" You know from the script what the objective of the scene is and you can work your way through a massive scene that way, a shot at a time. You get a rough assembly, but at least there it is, you've got something with a beginning and it works its way through to the end. Then I go through the process of examining all of the existing material very carefully and weave it into that basic framework.

Were there big master scenes of the battle? How do you know what is going on in the scene?

The master is more valuable as information about the general scheme of the scene, but in action scenes you can't stay in a master for very long. You have to cut; things have to be happening editorially. Scenes of large scope can only sustain so long and then you have to get in close. This is a generalization; in *Lawrence of Arabia* there were big master scenes that really played.

Because of tight schedules, many producers are putting more than one editor on a film. How do you feel about that?

It works better than I would have anticipated. People have said to me, "How do you reconcile different editorial styles?" The way a director shoots tends to dictate the editorial style, and consequently, the styles of two or more editors don't diverge that much.

Where do you think the future of film editing is heading?

Technically, I suppose it's going to tape. At one point it seemed as if it was going to tape much more quickly. I imagine it's going to lead to even more complications with directors who aren't sure what they want. It's going to be that much easier to press buttons and experiment with the editing. They're going to drive you up the wall, I know! Schedules are getting shorter and shorter. When you start on a picture, the release date has already been set and you say, "We've got ten weeks of post-production, we should be able to do that." Then all of a sudden the start of the picture is delayed two weeks. You think they change the postproduction date? Not at all, you now have eight weeks of post-production, and that's happening all the time. That's why more and more films are using more than one editor, because of the time element.

To what do you attribute your great longevity as an editor?

I guess it's a case of getting along with directors. I've liked the directors I've worked with, and consequently, they want me back. I think that's what really works with any editor; you get an association with a director. I've cut six, seven, or eight films for Bob Wise, I've done a whole series with George Roy Hill, Herb Ross, and a number of directors. I think if you are in demand, that's what keeps you going.

3

Rudi Fehr

Rudi Fehr emigrated from Germany in 1936 and ventured to Hollywood, where he became a film editor at Warner Brothers. At the studio he formed a close relationship with Jack Warner and collaborated with many of Hollywood's finest directors, including Alfred Hitchcock, John Huston, King Vidor, Michael Curtiz, Raoul Walsh, Howard Hawks, and Jean Negulesco.

In 1952, Jack Warner gave Fehr producer status on *The Desert Song*. Subsequently, he was made executive in charge of postproduction, a position he held for 22 years.

After a mandatory retirement in 1976, he was rehired in 1977 as a consultant and went to Europe to supervise foreign-language adaptations for Warner Brothers.

In 1980, he was hired by Francis Ford Coppola as postproduction consultant for Zoetrope Studios, where he returned to the cutting room to work on *One from the Heart*.

In 1984, Fehr was reunited with director John Huston as editor on *Prizzi's Honor*. He worked on the film with his daughter Kaja, and they both received Academy Award nominations.

1931	*Der Schlemihl*
1932	*The Unlucky Mr. Five*
1933	*Invisible Enemies*
	The Tunnel
1935	*An Old Spanish Custom*

1940	My Love Came Back
	The Great Mr. Nobody
	Honeymoon for Three
1941	Million Dollar Baby
	Navy Blues
	All Through the Night
1942	Desperate Journey
	Watch on the Rhine
	Devotion
1943	Between Two Worlds
	In Our Time
1944	The Conspirators
	Nobody Lives Forever
1945	A Stolen Life
1946	Humoresque
	Possessed
1947	The Voice of the Turtle
	Romance on the High Seas
1948	Key Largo
	The Girl from Jones Beach
	The Inspector General
1949	Beyond the Forest
	The Damned Don't Cry
1950	Rocky Mountain
1951	Goodbye, My Fancy
1952	I Confess
1953	House of Wax
	Riding Shotgun
	Dial M for Murder
1954	Land of the Pharaohs (supervising editor)
1982	One from the Heart (with Anne Goursaud and Randy Roberts)
1985	Prizzi's Honor (with Kaja Fehr)*

*Academy Award nomination for best achievement in film editing.

How did you become a film editor in Germany?
In 1926, I fronted one of the most popular dance orchestras in Berlin.

One day I sat down and said, "What do you want to do with your life?" I figured a diplomat made trade agreements with other countries and kept the peace between countries. Because I am Jewish, my dream came to an abrupt halt. I was crushed when I learned that because of my ethnic background, I was no longer allowed to work in the country I was born in. I was born into a well-to-do family. My family went back to the sixteenth century in Germany.

When I realized I could not be a diplomat, I turned to my second love—music. I wanted to become a conductor in the tradition of Toscanini. After six months of studying, I got a call from Dr. Guido Bagier, the president of Tobis-Klangfilm, the second biggest film company in Germany. He asked me if I would be interested in becoming a film editor. He had heard about me and knew that I studied music and spoke English and French. In those days the editor not only had to be able to cut the picture, but he also had to be the sound effects editor, the music editor, and be qualified to edit trailers and montages. I told him that I had just started to study music, was enjoying it, and did not want to stop and do something else. He said, "You're only 19, why don't you see what it's like in the world of motion pictures? How about observing film editing for six months?" I still said no. He said, "Well, I'm going to make it attractive for you, I'll pay you 100 marks a month." I still lived at home with my parents and wanted to become independent. I said, "All right."

I was to learn editing for six months and then tell him if I wanted to stay in motion pictures. In exactly three months, Dr. Bagier came to the cutting room and said, "Rudi, we're starting another picture. We have no editor available, are you ready?" I was stunned. Of course, I wasn't ready. I always talk to myself at those moments: "If I say I'm not ready, then he won't ask me again for a year or two and I will lose that time out of my life. If I work very hard, seven days a week, night and day, I can swing it." I said, "I'm ready!" He said, "You start Monday as an editor." That's how I cut my first picture, *Der Schlemihl*. I was very lucky. Somebody liked my work. I jumped from 100 marks a month to 1,200 marks a month.

In 1933, I edited *Invisible Enemies* in Vienna. After that, I worked in Munich and edited the French version of *The Tunnel*, but the Nazis would not permit me to work on the German version. Another editor was hired and instructed to edit the German version by matching my cut of the French version. Then I came back to Berlin. My father passed away in June of 1934 of a broken heart. My mother still lived in the big house we had.

How did you come to America and begin your Hollywood editing career?

I was very popular with the young crowd in the diplomatic corps, and with the children of the ambassadors and the Consular Corps. I

frequently heard members of the diplomatic corps say they had information from reliable sources that Hitler was targeted for assassination.
Even if he would have been killed, his successor would have been just
as bad. So one day, early in 1936, I got a call from the daughter of the
American ambassador. She said, "Rudi, after the Olympic Games, things
are going to get worse—get out!" I told her that I would need a visa in
order to enter the United States. She simply said, "Give me your passport." A few hours later a messenger returned my passport with the
visa. I was all set to go.

I arrived in New York May 1, 1936. I met William Morris, Jr. He said,
"What can you do?" I said, "I can do two things. I can lead a band and
I can cut film." He said, "Cut film. If you lead a band you're going to
have one-night stands and be living out of a suitcase. You can't have a
family life." I felt that I owed it to myself to try my luck in Hollywood.
I didn't know a soul in Hollywood and all of the friends I had made in
New York said, "Don't go to Hollywood. There are a hundred people
more qualified than you waiting for an opening." I told them I had
enough money to get by for six months without working. If I should be
unable to find a job, I would return to New York and work for Macy or
Gimbel, but I'll never forgive myself if I don't try my luck in Hollywood.

So I took the train, three days and three nights from New York via
Chicago. I arrived here—beautiful blue skies, palm trees; it was heaven.
Everybody was so friendly. I bought a 1934 Ford convertible for 450
bucks and I made the rounds. I had collected ten or 12 letters of introduction from bankers and attorneys in New York who were friends of
my father. One was to George Oppenheimer, who was a very sophisticated writer at MGM. He wrote *The Thin Man*. He invited me to have
lunch with him in the private dining room at MGM. I'll never forget the
day. I looked to my left and there was Clark Gable, and on my right
was Spencer Tracy.

How did you become a film editor at Warner Brothers?

Exactly five weeks to the day I arrived, I came home to my little apartment near the Ambassador Hotel and there were three messages rolled
up in my mailbox. I grabbed them and went to my room. Call Cedric Gib-
bons at Metro Goldwyn Mayer, call Fritz Lang at United Artists, call
Henry Blanke at Warner Brothers—all in one hour! Everybody wanted to
work at MGM; it was the best studio. So I called MGM first. Cedric Gib-
bons was in charge of the art department and the montage department.
He said, "We read your resumé. We noted that you have done montages.
We're not very happy with the man we have now, we'd like you to do it
the next time we need a montage." I was very excited about it. I said,
"That's awfully nice, about when would that be?" He said, "About six or
eight weeks, we'll call you." Then I called Fritz Lang at United Artists. I
had met him once in Berlin, but I don't think he remembered. I had a very

prominent uncle, Oscar Fehr, who was the finest eye surgeon in Berlin. Fritz Lang was in the Austrian Army during World War I and he got some shrapnel in his left eye. My uncle removed the shrapnel without hurting anything in his eye. He never forgot that. He said, "This is only out of gratitude to your uncle. I'm offering you a job to be the assistant editor on a film called *Fury*, with Sylvia Sidney." I said, "That's awfully nice, Mr. Lang, when do you start?" He said, "Oh, in about six weeks." Then I called Henry Blanke at Warner Brothers who was also from Berlin. He came here in 1922 as Lubitsch's translator and right-hand man. He said, "We just bought two films, *Episode* and *Mazurka*. We only have the prints, no scripts, no paperwork. We want someone to take the German dialogue off the sound track and translate it into English. Can you do that?" I said, "Certainly." He said, "Great, how much money do you want?" I heard about these fabulous salaries in Hollywood. I said, "I wouldn't work for less than 100 dollars a week." I thought he would say yes or no right away. He said, "I'll call you back." Twenty minutes later the phone rings. He says, "Will you do it for 60?" I said to myself, "Yes, sir!" Anything to get into a major studio, even if I had to pay them. "When do I start?" He said, "Tomorrow morning."

This job was supposed to last for six weeks. On the last day, the head of editorial, Harold McCord, came to me. He said, "I have an opening as an assistant editor." I said, "It's better to be a working assistant editor than a nonworking editor, if I have the understanding that if I get a job as an editor, I can leave." "Certainly," he said, "anytime." So I took it and I was an assistant editor for three years with a very fine editor, Warren Low.

The first picture I worked on was *The Life of Emile Zola* with Paul Muni. Then I worked on *Jezebel* with Bette Davis and Henry Fonda, and *Juarez* with Bette Davis and Paul Muni. I worked on one picture after another. My break came in 1940 when I edited *My Love Came Back* for director, Curtis Bernhardt, the same director I worked with on *The Tunnel*. It was a remake of *Episode*, a film written and directed by Walter Reisch in Vienna, which I had translated in the 1930s. At this time, every studio made 60 movies a year and there was a standing cutting department of 22 editors and 22 assistant editors. There were two words not in the vocabulary: layoff and overtime. You were never laid off, but you never got overtime. If you worked overtime you got a meal ticket, which got you a free lunch the next day—that was it.

How did you approach the editing on Watch on the Rhine?

This film was directed by Herman Shumlin, who had never made a movie before. He was very close to Lillian Hellman, who had written the play, which Shumlin directed for the stage. I was assigned to the picture. When I first met him he told me, "I don't know the first thing about set-ups, you have to help me." He had no idea when to use the close-up, when to move the camera, when to pan, when to dolly. We spent many evenings together laying out the camera set-ups for the next day. I had no social life. I was on the set most of the time advising him. Shumlin was so grateful to me. I did the same for other directors.

Were you making directorial decisions?

I did not contribute to the acting. I only contributed to what shots to take, when to shoot a close-up, when to move the camera.

You used wipes and dissolves very effectively in Watch on the Rhine. *Were they part of the Warner Brothers style or did they come out of your own editorial ideas for this movie?*

That was absolutely up to the individual. I ordered them, showed them to the director, and he approved of them. You give a lot of thought before you do something in a big picture. Is this right for the film? Is this right for the story you are telling? I'm a firm believer in time lapses. If it is a week, a month, or a year later and you make a direct cut, it tends to confuse audiences. I believe in the dissolve—slow dissolve, fast dissolves, it depends on what the situation is. If somebody says, "I'll see you tomorrow morning at nine," and then you cut to a clock showing it's nine o'clock, the audience can follow, they know what is happening and you do not need a dissolve.

Because it's an adaptation of a stage play, Watch on the Rhine *is a very talky picture. Did you have to resist overcutting?*

I avoid overcutting at all cost. I only cut to reactions when it is essential. I was the assistant editor on *The Life of Emile Zola* in which Paul Muni made a courtroom speech that ran over eight minutes. The entire speech was on him. There were no reaction shots and the scene held beautifully. When somebody says something startling like, "I'm going to kill you," of course you cut to the person who is threatened to see their reaction. Or sometimes when the performance is not up to par, you cut to people listening. If the director made a shot where the camera was moving, either a pan shot or a dolly shot, I used it. It somehow makes the telling of the story more fluid. I do not make arbitrary cuts; every cut is motivated.

In Key Largo *there's a wonderful atmosphere of tension. How did the editing contribute to that?*

The director John Huston gave me beautiful coverage, an editor's dream. One quality an editor has to have is to be very conscientious. I looked at the footage again and again before I decided which footage I would use. An editor should follow his own instinct when it comes to editing, unless the director has given the editor certain directions or instructions. When I screened my cut for John Huston, he was pleased with my work, he asked for very few changes.

What was the coverage like? Did Huston give you many choices?

Yes, he gave me many set-ups, master shots, medium shots, over-the-shoulders, and close-ups of all the characters involved in the scene. It was not too difficult for me to figure out who I should cut to. I was very fortunate to be working with John. It was a memorable experience.

In Key Largo *there are so many characters in one room. Did that cause any particular continuity problems?*

No, it just causes you to think a little harder. Who am I going to be on at this point? You have to keep every character "alive." You have every possible choice. Cutting is so flexible, you can do so many things.

Did Huston work closely with you in the cutting room?

I'm a very lucky man. I never in my entire career had a director in my cutting room—never. Huston never came to the cutting room on *Prizzi's Honor.* Hitchcock, Vince Sherman, King Vidor, Mike Curtiz never came to the cutting room. Lloyd Bacon never looked at the rushes. Raoul Walsh never looked at any cut. He saw the picture at the preview, came up to you, patted you on the back and said, "Good job, boy." That's all.

What was your relationship like with Alfred Hitchcock? Is it true that he liked to cut scenes in the camera?

No, especially not in *I Confess.* He shot the picture in Québec and in those days they didn't send the editors on location. The editor was at the Burbank studio. Hitchcock knew that he couldn't go back to Québec to pick up shots in case he missed anything. He protected himself by covering everything the way it could possibly be covered, especially the flashbacks. I had everything to work with. I believe Hitchcock exposed more film on *I Confess* than he did on most of his other productions. Of all the directors I have worked with, Alfred Hitchcock was my favorite.

You worked on two films released in 3-D, House of Wax *and* Dial M for Murder. *What was it like to edit movies shot in that process?*

It was not really much different than editing regular film. When I screened the rushes on *House of Wax,* I made notes whenever the 3-D effect stood out. For instance, the scene where the ping-pong ball hit the audience in the eye. I held on to that shot longer than I would have if the film were not in 3-D. Three-D is shot with two cameras, one for the left eye, the other for the right eye. The editor cuts one eye only, usually the left, then his assistant matches the right eye, which is not too difficult because the film has been coded. All the assistant has to do is match the code numbers. When 3-D was first shown in theaters, two projection machines ran simultaneously. They had to be lined up perfectly. If one frame in one of the projectors was a little higher or lower, it would pull the spectator's eye right of the socket. Nowadays, theaters don't use two projectors, both strips are optically put on one strip; therefore, only one projector is required. The *House of Wax* was made because the theaters were empty, people were staying home to watch television. In order to lure the audiences back to the theaters, Warner's came out with 3-D and Fox introduced a new process, CinemaScope, which threw an elongated image onto the screen. Their picture was *The Robe*.

Jack Warner called me and said, "Rudi, I want you to be the editor on this show, but it has to be in the theaters five weeks from the day we finish shooting." I said, "Mr. Warner, I guarantee you'll have your picture in the theater five weeks from the day we stop shooting, if we start shooting on page one and shoot in continuity. Then I can assemble the reels as they come from the director, show it to you and the director, and turn it over to the composer and sound editor a reel at a time." He called his production manager and said, "Change your whole shooting schedule on *House of Wax*." "Why?" "We have to have it in the theaters and Rudi says . . . " "Oh, Rudi says!" the production manager replied. "It will cost you more money that way." Warner said, "I don't give a damn, we shoot it that way!" Five weeks from the day we finished shooting it was in the theaters.

What involvement did Jack Warner have with the editing of Warner Brothers films?

Jack Warner's favorite department was editing. He had an instinct for editing. He was very helpful. Every day after lunch he went to the projection room and looked at the film that was shot the day before. I had to be there. In the evening he always ran a film. After the previews, there were printed notes from Mr. Warner's office making suggestions for changes.

How did your relationship with Jack Warner shape your career?

From 1940 to 1954, I was an editor. One evening the phone rings, it was Jack Warner's secretary. He said, "Rudi, there is going to be a story about you in the trades tomorrow. The boss said don't sign with any agents." So I dash out the next morning and here on the front page is, "Jack Warner gives Rudi Fehr and Dave Weisbart producer status."

I made an appointment to see Mr. Warner at eleven o'clock the next morning. I said, "I want to thank you, Mr. Warner, for thinking so highly of me to make me a producer. I'm very flattered, but I must be honest with you, I never dreamt of being a producer." He said, "Rudi, as long as I am here, you're here." He kept his word. I loved the guy, he was so wonderful to me. I knew how to handle him. I was even there ten years after he left. I was the only executive that was carried over by the new regime.

How did you come to work with Francis Coppola at Zoetrope Studios?

Francis Coppola directed two pictures for Warner Brothers, *Finian's Rainbow* and *The Rain People*. I was in charge of postproduction at that time and Mr. Coppola and I hit it off very well. When he heard that I was leaving Warner Brothers because of the mandatory retirement at age 65, he called me and said, "I am more interested in your ability than your age." He asked me to run postproduction for him at his newly acquired Zoetrope Studios in Hollywood. "You worked very closely with Jack Warner," Francis said, "I want to run this studio the way Jack Warner ran Warner Brothers." Occasionally, he would ask me how Warner did this or that.

How did you become an editor on One from the Heart?

Coppola was not crazy about the editor initially brought in to edit this picture. Without saying anything to him, he brought in another editor at a somewhat higher salary, which motivated the first editor to quit. Since we had to meet a deadline, it was necessary to bring in another editor. I presented a list with eight editors who were available at that time. Coppola looked at the list and he looked at me: "Rudi, you are an editor." I responded by telling him that I had not edited a film in 28 years. The next thing I knew I was in the cutting room. He's very talented, very insecure, very self-indulgent. I felt so badly that he lost everything he ever made. *One from the Heart* wiped him out. He got so burned when he took *One from the Heart* to a sneak preview in Seattle without titles, dissolves, the final music, or an ending. I said, "Francis, you're making a big mistake. You always want to know what Mr. Warner did. Mr. Warner said not to show the picture to anyone until you can put your best foot forward, when you have everything ready. You can't ask an amateur audience to tell you what's wrong with the picture. If you and I don't know what's wrong with the picture, we shouldn't be in this business." There was a reviewer in the audience and it was a devastating review. Theater owners wouldn't book the picture.

How did you get the job of editing Prizzi's Honor?

Paul Kohner, who was John Huston's agent, told me that Huston was looking for an editor for *Prizzi's Honor*, and he asked me if I could recommend somebody. I told him that whoever got the job would be a lucky guy, because it is a great experience to work with Huston. I explained that I had edited *Key Largo* for John and that it was a wonderful experience. He mentioned this to Huston and the next day I received a call from Paul. He said, "I think you've got yourself a job." I always wanted to work with my daughter, Kaja, who was following in her father's footsteps. I asked her if she wanted to be my assistant and she responded with an enthusiastic yes. After a few weeks of working together, she asked if she could edit a sequence. I had no objections and by the time we were ready to show the first cut to Mr. Huston, I realized that she had edited quite a few scenes. I therefore arranged for her to receive screen credit.

Would you consider yourself fast as an editor? Do you work quickly?

Yes, I am fast. I usually showed my first cut to the director within a week after he finished shooting. Action pictures take a little longer. It also depends on how many takes the director prints. I edited one film where I had to deal with up to eight prints on some scenes and they were long takes, running eight minutes. I am very conscientious; before I make a cut, I look at the material at least twice and that is time-consuming.

What equipment do you work with?

I work with a Moviola. Man is a creature of habit, and like many of my colleagues, I find the Moviola is the fastest of all the editing machines now available. I cut on two Moviolas. The first holds the scene I want to cut away from, and the second the scene I want to cut to. It is ideal for finding a match.

Do you start to feel the editing rhythms when you read a script?

I have the greatest respect for writers, their contribution to a movie is of utmost importance. Of course, I visualize the story when I read a script. Do I feel an editing rhythm? Not really. The director's concept of how to tell the story and mine may differ. Once I look at the film shot by the director, I can tell pretty much how I am going to edit the film. Writers suggest when there should be a close-up or a medium shot or a dissolve. That does not always work out. Sometimes the writer's suggestions coincide with my concept of what set-ups I should use, and sometimes they do not.

Have you ever discovered an error in a film after it was completed?

On *Helen of Troy*. We finished the picture. We ordered 800 prints, 400 were already made, when we get a telegram from a spotter doing the subtitles in Norway. The telegram read, "Is it intentional that in reel six at 820 feet, a plane flies through the scene?" I said, "The guy must be drunk. I've seen this picture at least 50 times, I never saw a plane." I run down the reel and sure enough there's a very short cut, maybe three feet, where a guy blows a trumpet fanfare to signal the start of the war, and a hundred pigeons fly off in all directions—way on top is an airplane. I never saw it, these things can happen. The first 400 prints went out with the plane. The next 400 didn't have the plane.

Do you think that an editor can have a style?

Editors interpret the director's style. No two directors would shoot a script the same way; therefore it is the editor's job to interpret the director's style, which makes it unlikely for an editor to develop his own style. For example, John Huston did not like to cut in motion. If somebody started to sit down in a medium shot and completed the sitting down in a close shot, Huston preferred for the person to sit down in one shot and to cut closer after he completed that motion. Other directors prefer cutting in motion.

Do you think there are major differences between the way editors in Los Angeles and editors in New York work?

Of course not. Editors get film created by the director and there is only one way to put a film together—that's the right way. You must know the values of the various shots that the director gives you. I haven't had many dealings with New York editors, but what I see on the screen is edited like any picture would be in London, Hollywood, or Munich.

What personality traits do you think are necessary to be a good editor?

When you edit a picture you should be happy with what you are doing. Don't become an editor if you're short-tempered. You need to have the ability to please the director, to get along with people, to listen, to express yourself. If the director wants changes and you think they are bad changes, you have to explain very clearly why you think they are not good for the picture. No editor should ever say, "I can't do that." You never say that, even if you can't do it or don't like it. Don't throw cold water over the ideas of the producer, director, or the head of the studio. Say, "That's great, I'll try that." Then you come back and say, "I tried it and it doesn't work." But don't arbitrarily say it doesn't work. You must always make them feel that it's their idea. That's where my diplomatic background comes in.

4

Ralph Winters

Ralph Winters' extensive career began at age 18 when his father, a tailor at MGM, helped him land a job as an assistant in the studio's editing department.

An MGM editor for over 30 years, he cut many of the studio's most prominent features, including *Gaslight*, *King Solomon's Mines*, *Seven Brides for Seven Brothers*, and *High Society*. His greatest achievement for MGM was *Ben Hur*, directed by William Wyler. The chariot sequence, which runs for eight minutes and took three months to construct, still thrills audiences three decades after its release. George Cukor, Billy Wilder, Fred Zinnemann, Stanley Donen, Robert Wise, Vincente Minnelli, and Norman Jewison are among the renowned directors with whom Ralph Winters has worked. He edited 13 films for Blake Edwards, including *The Pink Panther*, *Victor Victoria*, and *S.O.B.* The famous pie-throwing sequence in *The Great Race* is a sublime revelation of an editor's contribution to the filmmaking process.

Ralph Winters earned Academy Award nominations for *Quo Vadis?*, *Seven Brides for Seven Brothers*, *The Great Race*, and *Kotch*, and won Oscars for *King Solomon's Mines*, and *Ben Hur*.

With over 70 films to his credit, Winters is entering his sixth decade as a feature film editor.

1941	*Mr. and Mrs. North*
	The Penalty
	The People vs. Dr. Kildare

1942	*The Affairs of Martha*
	Dr. Gillespie's New Assistant
	Eyes in the Night
	Kid Glove Killer
1943	*Cry Havoc*
	Young Ideas
1944	*Gaslight*
	The Thin Man Goes Home
	The Youngest Profession
1945	*Our Vines Have Tender Grapes*
1946	*Boy's Ranch*
1947	*Killer McCoy*
	The Romance of Rosy Ridge
	Tenth Avenue Angel
1948	*Hills of Home*
1949	*Any Number Can Play*
	Little Women
	On the Town
1950	*King Solomon's Mines* (with Conrad Nervig)**
1951	*Quo Vadis?**
1953	*Kiss Me Kate*
	The Story of Three Loves
	Young Bess
1954	*Executive Suite*
	*Seven Brides for Seven Brothers**
1955	*Jupiter's Darling*
	Love Me or Leave Me
1956	*High Society*
	Tribute to a Bad Man
1957	*Jailhouse Rock*
	Man on Fire
1958	*The Sheepman*
1959	*Ben Hur* (with John W. Dunning)**
1960	*Butterfield 8*
1961	*Ada*
1963	*Dime with a Halo*
	Soldier in the Rain

1964	*The Pink Panther*
	A Shot in the Dark (supervising editor)
1965	*The Great Race**
1966	*What Did You Do in the War, Daddy?*
1967	*Fitzwilly*
	How to Succeed in Business Without Really Trying (with Allan Jacobs)
1968	*The Party*
	The Thomas Crown Affair (with Hal Ashby and Byron Brandt)
1969	*Gaily Gaily*
1970	*The Hawaiians* (with Byron Brandt)
1971	*Kotch**
1972	*Avanti!*
	The Carey Treatment
1973	*The Outfit*
1974	*The Front Page*
	The Spikes Gang
	Mr. Majestyk
1976	*King Kong*
1977	*Orca* (with John Bloom and Marion Rothman)
1979	*10*
1980	*American Success Company*
1981	*S.O.B.*
1982	*Victor Victoria*
1983	*The Curse of the Pink Panther* (with David Beesley)
	The Man Who Loved Women
1984	*Micki and Maude*
1985	*Big Trouble* (with Donn Cambern)
1987	*Let's Get Harry*
1988	*Moving*

*Acadamy Award nomination for best achievement in film editing.
**Academy Award for best achievement in film editing.

Do you think the general public understands what an editor does on a feature film?

The general public doesn't understand a thing about editing and I don't think they should. They can sit down and look at a movie and say, "What a beautifully photographed picture!" or "Those are beautiful sets!" They couldn't go and do it, but they recognize it, so they can make a judgment. As laymen they don't know anything about how the picture went together or what contributions the editor, director, producer, or executives may have made to the editing.

When an audience is watching a film, should they be aware of the editing?

I don't think that people should be too aware of the editing process. When you sit down to look at a movie you should be able to look at it as one piece of cloth, one piece of film. You shouldn't be conscious of cutting any more than you would be of a fine underscore. Certainly, people who want to get into the industry, and moviemakers themselves, should be interested in the editing process. All people who start to make movies know they can't photograph a scene, score it, write it, art direct, or set-decorate it, but they all suddenly become editors. There are some people who don't do that. They let the editor do his work; that makes the editing process a little more interesting and challenging. You're constantly dealing in personalities, politicking with them, ingratiating yourself, liking people, disliking people, trying to find compatibility. Those are all important parts of editing a film.

How did you become a film editor?

I worked at the old Consolidated film lab at Melrose for a few months. My father was a tailor at MGM. He became acquainted with the head of the editing department and got me a job as an assistant editor. I was only 18, so you might say I was born and raised there. I learned my craft and spent over 30 years there. My craft has been good to me. I've raised my family, earned my living, and always enjoyed it, especially when I'm working with nice, talented people. Then it's a real kick, a lot of fun.

During the studio era the dissolve was commonly used as part of the editing style. Was it up to the editor to decide if a dissolve should be used?

The editor had a big hand in it, but it was never left up to him 100 percent. If the script read "Dissolve to" because it was passage of time, or to get somebody from here to there, then you put a dissolve in. Today they cut a lot, they don't dissolve. I was looking at an old picture of mine last night that had a lot of dissolves. If you were doing that picture today, you wouldn't put dissolves in. Audiences are smarter today, they're wiser and accept things. It's from looking at a lot of television.

In Gaslight *Charles Boyer alternates between tormenting Ingrid Bergman and being kind to her as a way of driving her mad. As the editor, was it a concern of yours to keep this balanced and not go over the top?*

I don't think it was very much of a concern. That material pretty much played itself out and was developed more in the directing than in the cutting room. You can emphasize and de-emphasize emotional scenes, not use a close-up if you were going a little too much this way or that, or use one if you need a little bit more. It was easily discernible in putting together the picture if you were going over too much one way or the other. If two people were playing a scene and that held up, then there was no need to cut into close-ups or intercut to emphasize it. *Gaslight* was pretty much a director's movie.

How did you work with George Cukor? Did he pretty much leave you alone to cut the picture?

Yes, certainly for the first cut. Then, of course, we went in and started to fool with it, changing and moving. I've been lucky in that respect; most of the directors I've worked with left me alone. I put the picture together. I'm not going to show anything to anybody unless I feel it's presentable. Sometimes I've had to keep people waiting. Once I have done that, I'm certainly going to give the director everything he wants. I've had my shot.

How long does it take you to complete a first cut?

It depends on the quality and quantity of the picture. First of all, you cut a sequence, it might go into the middle of the movie. When you put it together you're looking at a vignette, a tiny short subject. When that sequence goes into the middle of the picture in its proper continuity, it takes on a little different look. It may be a little long, some of the things you did now didn't work because of things you've forgotten in the earlier part of the picture. Maybe you don't need to hit this moment quite as hard, you can pull back and play it out more. It really is a question of put and take. Otherwise, you could take a picture when they finish shooting, run it for the director, stick it right in the lab for sound effects, music, and negative cutting, and you'd be finished in two or three weeks. The fastest picture I ever worked on took three months. It takes time, you've got to stop and do it. Somebody gets an idea of how to do something and that idea might take a couple of days to do, and then it might not be any good. I have put sequences together that are never touched, but if I've had one sequence a picture where they left the cutting alone, I'd say I was batting very high.

How does the material influence the final shape of a sequence?

Take *King Solomon's Mines*—there was a stampede in that picture which really earned the Academy Award. One of the cameramen was fooling around and shot a lot of 16mm stuff on his own, all kinds of wonderful pieces of film of the animals running. We looked at it and the producer, who had been an editor at one time, said, "Gee, we could have a stampede here." It was 16mm that we blew up and it developed into something really great. That was a picture that was really made in the cutting room and put together with spit and baling wire. I'll take my share of the credit but no more, just my share.

In High Society *the cutting seemed minimal. You used a lot of master shots; was there a lot of coverage?*

A lot of the material that you were looking at in *High Society* was not covered. Chuck Walters directed it. He didn't print a lot of film, but he was a good director and did well with people. He rehearsed quite a bit. Because of the quality of the story and the music, it carried out pretty well. He rarely shot close-ups. In a picture like *High Society*, which is a people picture, not an action-filled picture, Chuck Walters played out many scenes in full shots or two shots and they played. He never went in and made close-ups. That's a pet theory of mine. I say to the younger directors that the thing to do is work on a scene and get a performance; never mind about how you are going to cover it and how it's going to get cut. Take Billy Wilder, who camera-cuts. He will stage and shoot a scene in such a way that the important action is taking place near the camera all the time; it's all on one piece of film. Then he'll cut to somebody over here, start a whole new thing and bring them over to join that person. It's all in the staging, isn't it? Another director may stage it differently.

Is it wrong to believe that all editors want to make a lot of cuts?

A good editor will choose the path which gives him the most amount of material. It depends on the way it was shot. I've had sequences that had three, four, or five angles and we played it all in one angle, because when we looked at the film everyone felt that the scene sustained itself. Any time a scene sustains itself, you want to let it play, because the people in the audience have a chance to relate to whomever they want up on the screen. I can have my eye shift back and forth where it wants instead of being directed by close-ups. If you are playing a two-shot and you can make it better by intercutting close-ups because those performances are better, then you should do it. If you're given a mediocre scene and you have no coverage, that's the way it's going to play.

What was it like to work on Ben Hur?

That picture was out of the ordinary. We're not talking about the normal kind of movies that are made every year. *Ben Hur* was a big project, it took five years to prepare it for shooting and 18 months to do.

Were you involved in the preproduction?

I was involved a lot in the shooting. One time Wyler called me down to the set. He was getting ready to shoot the moment in the picture where the two friends, Messala and Ben Hur, threw spears into the wall. Willie said, "How would you shoot this?" I said to myself, "Jesus, the great Willie Wyler is calling me down to ask how I would shoot it." So

I made some suggestions, I said shoot it this way and that way. He thought about it for a minute and he said, "That stinks," but he shot it that way and other ways, too. He shot a lot of film. Wyler had a tremendous amount of drag in the industry. He already had been an extremely successful director. He didn't have anybody sitting on his shoulders from upstairs telling him he was spending too much money, because he didn't care. He went along and shot the picture the way he wanted. He shot many sequences with different staging and coverage. He shot and printed a lot of film. Wyler would throw one version right out if he didn't like it when he looked at it. So that was an unusual picture, in that respect. We had a lot of film, about 600,000 feet of rushes.

Ben Hur *was co-edited with John W. Dunning. How did you work together?*

I started first. I fell so far behind and there was so much other material to be cut that we called him over to help. John and I knew there was going to be a lot of pressure put on both of us and perhaps Wyler was going to pit us against each other. We discussed this before he came on and decided that we weren't going to let anything get in our way. If somebody tried to start something between us, we would discuss it further. He had his sequences to cut and I had mine. As we went along I would say, "You take that one and I'll take this one." We worked very well together personally. We were always behind, even when we came home from Rome. There was something like 30,000 feet of film on the picture that needed to be cut together.

The chariot race is a tour de force of action cutting. How did you put it together?

Yes, that was really something; the material was there. I worked on that sequence for three straight months, I never touched another piece of film on the picture. I had a big chart, about the size of the wall, with the laps of the race. I entered the shots as I got them so I'd know where in the hell I was, because they didn't shoot it in continuity. It was extremely rough on the first go together which was around 1100 feet. We got all the elements in it and we pared the actual race down to eight minutes—that's a little over 700 feet.

What did that long version look like?

All of the elements were there but it didn't have the pizazz, the tempo, and pacing. You have to start to build the rhythm. The cuts would start to get shorter and shorter. You might wind up with an insert of the spokes that was a few frames long, a split second on the screen. Certainly, the first time you put it together, you wouldn't put it in that short. There was a lot of trial and error. There was a lot of coverage that wasn't used, because it was mainly a duplication of a particular action. They shot material with the doubles, then they found that both the actors could drive the chariots, so they went in and made closer angles where we could actually recognize the principals. That created a lot of extra footage. I started pruning out the shots with the doubles and started putting in those with the principals.

Did you work with sound as you were cutting it?

The race itself was shot without sound, but we had a big sound track of 5,000 people yelling that we used to run against it. It would give us a feeling of sound until all the other elements of the race were built into it. There were a lot of units, a lot of tracks.

Do you have any theories on how to cut action scenes like this? Are there basic principles?

Yes, I do. The man who produced *Ben Hur* and *King Solomon's Mines*, Sam Zimbalist, was one of the greatest editors of action sequences that I have ever known. I learned things from him which through the years have held me in good stead, so that I could put an action scene together, assuming that I had the proper material to work with. It's got to be dramatized with the actors. You've got to hook the audience by making them pull for or against something. That's dramatization and that's the secret. It's having conflict between two people; that's a very important element in entertainment. You just don't want to look at a thing blandly. In the chariot race, it's just a bunch of chariots running around the track, but you had elements there. First of all, you have two men who were great, great friends and became great, great enemies. Then you had the sheik up in the stands and he brought the humor and the counterpoint which made that such a great sequence.

For the stampede in *King Solomon's Mines* you were involved with people in danger, we were worried and concerned for them. Every time an animal jumped, it made you worry a little bit, as opposed to putting the camera on and seeing animals running through the jungle without somebody being in danger. If you can introduce that element in your sequence and dramatize it with intercutting the proper way, then you've really got something good going and that's what you have to strive for. It takes years to learn to do that.

Was it especially rewarding to have won an Academy Award for editing Ben Hur?

Yes, it was very rewarding. I once had an argument with a friend of mine who was president of the Academy. My argument is that an award is really the achievement of the picture. He claims that it is the achievement of the individual. I still think that I'm right. A picture like *Ben Hur* won 11 awards out of 12. I can speak for the editing. It's safe to say whoever may have edited that picture would have won an Academy Award, but I'd like to think every picture I work on is better because I worked on it. I have too much experience and I've made too many contributions for it to be otherwise. I would entitle myself that much ego. I don't need to keep patting myself on the back and I don't need people to be telling me; I know.

You had a long association with Blake Edwards. What was that relationship like?

I did 13 pictures for Blake. We had a great relationship. He's a very bright, astute, talented man and he understands your problems. Blake will make some suggestion that will get you off the spot in terms of getting the picture together. I looked at the rushes one day and went down to the set and said to Blake, "I think you need close-ups in this scene." He said, "Okay, I'll shoot them." I said, "We'll look at the rushes." He said, "No, I don't have to look at them, I'll go ahead and shoot the close-ups." He was in that set, so he shot them. He had confidence in me. Later, if I said, "I was wrong, we didn't really need the close-ups, so let's not use them," he'd say, "Fine." That's the way to make movies. Where his editor was concerned, he had no ego, and where he was concerned, I never had any ego. He is a very dispassionate guy when it comes to cutting. That's very important in a director: to be able to wear another hat, and no matter how much he killed himself shooting something on the set, to say, "It doesn't work in the picture, let's take it out."

In The Great Race *there is a pie fight sequence with multiple action. Was it difficult to maintain continuity?*

That was very, very tough. A couple of things we did weren't planned for in the shooting. There were so many elements in the sequence. It was starting something, going away, and then coming back for the finish, to develop it a little bit. This one was throwing pies, that one was throwing pies, this one was getting them in the face. It was all kind of happening at the same time. Trying to get the timing in its proper form so that you could keep everybody "alive," as we say, was tough in that sequence.

How do you edit a sequence that involves intercutting?

When you've got the film in your hands and you're first putting it together, intercutting is a very difficult thing to do. Sometimes I'll put a sequence together knowing it has to be intercut with another person or location. I won't intercut until I get the main body together. If you try to intercut when you're first putting it together, you can get so bollixed up you don't know what you're doing. There was a sequence in *Orca* where there was a house built out onto the water. Part of the house was on stilts and the whale was swimming back and forth smashing it. There was a long shot where you could see the whole house and the whale. In those pieces you could see the house slowly disintegrating until finally the whole house fell into the water. I cut what was going on inside the house and never cut to the outside at all. After I got that the way I wanted it, I ran the sequence and spotted the long shot. I let the house slip so much in a cut here, then later let it slip a little bit more, so that it timed in just right. That's the way you should work something. It's like a boxing match, if two fighters are in the ring and they're fighting, you know you've got to use doubles and close-ups. You've got one of their sweethearts sitting in the audience. You've got to cut to that sweetheart once in a while and you don't do that right away. You cut the best pieces of the fight and when you really get in a jam, maybe that's the place to cut and do it. You introduce those kinds of things later in the process. I think editors who intercut right away sometimes find they're going up a blind alley and get trapped.

Did the chess sequence in The Thomas Crown Affair *follow the script or did you heighten the sexual tension in the scene by the way you cut it?*

I'm sure the director, Norman Jewison, had it in mind, but maybe not cut for cut. That sequence had no continuity at all. You could have used any piece to open or to close it. I studied the film very carefully for a day or two before I even cut a piece of film, because I knew if I didn't do it in a very organized way, I could get trapped. I probably got lucky with it in trying to get the most erotic and suggestive things at a point where they began to mean something and not to have shot my wad at the beginning. That's a very erotic sequence. I was not really the editor on that picture; the editor was Hal Ashby. The one sequence I did do was the chess game. Norman Jewison was so happy with it that he insisted that I have a credit on it.

What does the term "cheat" mean in editing?

Most of the time things are shot with one camera. Nobody does anything twice the same way, so the trick is to get in and out at those times when you don't think an audience is going to be disturbed. I've jumped people clear across the room, the audience doesn't even blink an eye. It takes a long time to learn this. Young editors say, "I couldn't cut there, because I didn't have a match." I say, "What match are you talking about? I don't see that and the audience doesn't see that." You've got to learn where the audience's eye is going to be. I once had a young apprentice, a little smart-ass, wonderful kid. He'd sit in the projection room and start picking on all of the cuts: "That doesn't match, Ralph." I said, "If you're going to study the corner of the screen, a lot of things are going to change. There's going to be a cigarette in the right hand and in the next cut it will be in the left hand." In a particular scene, I went from the long shot to a closer angle, and on that cut the character completely turned around, but you weren't watching and I knew it would never disturb an audience because their eye was on another part of the scene; it had to be. Try pulling your eyes off of movement—you can't do it. It's as if somebody shoots a gun outside this door, you and

I are going to look off, and nothing in the world is going to keep us from doing it. Movement attracts the eye, sound attracts the ear. So I ran the sequence and asked him what he thought of it. He said, "I think it looks pretty good." I said, "How about where he jumps around?" I had him look at the sequence again and he couldn't believe his eyes. I said, "Now there's a lesson for you in learning where the audience's eyes are going to be; you put them where you want them to be. They'll watch action, they'll watch movement."

Young editors will make matches on a small movement, you can't do that. You've got to make it when somebody does a broad movement. They can have a wig on and you won't know it. In *Victor Victoria* there was a scene where Julie Andrews has dinner with Jim Garner. She puts a cigar in her mouth and he lights it. Then we cut because she's going to cough and we wanted to be in a close-up for that. In one cut she had the cigar in her fingers and in the other cut she had it in her mouth. It was a bad cut and I never saw it because of other movement in the scene. One day one of the sound fellows came to me and said, "Would it worry you if she had the cigar in her mouth now?" He was being very careful because he didn't want me to get upset with him. I said, "It would worry me to death." He said, "That's what you got." I ran to the cutting room and I couldn't believe my eyes, Blake and I never saw it. It's the secret of movement. You have to learn to recognize when you try a cheat and you get knocked out of your own seat, that it's not going to work and you can't get away with it—but you'd be surprised how much you can get away with.

How do you handle interpersonal relationships in the cutting room?

I don't have to negotiate with my assistant editor every time I want something done a certain way in the cutting room, and I don't think that producers or directors should have to negotiate with me. They have ideas, good or bad, and you've got to bow to their judgment. If you don't have any respect for them, then you're not going to do good work and you're not going to get the best out of them. That's a very important thing about cutting.

How would you define the editor's contribution on a film?

I don't think the editor has as much to say as he thinks he has. An editor doesn't make a picture, the material really has to be there. Somebody has to make it and when I hear some of my colleagues say, "Well, gee, the guy wouldn't let my adrenalin and creative juices flow," that's a lot of malarkey, because what you've got in your hand is work that somebody else has already done, good or bad. There are no miracles in film. You're working with material you have been handed. I have worked, striven, and beat my brains out, and sometimes I can't make a sequence look good, because it just isn't there. Maybe I can take it, cut it, and present it a little bit differently than the next editor. That's where you can bring your talent in, getting the most out of what you are given.

When you're running a picture, the editor might see the chance for a switch in continuity quicker than the producer or director who are involved in the original writing. The editor has the chance to study the film, to know and learn it a heck of a lot better than the director or the producer. If the editor really wants to put his mind to the project and think about it, that's where he can make wonderful contributions and embellish what has been done. That to me is creativity. You are working with something that is already there, but when you can take a sequence or a section of the story and switch it around, put the sunset here instead of there, even with minor things, the whole piece begins to take on a glow. That's the creative part of editing.

What advice do you give people about editing?

One of the things I tell young people is that it's important to have a personality, you cannot be a lump. You've got to have something to say. You've got to teach yourself to think about the movie and make ongoing suggestions. If they refuse nine of them, don't be abashed, because the tenth time they'll say, "That's a great idea." You have to ingratiate yourself with people because if they like you, your mistakes are laughs, but if they don't like you, you can't do anything right. If you're going to become an editor and you're not that way, you have to recognize it, teach yourself, or get help. "Hey, tell me what I did, did I say something wrong?" I used to be on the phone with the director, he'd call me at night or we'd kick something around over the weekend. I'd tape the conversation and I'd listen very carefully to the tape later to see if I behaved myself properly, if I expressed myself properly. I did it because I wanted him to be open to what I was going to say. When you don't talk properly to people they get closed up. That's all part of the job. You have to deal with just terrible frustrations. On the other hand, there are times when you're not hitting it right, and if you can sit and really work it out, maybe there is a solution. One of the secrets of a good editor, when he puts a scene together and takes it into the projection room, is to recognize if there's a problem with it, or that it's not as good as it can be, or that it is good, and not to start fiddling with it. Editing is very tough, challenging work. When it goes well, it's very gratifying, especially when you have made good contributions to the film.

5

David Bretherton

David Bretherton began his career in the 1940s at 20th Century–Fox where he assisted many distinguished editors, including Robert E. Simpson and William Reynolds. On returning from the service after World War II, he became the youngest member of the Fox editorial team.

After 20 years at Fox, Bretherton cultivated a highly successful independent career, cutting such films as *Save the Tiger*, *Coma*, and *Cabaret*, for which he received an Oscar. In the 1970s he also developed a strong reputation as a film doctor and frequently is called in to recut films in trouble.

Bretherton's accomplishments have spanned decades of notable collaborations with George Stevens, Henry Hathaway, George Cukor, Vincente Minnelli, John Frankenheimer, Bob Fosse, John Avildsen, and Michael Crichton.

David Bretherton's long and varied career is testimony to his tenacity and versatility.

1955	*The Living Swamp* (with Robert Fritch)
1956	*The Bottom of the Bottle*
	Hilda Crane
	The King and Four Queens
	The Dark Wave
1957	*Bernardine*
	Peyton Place
	Three Brave Men
	Valerie

1958	*Ten North Frederick*
1959	*The Diary of Anne Frank* (with William Mace and Robert Swink)
1960	*The Facts of Life* (with Frank Bracht)
	Let's Make Love
1961	*Return to Peyton Place*
1962	*State Fair*
1963	*Empire*
1965	*The Sandpiper*
	The Train (with Gabriel Rongier)
1968	*Villa Rides*
1969	*On a Clear Day You Can See Forever*
1970	*Lovers and Other Strangers* (with Sidney Katz)
1971	*Fool's Parade* (with Robert E. Simpson)
1972	*Cabaret***
	No Drums, No Bugles
1973	*Save the Tiger*
	Slither
1974	*Westworld*
	Bank Shot
1975	*The Man in the Glass Booth*
	High Velocity
1976	*Harry and Walter Go to New York* (with Don Guidice and Fredric Steinkamp)
	That's Entertainment, Part 2 (with David Blewitt, Bud Friedgen, and Peter C. Johnson)
	Silver Streak
1977	*Silent Partner*
1978	*Coma*
	Stoney Island
1979	*The Great Train Robbery*
	Winter Kills
	Caddyshack (supervising editor, with William Carruth)
1980	*The Formula* (with John G. Avildsen and John Carter)

                        The Big Red One (with Morton Tubor)

1982   *Cannery Row*

                        The Best Little Whorehouse in Texas
                            (with Nicholas Eliopoulos, Walt
                            Hannemann, Pembroke J. Herring,
                            and Jack Hofstra)

1983   *Man, Woman and Child*

1984   *Love Lines* (with Fred Chulack)

1985   *Baby—Secret of the Lost Legend* (with
                            Howard Smith)

                        Clue (with Richard Haines)

1986   *Lionheart*

1987   *The Pick-Up Artist* (with Angelo Cor-
                            rao)

1989   *Sea of Love*

**Academy Award for best achievement in film editing.

How did you become a film editor?

Mowing lawns. I had just gotten out of high school and I was mowing a lawn for a guy on Motor Avenue in Cheviot Hills. He came out and paid me 25 cents and said, "Ever think about being in the motion picture business?" I said, "No, not really." He said, "If you show up Monday at 20th Century–Fox, they are going to have an interview for somebody to work in the editing department." So Monday I was there bright and early. I knocked on the door, the secretary said, "Come in," and I said, "I'm here for the interview." As I came in, the man who I had been mowing lawns for came in the other door. His name was Hector Dodds and he was the head of editorial. He said, "You've had your interview, you start right now." I was there for 20 years almost to the day.

How was the editorial department at Fox set up?

We had 18 editors. Nine were on the A side doing color pictures for Zanuck and nine were on the B side doing black and white pictures for Lou Shriber. It was very well organized. We had a screening once a day. All the executives would come and see their dailies. All of the production managers, unit managers, and editors were there. You had some very fine editors. They called me "The Kid" because I was the youngest one there. I worked with the musical editor, Bob Simpson, for a long time. He would let me cut scenes. He would say, "Don't touch anything you've cut, just move the track four frames." I was waiting until somebody stopped talking before I cut. By retarding the track, the tail end of a word could carry over the cuts. It was the same length, but it looked faster and better. That doesn't work all of the time, but he told me when it did and when it didn't. We never saw a director or a producer in the editing room. If you got more than four or five notes for changes on the whole picture, you weren't doing your job. You would run that for the director, then the producer, and they would have their arguments. Zanuck told me never to get in the middle, and I never got in the middle.

How were musical scenes cut at Fox?

We had a complete music department. You prescored every musical number; it was a complete, final arrangement. Very seldom did we do anything with a click track or a simple instrumental. The playbacks were established with singing voices as well as the background. You would get a combine track of that with your dailies. On occasion you would have a click track when they were going to add dialogue or if they were going to extend the scene.

What is a combine track?

The voice was mixed with the music at the correct level.

What is a click track?

A click track gives you the beat in the same tempo.

Like a metronome?

Sure. I used a click track when I didn't want to waste the time with an extra track. You find sync and you hit it from there.

What is your approach to cutting scenes with music?

You have to know where you want to start and stop and for what reasons. What story am I telling? What emotion am I going for? Is it a waltz? Is it a tango? That has to be established. In ballroom dancing, it's the smoothness and the sweep of it. After you've first established it, you go in close, you're in faces. A lot of actors are not great dancers so it makes you more inventive as an editor. My basic approach to cutting music is, I don't want anybody to see a cut. I don't want them to be aware that the picture is edited. You want to get it on the swing. You don't see where I cut. When you cut a musical, you cut ahead of the beat, just one or two frames, because your ear is instantaneous, your eye takes three or four frames to adjust. I don't want to match the face, only the movement. She turns her head, then he turns his head, and we're into the next cut without even noticing. It's beautiful and graceful.

You worked with George Stevens on The Diary of Anne Frank. *How was the opening montage accomplished?*

George Stevens gave this to me as a challenge. I had seen hour after hour of stock footage of the occupation and the concentration camps. It took Stevens about two weeks to make a selected run of 147 feet. I had 22 shots in the montage. There were as many as five images on the screen at the same time. I had to draw up yellow sheets for the optical man. I marked where I wanted this shot at 10 percent to here, the dissolve was to be 20 feet to get out of it, that one would fade out in X number of feet, this one we would fade in at this point. I had 10 percent of this one, 20 percent of that one, and 40 percent of that one. It ended up to be 100 percent, all different layers coming in and out of each other. I am very proud of it because George Stevens never touched it, he never moved one sprocket. The optical man, Armand Allen, could hardly believe it. I was thrilled that he bought it the first time out.

George Stevens was known as a director who shot a tremendous amount of film. How did this challenge you as an editor?

Stevens would shoot the master and all the corresponding elements of everything around the clock from twelve, three, six and nine; then you had to figure it out. I would cut four versions of the scene, each one utilizing what I could, until he said, "I like the beginning of this, the middle of that, and I like the end of that." I'd say, "That's a direct reverse," and he would say, "Find a way." So he would leave it up to me to find a way to get to the direct reverse. It could be a head turn or a lot of things. It taught me how to do it. You absorbed all the things you'd learned. He told me that every scene had to be interesting and had to have a challenge. In the Hanukkah sequence, Stevens purposely put a candle on one side of the table. Now how do you not make the candle jump from one side of the scene to the other side? It drove me out of my gourd. I had to figure out a way to meet those kinds of challenges.

What systems were used to keep track of all of the coverage?

We had a projection room and an editing room on the set. Every day you'd have to run a master for Stevens of each angle of the scene he was working on: twelve, three, six, and nine o'clock. This was to give him an orientation so he could shoot a tie-in to the scene. The editorial secretary had to keep notes. One of our assistants did nothing but take the head and the tail of each scene and mount them in a book. We had light boxes in the projection room to check them. We had so many dailies, anywhere from 11 to 19 reels a day. We projected two reels at the same time on one screen with counters. Stevens would say, "Gee, that looks great!" and you would say to yourself, "What was great? Was it the seagull flying, or was it Anne Frank's close-up while she's writing in the diary, or was it the combination of both?" You would take down the footages so you'd know that was a good piece of film. It was a wonderful experience to work with a man who was so absorbed with the film.

What was it like to work with Bob Fosse on Cabaret?

Bob never really spoke to me through the shooting of the whole picture. He had to leave Germany the day he finished shooting, otherwise the picture was going to be taxed by the German government. He said, "I'll see you in New York." I got my assistant, David Ramirez, to join me in New York from Los Angeles. Everything was edited except for one dance number. I had done the best I knew how. Fosse came in after we'd been there two or three weeks and said, "Well, we'd better look at this stuff." The next morning we put the film down in the projection room and he said, "I'll sit back here." I sat in front, I didn't want to disturb him. We ran the picture. When it was over he got up and as he was going out the door he said, "My God, I feel sick," and he walked off. I turned to David and said, "My God, I must have really screwed up. I don't know what to say to you, Davy. I'm so sorry to have brought you all the way out here, maybe this is it." The next morning I was in the cutting room waiting, I didn't know where else to go. Bob showed up and said, "Look, did I disturb you yesterday? I didn't mean to say that. I thought I was going to see dailies." I said, "What the hell was I supposed to be doing in Germany for six months?" He said, "Can we run it again?"

What were some of the changes Fosse made in your first cut after you looked at it together?

At one point he said, "In this dance number, why did you use those takes?" I said, "Well, it's a schlocky, third-rate German nightclub, and the script said the girls would kick too high or too low and they would miss steps, so I used those takes for the effect of the story." He said, "The most important thing to me as a choreographer, is for *that* toe to hit *that* floor at *that* particular split second. Can you fix it?" I said, "Sure, I've got all the takes." I marked them one, two, three, four, five, and I used five because one was perfect. That was stupidity on my part, I should have used the perfect takes, then he would have said, "Let's slop it up a bit." From then on he never came in the cutting room. I didn't understand this man because he didn't communicate, he didn't try to talk to me. He would just be this panther pacing back and forth in the halls for six hours. After we'd been there for about three or four weeks I said, "Bob, I just wish you'd come into the room and sit down and talk to me, because sometimes I might need a little back-up. You can make a quick decision. I'm fiddling with three or four pieces of film and I don't know which one you really prefer." He said, "Can I tell you something? The reason I don't sit down is that I've got the worst case of hemorrhoids anyone ever had." All of a sudden, all the walls, all the noncommunication just dissolved. God, I loved that man. I respected him, but I was afraid of him. When he told me that, he became human.

What were the editing facilities like while you were in Germany?

The difficult thing was that Germany had no facilities for coding the film so I had an apprentice hand-code the film every two feet. She couldn't sync it up musically, because she didn't have the time. She used to be there until three o'clock in the morning. She was my right arm, she saved my ass, because the film had code numbers on it in yellow ink. Nothing was coded to playback. I had no clue other than the set track. It was mostly instrumentals. Any time I started anything, I had to get the same instrumental beat as the set track to get it in sync.

It came out well, that's the main thing. You rise to the competition. You don't say, "I can't do this," and get yourself into a frenzy. You say, "This is what I've got to do," and you do it. It's no big heroic thing, you just accept it.

Throughout the film there are close-ups of Joel Grey intercut with dramatic scenes to comment on the action. Did the use of those shots come out of the editing process?

Joel Grey was brilliant in his performance, but there were some things which were pretty vulgar to me. Like he would cop a feel off Sally Bowles as she went on stage and he would wag his tongue. It seemed too crass and a bit much, so I used a close-up of those shots as opposed to the whole scene, as a comment, just to keep him "alive." It became a scene that had importance, it was a piece of evil as opposed to being a graphic vulgar thing.

Did any of the musical scenes go through substantial changes during the editing process?

The slap dance originally only lasted for 20 seconds. When Fosse saw the scene with the Nazis beating up the manager of the club, he said, "There's too much of the fight. Do you think there is any way we could use the slap dance again?" Without thinking I said, "Sure, we'll give it a shot." Fosse always shot with more than one camera and I figured there must be other angles you could do something with, so it wouldn't look exactly the same. Instead of just having the fight, we intercut it with the slap dance; that made it more important. The slap dance is over two times its regular length, using different angles of the same film. I doubled, tripled, and quadrupled up the track; it's the same music.

There is a very effective cut at the end of the film when Liza Minnelli sings the title song. You go from a long shot of her holding the last note of the song with her head thrown back, to a great close-up with the colored lights spinning.

You find the button. In that instance you mentally cut the end before the front. You know where you want to end up. You know you've got to drop back for the impact when you cut in. You think about it. You say, "What would satisfy me?" It's not to satisfy the director, it's to satisfy me; that's what you're paid to do.

You had done many musicals before doing Cabaret. *What did you learn about musicals from Bob Fosse?*

He was thinking so far ahead of me. On the musicals of the Fox era, you would have a music start mark and a playback from the set. It would pick it up on a certain thing and the take would go on for 35 to 55 feet. Fosse shot Liza Minnelli with five cameras. You had to cut away to something to sustain it. He was so intelligent and well-versed, that he gave me all these cutaways. There would be a close-up of a girl or one of the dancers, there was all this coverage. First you cut it normally, the simple graceful way, because I believe that simplicity is the key for most pictures. The dances looked dull, you're trying to build up Sally Bowles and make it more exciting. All of a sudden I would say, "I'll cut on the half beat," and then Fosse says, "That's not enough. That was a good look that guy had with the flash of his head." You'd cut that in. Every cut you make changes another cut. Then all of a sudden this opens up a new way of doing something. I learned that nothing is impossible. Film is so flexible and all of a sudden something happens not in your head, but in your stomach, and you just know that it's good.

Have you ever removed a scene for content rather than technical reasons?

Early on in *Save the Tiger*, after the scene where Jack Lemmon talks with his wife about his kid going to school in Switzerland, he gets in his car and goes and sees his mistress. My response to it was that I didn't want to see him going to a mistress, because it made him some-body I didn't like, and I wanted to like and understand him. It just said, I don't like him. When I looked at it I just turned around and said, "I can't take that scene." I guess I was not alone because we took it out.

You have a reputation of being a film doctor, an editor who comes on to projects that are in trouble. How did this begin?

The first film I did as a film doctor was *Lovers and Other Strangers*, directed by Sy Howard. David Susskind was the producer. A wonderful editor, Sidney Katz, was editing it, and he had three versions of the same picture in the script notes, one in red lines, one in green, and one in black. He was listening to both Susskind and Sy Howard. It was a conglomeration of junk. Sid was doing his job and they called me and said, "This picture doesn't make sense, do something about it." I went back to the original script they bought. Simplicity. You make the best story out of that script. I don't give a damn whether it's this guy's version or that guy's version. I took everything apart. I didn't want to be biased by something, because it's easy to get lazy and say, "Oh, that works pretty well." I had it all spliced back as dailies would be. I took every scene apart and went back to basics. I went through it in my way because all editors' rhythms are different. If you change one cut, it affects every subsequent cut; you end up changing three or four. All of a sudden, my reputation as a film doctor began, because it went out and made all of this money, then somebody else gave me a picture and another picture to doctor.

Does a good script make your job easier?

Oh, sure. Don't get in the way of the storytelling; make yourself as unobtrusive as possible.

What is the hardest kind of scene to cut?

For me, reaction scenes take the longest time because I want it to be perfect. There will just be something that disturbs me and I say, "Why can't I get that?" It's not in your head, it's in the gut. From my head I know there's a problem; from my gut I feel when it's right.

What equipment and techniques do you use?

When I work, I stand up at the Moviola because I feel it through my hands. It goes through my hands. I have a brake. I can almost close my eyes, listen to the dialogue, and I'll hit the mark where I've got to be on the next cut. While the KEM is a marvelous thing to re-edit on, the button may be one or two frames away from where I want to be; that isn't good enough. When you look at it on the KEM or the Steenbeck, it's so smooth, it's a fait accompli. I have to start a Moviola physically with my hand on the brake and my foot on the pedal, I'm not just standing back there and looking at it. I don't put it on automatic when I'm running it. I put it on my foot. When I say, "No, that's no good," I fix it right there. I won't go past that cut until I've got it fixed. I don't cut ahead of myself. I don't cut the end of a scene, then the beginning, and then cut the middle, because it has a flow and I've got to make that transition from first gear to second gear. What cut do I use there? How am I going to get into it?

I reconstitute all of my own trims, because sometimes I get my best ideas when I'm doing it. I roll all my own trims, because I want to say, "I'm finished with this shot. I've gotten everything I can out of it." This is kind of a psych job I do on myself. Yes, that's everything I can do with that one and I let it go. I just do it automatically. I think about what it is I'm holding. I'm thinking about every piece as I put it back. I cut a sequence, then I put it away for three days, five days, sometimes a week. I'll cut seven or eight sequences and I'll have them all up on a rack, numbered. I'll run through them and I'll keep all of the trims for that scene in my room. As soon as I've gone through it that second time, all of the trims go back to the assistant's room. Then all of the new stuff comes into my room. That way I know I've done my best.

What are your feelings about how the film editor is treated in the industry?

I don't think that the editor has the respect that he deserves. I have it written in my contract that I get exactly the same treatment as the cinematographer. If he gets class A–1 transport, I get class A–1 transport. If he gets a room in a decent hotel, I get a room in a decent hotel. I know the hell I go through internally, on a daily basis, because what I do is going to be seen on the great big screen just the same way as his stuff is going to be seen. I can't say, "Oops, can we have another take of that?" What they see is what they've got; I have no room for mistakes because I've had the chance to fix all of my mistakes. I may not get the same salary, but I want to be treated and accepted the same way. I think we both contribute exactly the same amount to what you ultimately see on the screen. The responsibility is certainly more long-lived for the editor. When I see that the secretary has a better office than three people in a normal editing room, it makes me furious. My contract calls for a room with a window and I work alone. My assistants are equal to me in every respect, they get a room of their own. I do not have a director, producer, or a star in my cutting room when I'm working. If they want to see film, I'll give them my twin KEMs and they can go play to their heart's content. I'll watch it with them, but I will not edit with them. My magic is my magic. They don't ask the cameraman, "Why did you put the light up there?" They'll say, "You've got too much light." They don't go up there and watch him change the goddamn light. I don't want them to come in and watch me change a cut. If I've got a brain in my head I'll do it, if I don't, get rid of me or don't hire me.

I never work for money. I have never, ever asked how much I was going to get—never. Many years ago I got an agent and I said, "Don't tell me how much I'm making, I don't want to know. You make the best deal you can; I'll tell you if I want to do the picture." The bottom line is I want to be wanted. I'm not unique. I'm nothing special. I'm diligent as hell. I'm a workaholic. I love my work. I've never had a day where I said, "I wish I wasn't here."

6

Anne V. Coates

Born in England, Anne V. Coates began her career working for a company that produced religious films. A year later she joined the union and became an assistant editor at the prestigious Pinewood Studios.

As editor, Coates cut many major English films, including *The Pickwick Papers*, *The Horse's Mouth*, and *Tunes of Glory*, before editing David Lean's masterpiece, *Lawrence of Arabia*, in 1962. Her contribution to this epic film earned her an Oscar. She returned to the film in 1989 to supervise the restoration of the original director's cut, which toured the world to great acclaim.

A versatile and dynamic editor, Coates received Academy Award nominations for her affinity for literate films, as displayed in *Becket*, and her ability to achieve poetic beauty in David Lynch's haunting film, *The Elephant Man*.

In the 1980s Coates moved to Los Angeles and has edited such films as *Raw Deal* and Lawrence Kasdan's *I Love You to Death*.

1952	*The Pickwick Papers*
1953	*Grand National Night*
1954	*Forbidden Cargo*
1955	*To Paris with Love*
1956	*Lost*
	Mondango
1958	*The Truth About Women*
1959	*The Horse's Mouth*

1960	*Tunes of Glory*
1961	*Why Bother to Knock?*
1962	*Lawrence of Arabia***
1964	*Becket**
1965	*Young Cassidy*
	Those Magnificent Men in Their Flying Machines
1966	*Hotel Paradiso*
1968	*The Bofors Gun*
	Great Catherine
1970	*The Adventurers*
1971	*Follow Me*
	Friends
1973	*Bequest to the Nation*
1974	*Catholics*
	11 Harrowhouse
	Murder on the Orient Express
1975	*Man Friday*
1976	*Aces High*
1977	*The Eagle Has Landed*
1978	*The Medusa Touch* (supervising editor, with Ian Crafford)
1979	*The Legacy*
1980	*The Elephant Man**
1981	*Ragtime* (with Antony Gibbs and Stanley Warnow)
	The Bushido Blade
1983	*The Pirates of Penzance*
1984	*Greystoke: The Legend of Tarzan, Lord of the Apes*
1986	*Lady Jane*
	Raw Deal
1987	*Masters of the Universe*
	Farewell to the King (with C. Timothy O'Meara and Jack Warden)
1989	*Listen to Me*
1990	*I Love You to Death*
1991	*What About Bob?*

*Academy Award Nomination for best achievement in film editing.
**Academy Award for best achievement in film editing.

How did you become a film editor in England?

When I was at school I decided I wanted to become a film director. At that time there weren't many jobs open for women. Today, women can do almost anything in the industry, but then you could be a secretary, a script girl, or work in the cutting room. I decided it would be interesting if I could get into a cutting room, but it's a completely closed shop in England, it's totally unionized. There are no non-union films like over here. I had an uncle who eventually helped me because he was doing religious films. He thought I was only getting into films for the glamour. He thought if he put me in religious films, it would take all that away from me, but I was actually very serious about making movies. I started at a company called GHW which made religious films. I sent films out to churches for Sundays; I was a projectionist, and did all sorts of odd jobs. I worked in the cutting room on a little hand splicer. I worked there for nine months and got to know the people next door at GBI who were making instructional films. I hung around their cutting rooms. Then one day the union came round and said, "We don't want this little outpost that's not unionized, we want all of you to join the union." Most of the people were kind of religious and they said no. I said, "Give me the form," and signed it. Once I did that, it wasn't that difficult getting transferred to Pinewood as a second assistant in the cutting rooms.

Have you experienced any discrimination as a film editor because you are a woman?

No, not really. I never think of myself as a woman, I just think of myself as an editor. I expect to get paid the same money as a man, that never entered my head. It wasn't until later on that I discovered that women aren't always paid equal money, because in films, for these kinds of jobs, they are paid the same money as men.

You've worked on a lot of films with strong male themes like Tunes of Glory, Becket, *and* Lawrence of Arabia.

Yes, I think often people employ you to bring a woman's point of view to it. I know that the director, Ronnie Neame, was particularly interested in my doing *Tunes of Glory* because I was a woman.

What do you think you brought to that film?

Maybe, subconsciously, I brought a certain warmth and sensitivity to the relationship between Alec Guinness and his daughter, and an understanding of the relationship between the two men that maybe a man would not have.

Did the performances of John Mills and Alec Guinness emerge easily?

All those things take a little nursing. They were very good performances but sometimes they both went a little bit over. When performances are very dramatic, you've got to be careful that you don't go over the top with them. You often play it a little bit down. I don't like overacting. I like really sincere acting. I think that you can tell the story much better with the little innuendos than the big bravados, and those were big bravado performances. It was very important for those two people to be absolutely real characters that you believed in. You have to choose very carefully on every performance. For instance, there were many takes on the scene at the end when Alec was breaking down. It was a lot of material, many different angles and slightly different performances. Ronnie Neame and I worked closely to pick the best bits out of that material to draw out the very best of Alec.

What sound elements did you have to cut the scene when Guinness breaks down? Did you have the music?

Mostly the music, the marching feet, and particularly the drum beat.

There is a wonderful scene with John Mills and another officer in a jeep, which is played in a single take without a cut. Was the decision made to let that play because he was so good? Was there coverage on that scene?

Yes, there was coverage on it. The single take played very well in dailies. First we cut it with the coverage several different ways and then we took it out, which I think is the correct way of doing it. If something plays really beautifully and it holds, you should play it. I think you should always hold it as long as you can; don't just cut to say you cut it, unless it's a very boring scene. If the emotion and interest is holding, I believe you should hold the shot. On the other hand, it is very important that you always shoot coverage so you've got it. Sometimes something that plays beautifully in dailies doesn't hold with what goes around it when you put it into the finished film.

Many of the scenes in Tunes of Glory *are full shots with several characters in the frame. Was there over-the-shoulder and close-up material available on these shots?*

I don't know that there was coverage on all those scenes, because I think what Ronnie was aiming for was the feeling of being at an officers' mess with people who lived together, not in isolation. So in the group shots you can see them all together. They rehearsed for several weeks before we started shooting. They would live together and we would eat together—Ronnie had me in on it as well. It was great for the editor to be involved on that level. We all lived together, as it were, like an officers' mess, so they got to know each other. They laughed, joked, and played the scenes, so they were easy with each other. He very much wanted to get the feel that it was a group of people who were used to living together, and that's why he didn't always go for the single shots. He used single shots in the more dramatic moments like the scene when John Mills and Alec Guinness confront each other in a room upstairs.

You have a marvelous ear for dialogue. The Scottish accents in this film have such a melodic lilt to them. Do accents affect the way you cut a scene?

Yes. You're very aware of when the actors come out of their accents, too. We always loop a little afterwards. We did a little looping on people if their accent slipped a bit. So much of editing is rhythm, so the way they talk is important. You just flow along with it. On *I Love You to Death*, we had a lot of accents. We were careful to clean up anything we thought was out of character or where the accent was lost a little bit.

How did you get the job of editor on Lawrence of Arabia?

Originally, David Lean did a whole week of tests for the part with Albert Finney. I just happened to get the job because I bumped into a friend of mine in Harrod's one Saturday morning with my husband, and I said, "What are you doing?" He said, "I'm going to do these tests with Albert Finney." The film was called *Seven Pillars of Wisdom* then. I said, "Have you got anybody cutting them? I'm not doing anything at the moment," and he said, "I don't think we have, ring up on Monday morning." So I rang up on Monday morning and then checked with David, and he said he had nobody especially lined up, so I went down and cut those tests. He did them in two complete sequences. He did one of Albert in the map room with other actors, and then he did a scene with him as an Arab in the tent talking to Ali. I cut them together. Albert actually turned it down. David liked the work that I did on them so much that he and Sam Spiegel offered me the movie.

What was it like to work with David Lean?

He loves the cutting room. I find him very easy and clear in communicating what he wants you to do. The assistants adore him, he really works well with them. David thinks a great deal like a cutter, but, like every director, he gives you a lot of cover because he knows that you always need cover. He fell in love with the desert, so we had thousands and thousands and thousands of feet of desert and mirage. There was a lot of argument at the end when it came down to color timing the film, because Technicolor was busy trying to make all of the sand look yellow, and David had gone to these deserts especially because the sand had that pink tinge. It was very important to get that, so we spent quite a lot of time getting the colors correct, and we cut them so that the colors went from one shade to another and the shadows matched with each other.

Does David Lean storyboard sequences or are they just very worked out in his mind?

They're very worked out in his mind; he doesn't really storyboard. Sometimes he'll storyboard it, if it's a special effects sequence, but he doesn't for ordinary scenes. He works it out carefully with John Box, the designer who has done all his films. They design the sets with David knowing where he's going to put the camera before he gets there.

The transition from the shot of Peter O'Toole blowing out the match to the shot of the sunrise in the desert is so visually effective. How did that come about?

Robert Bolt, the writer, says it was his cut; David Lean said he did it. The actual timing of the cut is mine. Robert Bolt described it in the script;

it went from the match blowing out to the sunrise, but it's the actual moment that you do it that makes it special. David said, "Try cutting it when he's actually blowing it." I only did about two cuts on it and got it more or less right.

What was your approach on the sunrise shot?

We timed that several times to see how long we could hold it before the sun came up. It always seemed like we held it a bit too long, but once the music was on there, it seemed perfect. David taught me a lot about holding on to shots. He was much braver than I was in those days. I would say, "It's really too long, David." "Nonsense," he would say, "it's perfect." When you got the music on he was quite right. I learned such a lot from him: to be brave, and to throw stuff out, too. You've got to be ruthless to get down to the actual core of a picture and he was ruthless. He threw a whole heap of stuff out that broke my heart and he was right.

Omar Sharif's entrance almost has a magical quality. He seems to appear out of nowhere in the desert and slowly rides straight into the camera. Was there a lot of coverage on that scene?

Oh yes, masses of coverage. The scene had been longer, it only got shorter. It was difficult to cut just the right moment when Peter O'Toole and Tafas break away to run.

Tafas is shot by Omar Sharif off-screen. Was that because you didn't want to show the actual violence of it?

No, it was really just to do it in a different dramatic way. David likes you to try things differently. That's why we used direct cuts in the film, which he hadn't done very much. In the script it said dissolve, but I'd been to the French cinema quite a bit, and they were doing a lot of direct cutting. Opticals were becoming old-fashioned. It was also one of the first pictures to use presound, like on the charge of Aqaba where the bell starts ringing over the close-up of Lawrence from the previous scene. Also, in the tram where he says, "Who are you?" and then we start the tram and he comes back to civilization, the noise of the tram came before the cut. The manager of the theater where the premiere was held said, "I knew you were in a hurry, but you'd think they could have gotten the sound in sync." He didn't realize that we had done this on purpose. He thought that was an accident. We spent hours getting those right. Now, everybody pre-laps the sound, it's old hat, but in those days people hadn't started doing that.

In the battle scene, you cut twice to Arthur Kennedy, as he takes a flash photograph. How do you know where to have that happen and how many times to show him?

It's a feeling, an emotion. That's what editing is about: knowing how many cuts to put in and knowing when you've got it cut right. You're telling a story, so you've got to be sure that the audience knows what's happening dramatically, without boring them by telling them too many times. You have to build up something to just the right moment.

When you were putting that scene together, did you cut the battle first and then decide where the shots of Arthur Kennedy would go?

No. I'd look at all of the material and then I would decide to put in the cuts of him right from the start. Afterwards, you do add things, but I try to get those kinds of things right in the first cut; then you start changing and altering, but you've got the material there.

In the original roadshow presentation of this film and in the restored version, there is overture music that plays before the film. How is that prepared?

You just put it onto black film with a mag stripe. We had intermission music as well, and then we had playout music at the end. People don't do it very often, other than for a roadshow, but I like that. It's got some style to it.

How much film was shot for Lawrence of Arabia?

There were 31 miles of film.

How long did it take to cut the film?

From the time we finished shooting to the time we premiered it for the Queen was four months, which was very fast to cut, dub, and write the music for a film of that size. A normal film takes you six months. The first version of *Lawrence of Arabia* ran 3 hours, 42 minutes. David and I had never seen it from beginning to end before we ran it for the press. We'd seen the second half first, because we'd cut that first, and then we saw the first half; but we never saw the whole film. I've probably seen *Lawrence* less than any film I've ever worked on. We never had time to finesse some of the things we would have liked to. I think possibly one could have taken out quite a bit, just in trims, if we had more time. When the film opened, there was a general consensus of opinion that it was too long. With an intermission of 10 minutes, it was getting on to 4 hours. We took out 20 minutes. That was the first time we cut it down. Then about seven years later, they wanted to do a cut-down version for television, so we took out approximately another 15 minutes. David was assured that version would only be used for TV; then he eventually discovered that version was going out everywhere. If you saw the film after 1970, that was the version you would have seen. It was about 3 hours and 8 minutes.

Were the 35 minutes that were taken out of the film during those two cuts put back for the newly restored version?

Yes. It's nearly the first version that opened in that December. When we came to the restoration it wasn't a straightforward thing of just putting pieces back in. We had to restore it from two different cut versions. Some of the scenes taken out were very easy, because they were stored away in little sequences. Others had lines and shots that had to be all joined up. Once your negative is cut, you always lose a frame, so it really was a very complicated thing to do. When Bob Harris rang me and said they were going to do it, I was skeptical. I didn't think they would be able to find the negative. I didn't think they could do it. I didn't remember the film all that well, and I hadn't seen it for 15 years. Once we did the TV version, I never saw it again, because I didn't like the cut-down version at all; I really hated it. I thought they ruined the picture. I didn't like the first cut-down either; I liked it the long way, and that's the way everybody likes it now. It actually plays shorter as a picture, because now you know why Lawrence is doing things. Though it runs longer, it seems shorter, because you're more interested in him as a person.

In a film like Becket *where the language is so important, are you referring to the script more than on other films?*

Not really, because I cut very much from the material I am given. Obviously, one would check to see that they have said it properly, or if you haven't got it all, but usually there would be a note from the continuity girl. I like to run the material, listen to it, and think about what I'm going to do with it, how I am going to construct it on the Moviola. I go for the rhythm, the magic, and the music.

Did Richard Burton and Peter O'Toole give you a lot of choices in their line readings?

Richard played it nearly the same, a very disciplined actor. He could do it differently if the director asked him, but basically he thought his part out. When he was doing the excommunication scene he had a big gold medallion on his chest. As he took those big breaths and shouted, the medallion went up and down exactly the same on every take. Peter gave you more variance and did it differently.

What was the most difficult scene to cut?

The beach scene, which I thought was brilliant. It was very difficult to cut because neither of them could control their horse, so the horses were never standing in the same direction or angle from cut to cut. I had to get what I wanted out of the scene in spite of the horses, because it was a very important scene and I had to get it right. Then they didn't like the way they did it the first time, so they reshot it. They liked some of the first shoot and some of the second. It was absolutely crazy because there was no way that they were similar. It didn't match, it was a different sort of day. I don't know how I ever did it. I love the beach scene, it's one of my favorite cuts.

What was it like to work with David Lynch on The Elephant Man?

I went to have a meeting with him and this young boy came out of the back of the office. I was just about to say, "I'll have cream in my coffee, thank you," when somebody said, "This is David Lynch." He looked so young I really did think he was the office boy. He has this freshness about him and an extraordinary mind that's nothing like the way he looks. I hadn't seen *Eraserhead*, so I went to see it with the cameraman, Freddie Francis, and a couple of other people. We all sat and watched this film and when the lights went up we all went, "God, what have we let ourselves in for." I thought it was a brilliant film, but it didn't seem to go at all with this bright, pleasant, young man. He's a very interesting man. My appreciation of him evolved slowly as we went ahead with the film. I enjoyed working with him.

Was there a lot of discussion of how and when to show the face of the Elephant Man?

There were two ways of shooting the opening. David wanted to see him in the cellar, when Treaves first goes down and the tears run down his face. Then, there was the possibility of not seeing him, until the little nurse with the tray sees him and screams. When we had a meeting with Mel Brooks, who was the executive producer, he said, "It's your picture and I don't want to interfere, but I would like you to shoot it both ways, because I'm not absolutely sure how I would like it to go." I don't think David thought that Mel was really serious about that. David shot it the way he wanted. When Mel saw it he said, "I want to see it the other way." It hadn't been shot the other way. In the scenes after Treaves, you could see the Elephant Man very clearly, so I had to cut it the other way by blowing up quite a lot of shots so that the Elephant Man was blown out of the side. Because it was shot in black and white and very grainy, you really didn't notice. Just when you were about to see the Elephant Man, we cut away to something else. You didn't actually see him until the nurse sees him, and that took quite a tricky bit of cutting. Mel Brooks was right, it was better that way, but it was an interesting challenge to do. We did lose a couple of scenes, which was a pity, because we couldn't cut them without showing him.

There were several complex montages of surrealistic imagery in the film. How did you work with David Lynch on them?

It was fascinating work on those montages with David. Now by doing it with video, it would be easier to get inside his mind, but it was very difficult on film because he didn't know exactly what he wanted until he saw it. Something complicated like the mother and the elephant we did hundreds of times before we got it right. David would be telling us what he wanted, my assistant was very patient and kept ordering it over and over again, and it was always wrong. The montage when he goes to the theater was shot as a straight scene; that wasn't shot as a montage at all. It was shot with him coming into the box, the whole performance, the reactions, the crowd, and everything. Afterwards, it just didn't hold, so we made it into a montage. The extraordinary thing was that we had a piece of music that had already been recorded and we had to cut to it. We got it right the first time.

The whole first third of Greystoke: The Legend of Tarzan, Lord of the

Apes has almost no dialogue. It must have been a unique experience in cutting that material.

Telling a story with pictures is what editing is all about. It was fascinating. We had a great deal more of it—about two hours of that jungle material. It gave me a great opportunity to do some very interesting things, many of which were never in the picture, because it was much too long. I made vignettes from the ape material with the boy, their family life, their surviving, watching the apes, crying, and laughing. There was some lovely stuff. There was a lovely scene when the boy first goes swimming. He's diving off the waterfall and all the other apes are on the side looking in horror because they don't even want to get their feet wet, let alone plunge in like that, and they're so concerned for him.

What were the production tracks like on all that material? Was most of the material silent?

Yes, mostly silent. Sometimes the boy and the people in the ape suits grunted, but none of it was used. The final tracks were completely made up, we did a lot of work on them. We were very concerned not to make the jungle sound monotonous. If you noticed, it sounds different in different areas. We used various background animals and birds and those ape voices are made up. The sound editor, Les Wiggins, came to America, went to an ape farm up in Ohio, and recorded a lot of sound. Then we recorded human sounds and mixed them together to get the sound that we wanted. They're marvelous tracks, they sound right, and therefore you don't realize what went into them. You shouldn't be aware of them, or you've done it wrong. It should seem as if it's absolutely perfect, but they are, in fact, made up of a lot of different bits and pieces, equalizing, slowing down, speeding up, and all sorts of sound to make each ape's voice sound different.

The apes that Rick Baker created were wonderful. Did you have to pay particular attention in editing that material so that they appeared to come alive?

Yes, we very carefully picked out the best bits. There was some material that was not so good. There were shots where the apes were running along branches and swinging that didn't look at all real, so you had to be very careful that you got the dramatic bits you wanted to tell your story. When we finished the picture, we ran it for an expert on apes, to make sure I hadn't put in anything that didn't look absolutely real. We checked it very carefully. We were worried when we first went up to preview in Seattle they would all say, "What's Hugh Hudson doing with a film with people dressed up in ape suits?" but we got exactly the reverse. We had much more violent material that's not in the film now. We had a great fight between two apes and a scene where an ape mauls a woman. The audience was turned off, because they thought real apes were getting hurt. They didn't care about the humans getting hurt. They were horrified, so we had to tone down the whole thing.

Did you cut to music?

I didn't cut to music, but we laid a certain amount of music on the tracks. Hugh likes that. I always put music on a film. I think it helps a lot, particularly if you've got silent scenes. I don't cut to the music.

Did Arnold Schwarzenegger have any input into the editing of Raw Deal?

He wanted various inserts put into the film. We did a whole day of close-ups of hands clicking guns and gun barrels exploding, and all that sort of thing. They were really requested by him.

Masters of the Universe *was a complicated special effects movie. What was their impact on the editing process?*

I like doing different movies. I've always resisted doing effects movies because I knew there'd be an awful lot of boring stuff going on while waiting for effects to come. You can't finalize your scenes until you get them. People say you can just slot them; well, there's no way that you can just slot them in. You have to alter your cuts to make it work.

You have edited many epic films. Do you find they need a different approach than a smaller film?

Not really, it's just the same. You just take it sequence by sequence. It's not really very different. Obviously, it's going to take you a little bit more time, and you have more material to choose from, but you should remain calm at all times. If you've got a whole heap of material coming in, just take it step by step; work out in your mind what you want to get out of a scene. Whether you've got thousands of feet or five feet, it's the same thing. You work out very carefully what you want to say to the audience and how it fits into the rest of the story. So you can be panicked by the amount of the material, but you should just get calm and go through it slowly. It's very important for you to get to know your material.

Is there any particular piece of cutting that you are most proud of?

In *Aces High* I made battle scenes out of nothing. I made them out of footage from *The Blue Max*, *Darling Lili*, stock material, our own full-size flying planes, 20-foot miniatures that were electronically controlled, little baby miniatures that were flown, and real live people on the ground firing guns in machines that rocked about and had clouds rush past them. I made complete World War I dogfights out of them and that was really exciting. I cut from one of our planes being blown up to one from *Darling Lili* that was spiraling down. It was a different plane, and yet it worked because when you saw it exploding and falling, you thought it must be the same plane. When Malcolm McDowell, who was in it, saw the film, he said, "I saw this guy shooting down these planes and whirling about the skies; then I realized that was me." That was fun to do. The film wasn't successful so you get no credit for doing it, but I consider that one of the best editing jobs I've ever done.

What would you like to do that you haven't done as an editor?

I would like to do a really big musical and I would love to do a cowboy movie. I love editing. I think I'm just so lucky to be doing something that I like to be doing.

7

Dede Allen

Dede Allen is one of the best-known names in feature film editing. Her dynamic cutting on *Bonnie and Clyde* helped transform contemporary American film. Throughout her career she has been responsible for training many of the industry's most prominent editors, including Jerry Greenberg, Barry Malkin, Richard Marks, and Stephen Rotter.

Dede Allen became a feature editor the long, slow way. Starting at age 19, she spent ten months as a messenger for Columbia and three years in the sound editing department. In New York, she was a picture editor at Film Graphics, where she cut industrials and commercials. After working on several TV series supervised by Carl Lerner, he recommended her for a monster film, *Terror from the Year 5000*, which was her first feature. Her major break came in 1959, when she cut *Odds Against Tomorrow* for director Robert Wise.

Dede Allen has gone on to work with Robert Rossen, Elia Kazan, Arthur Penn, George Roy Hill, and Sidney Lumet. Her powerful editing has helped shape such challenging films as *The Hustler*, *America, America*, *Little Big Man*, *Dog Day Afternoon*, and *Reds*. Her work on *Dog Day Afternoon* and *Reds* earned Academy Award nominations.

1958	*Terror from the Year 5000*
1959	*Odds Against Tomorrow*
1961	*The Hustler*
1963	*America, America*
1967	*Bonnie and Clyde*

1968	*Rachel, Rachel*
1969	*Alice's Restaurant*
1970	*Little Big Man*
1972	*Slaughterhouse Five*
1973	*Serpico* (with Richard Marks)
	Visions of Eight—Arthur Penn segment, "The Highest"
1975	*Dog Day Afternoon**
	Night Moves
1976	*The Missouri Breaks* (with Jerry Greenberg and Stephen A. Rotter)
1977	*Slap Shot*
1978	*The Wiz*
1981	*Reds* (with Craig McKay)*
1984	*Mike's Murder* (with Jeff Gourson)
	Harry and Son
1985	*The Breakfast Club*
1986	*Off Beat* (with Angelo Corrao)
1988	*The Milagro Beanfield War* (with Jim Miller)
1989	*Let It Ride* (with Jim Miller)
1990	*Henry and June* (with Vivien Hillgrove and William Scharf)
1991	*The Addams Family*

*Academy Award nomination for best achievement in film editing.

How did you develop your interest in filmmaking?

My grandfather was a surgeon in Cincinnati whose whole life revolved around the theater. My mother was a stage actress who didn't stay in the theater when she married my father. She was a tremendous movie buff and we spent a lot of time at the movies. There was nothing I didn't see. If you go to the movies four times a week as a kid, you become pretty hooked. I saw a lot of theater because my grandfather went to see everything and I drove him. In 1943 I went out to California, where my grandfather gave me an introduction to Elliot Nugent at Goldwyn. He said, "Young lady, if you want to become a director, get into the cutting room." Well, I didn't know what cutting meant. I went to the studios and tried to get into the cutting rooms. I couldn't get in. In those

days, women were not considered as hireable as men because they didn't
support families. I was lucky to get started at Columbia as a messenger.
I was 19. I was in the first hiring of women; we were called "the girls."
I made some very good friends. When Carl Lerner became an assistant
picture editor, he helped me learn everything he was learning. I spent
every night and weekend working for the Actor's Lab. It had a lot of
people from the old Group Theater who started getting into films. I
learned a lot about theater, sound, props, lighting, and performance. It
became part of my background.

How did you get your first job as an editor?

I got in the long, slow way. I was a messenger for ten months. I
couldn't get into picture editing because they claimed I couldn't carry the
big cases for the synchronization room. Finally, I got into the sound effects department at Columbia, where I carried a great deal more film. I
pestered the people so much that they hired me to get rid of me. I was in
the sound effects department for about three years and became an assistant in sound. At the end of the war, everybody got bounced out. I had
seniority so I stayed and finally got to be a sound effects editor, but I
could never get into picture editing at Columbia. Verna Fields was a
sound effects editor for years before she got into picture editing. In Hollywood, most women of my generation did not get into picture editing
until they were well into their middle life. When I got out into the freelance field there weren't many jobs. I got into picture editing as an assistant and eventually I came to New York and was a script clerk on and off.
In the beginning I couldn't get into the union in New York. I started in
commercial spots. I was having my children and my husband was a freelance writer, so one of us had to have a staff job. I had a staff job for four
years at Film Graphics doing television work and some industrials. Carl
Lerner was in charge of a couple of TV series, so I went to work as an
editor for him. Then through Carl I got a monster film, *Terror from the Year
5000*, which was my first real feature. When Carl was doing *Middle of the
Night*, Bob Wise came to do *Odds Against Tomorrow* and Carl recommended me. Bob took a chance on me and that's how I really got my first
break. I was 34. I'd been in the business for quite a while.

*Robert Wise was the first of many important directors you have worked with.
What did you learn from him?*

He's a graceful, lovely man. Bob started out in music editing. One of
the reasons he hired me was because I had come out of sound. There
were a lot of people in New York with a lot more experience than I had
at the time. On *Odds Against Tomorrow*, the very first time Robert Wise
saw a scene I cut was on the Saturday after we started. It was a scene
with Ed Begley and Robert Ryan in a Riverside Drive apartment. It was
quite interesting, Bob's angles and Joe Brun's lighting were excellent,

but in order to make the scene play better, I tried different things. When I started working on *Odds Against Tomorrow*, we still didn't have tape splices. When you lost frames from hot splicing the picture cuts, you had to put slugs. I said something like, "I apologize that there are some slugs in it." The first thing he said was, "I see you've been working with it. I like that—never be afraid to put in slugs." That was a tremendous piece of direction for an editor to get, particularly if you are editing for Robert Wise and are scared shitless that you are going to fall on your face. I mean, how much better start can you have? The other thing I did was to bounce sound forward or backward to propel something. Bob loved that. He said, "I love you people in New York, you're not afraid of anything. I could never get editors to do that." I was the first woman editor that Wise had worked with. He found it fascinating that I saw things differently, everything from the way you approach material to the way you would play a sexual encounter. Later I discovered that other directors would have to get used to the number of slugs I put in, because many editors very carefully never let it be known that they had been struggling with a scene. I think I would have been terribly intimidated if I hadn't had that experience with Bob Wise. He's a marvelous director to work with.

Did director Robert Rossen know a lot about editing when you worked with him on The Hustler?

One day he said to me, "Kid, I want you to see this picture called *Breathless*, then tell me what you think." Next to Ames pool hall there was a crummy hotel where Rossen had a little suite where he would go for meetings. I went up there and said, "I saw *Breathless*." He said, "What do you think, kid?" I said, "In what way do you mean, what do I think?" He said, "Well, all that stuff, do you think it works?" I said, "No, I think some of it works very nicely, but it was totally accidental. The shot where it went round and round in circles in a car was a big mish-mosh, but that style worked wonderfully for that particular story called *Breathless*. . . . Why are you asking?" He said, "Everybody tells me I'm old-fashioned." I said, "I don't think you're old-fashioned; film is film—storytelling." He said, "Well, I just want to know whether you think we should incorporate some of that." I said, "I wouldn't know how. I have to do whatever I think is right for the scene." So he says, "I thought it was a crock of shit!"

When I started cutting *The Hustler*, I didn't use the dissolves that were indicated in the script. I was using cuts which Kazan enjoyed and Bob Wise loved. It gave it a different style. Rossen was very smart. If something was working he didn't fool around with it, but I think it came as a total surprise to him.

In preparation for the film did you try to learn about pool?

The prop man did black and white Polaroids of all the balls for me and called the pictures "Dede's Balls." I got a book on pool and Rossen said, "What's that?" And I said, "I'm trying to study up, I've got to know which ball is which." He said, "Kid, this isn't about pool, this isn't about billiard balls; this is about people, it's about character. You'll figure it out, that's just mechanics." But then, to Rossen, everything that wasn't story was mechanics. His point was that the game is a metaphor. Rossen was very, very strong on story, probably the strongest director on story that I've ever worked with.

Did The Hustler *go through many changes during the editing process?*

A lot of the scenes are the original cut. We never touched some scenes between Piper Laurie and Paul Newman because Rossen was always afraid of taking something that worked and damaging it. We threw out a scene Paul Newman always said cost him the Academy Award. It was one of his speeches in the pool room, a very impassioned scene, an absolutely brilliant performance. It was exactly like another scene that couldn't be gotten rid of because it was tied to the plot at both ends. Almost at the very end, we finally had to say, "It has to go." That's very painful. It didn't move the story. We had to throw out a scene that was probably the greatest part of his performance.

When did you first start cutting on two Moviolas?

On *America, America,* when Kazan went away for six months and I was left alone with a mammoth amount of footage. They couldn't pay any overtime to an assistant, so I was there alone for endless hours. I paid for the second Moviola on several films. It was never in any budget. I used it to compare takes and line readings. When I'm cutting, I'm mainly working on my left Moviola, but I don't keep the cut in the Moviola. I keep my cut on a reel and I just keep running it through. Now that I have video I don't need the second Moviola as much, but I always use a second Moviola because it saves time.

Why do you prefer cutting on Moviolas?

When people are working on an eight-plate flatbed, they are in effect working with two Moviolas, but they don't get their fingers on the bits and pieces. With the Moviola you're very close to the film. I find when you stop a KEM it doesn't stop right on a frame. You can't sneak it forward and back. It stops and then chatters on for a frame or two, which is very imprecise for me. The rhythm in which you cut on a Moviola is just easier. The physical aspects of the Moviola are much harder on your neck and legs. It's not as good to the fatigue factor as the KEM is, but you learn to adjust. I had to retrain myself to learn to sit at the Moviola after years of cutting standing up, because my neck began going. I found I had developed what I guess is called an editor's shoulder, which a lot of people have.

Were the films you edited in the 1960s influenced by the changes in film style that were coming from Europe?

There was a definite evolution in filmic style and it came from England. The "angry young men" films that Tony Gibbs cut, *Look Back in Anger* and *The Loneliness of the Long Distance Runner*, had more direct influence on me than anything. I loved the way those pictures were cut. It was incorporated in pictures cut in New York like *Bonnie and Clyde*.

Many people have credited you as the founder of the New York school of editing. How do you feel about that?

I call it the Arthur Penn school. For years we were lucky enough to be able to train a lot of people in New York. Directors like Arthur Penn came along and allowed us to have more people in the cutting room because he shot more film. It was a wonderful educational school for Stephen Rotter, Richie Marks, Jerry Greenberg, and many other people who came up through the Arthur Penn cutting rooms. It was a very rich period for New York. There was a vitality and an independence in being away from the studios.

Many editors have told me that they consider your work on Bonnie and Clyde *to be a landmark in film editing.*

It's interesting because at the time, in Hollywood, a lot of what I did was considered bad editing. The first time Jack Warner saw a cut he said, "You mean you're going to fade out and cut in?" Arthur Penn said, "That's right." "And in other places you're going to cut out and fade in?" Arthur said, "That's right." "I never saw such stuff in my life!" That was ridiculous to him. It came about because I made a temporary fade and the other side wasn't ready. Arthur liked it, so we began using it. It went faster. A fade out and a fade in has black in the middle which stops—it doesn't whoosh you into the next scene, which Arthur felt was so important for that story. Arthur gave it a special energy.

We were using shorthand in *Bonnie and Clyde* because of the nature of the story, and the kind of coverage and performances it had. We were able to go in with angles and close-ups and only pull back when we wanted to show what Arthur would call the "tapestry." Every time I went in a certain direction and Arthur liked it, he'd want more. He wanted the film to propel the drive of their lives. He never intellectualized it. I got to the point where I was doing things in the spirit of it. He'd say, "Go through the film, make it move faster." I did that two or three times, so it began to move faster and faster and it got better. I broke all of my own rigid cutting rules about story, character, and how a scene plays. I never got an Academy nomination for *Bonnie and Clyde*. I think it was truly because they thought it was badly cut. Later it became a mystique which everybody imitated. Even commercials have gotten into what's called the "energy cut," which *Bonnie and Clyde* supposedly help to start. Basically, they were all playing catch-up to Arthur Penn; it was his rhythm.

What does a first cut on an Arthur Penn film look like?

Arthur Penn directs everything full, in terms of performance. With Arthur, the performance is so interesting that you'll overexpand it. A first cut can be a nightmare of overabundance. I'm not talking about loose; it plays and it's tight within itself, but the whole picture is just cumbersome.

Arthur Penn is known as a director who covers his scenes very thoroughly. Can you describe the coverage on a specific scene?

The scene in *Little Big Man*, when Custer says, "You go down there" to Jack Crabb, looks like a very simple scene. Arthur staged it so Custer moved to various places and Jack Crabb was always sitting on the rock. I had so much coverage of Dustin Hoffman's every look. I had Jack Crabb on that rock in every conceivable way. A lot of directors would not do that. They would just give you a close-up of Jack Crabb looking generally in that direction. When Arthur stages a scene, he knows intuitively what he's got to get. He can't allow one close-up to serve for various eyelines. This gives an angle the nuances and eye contact that allow the character to be played more specifically.

How have other directors covered reaction shots?

Kazan will come in and do pick-ups. He comes much more out of the school where you learned to get what you needed. Sometimes that doesn't work. If the actor needs the preparation to get into the take, Kazan won't break it up. He'll just shoot the whole scene to get them into the mood, so that the character will be at the right emotional point for the section the director needs. There's a scene in *America, America* where I used a three- or four-minute lead-in which played endlessly on the back of a woman, because I found it very moving. Playing off somebody can be as moving as something that plays on somebody, because the other actor may be doing something that embellishes the character. You have to know how you're going to sustain the level of performance. If you're going to start breaking it up and shooting pick-ups in bits and pieces, you have to know how much lead-in you have to do to get the performance to the point where it will play for the section you need. Pick-ups are a very awkward way to cut unless you want that punch.

Many editors talk about the integrity of a shot. Do you feel that a shot has a natural in and out point that should be respected?

I never think in terms of that. Maybe it's because I don't start with the fear that a shot has such integrity that I have to observe it. You have to go with whatever the scene is trying to do.

What is your method for cutting a scene?

I don't cut the old way I was taught at Columbia, when picture editors would say, "Now, young lady, I'll tell you how to start. You always cut from a master to a closer shot, then you go over-the-shoulder, to close-ups." Well, that's bullshit. You don't always do that. You sometimes start with a close-up. I love over-the-shoulder shots and tight over-shoulders because that's where you often have the most related moments. I like to keep the feeling of both people in the frame, but I don't ever sit down and intellectually figure it. You go where the performance is. Suddenly, you may see a transition that will make the story point through a character by starting on a close-up. You are cutting it one scene at a time. A director directs a scene in beats. You might have a master of the whole thing, but then it breaks down into the various dramatic parts of the evolution of the scene.

Like the scene in the jockey club in *Let it Ride*. Richard Dreyfuss sits down and has his conversation with the Allen Garfield and Jennifer Tilly characters, and then he goes into the thing with Michelle Phillips and somebody else moves in. Those are all different beats in the same scene. If you have a great deal of coverage, you really can't just go plowing through the whole thing, you'd never remember all of it. So I break it into beats and cut it in the continuity of the scene. I make massive notes which I have if I need them, but I memorize the material so thoroughly that I seldom even look at my notes. It becomes almost automatic. Every editor really has to remember almost every frame. It's like chess; you have to be able to think ahead and think back. You have to know where that scene is going to go and how that character is going to evolve. If you just go for the snazzy cuts in the beginning, you get into a lot of trouble, because you're not following content or character. You lose something or you never develop it. You've got a bunch of great cuts but the story is dying.

So you don't rough out the whole scene.

I could never cut that way. I know a lot of people do. I think that the tempo and the timing of my cuts are different than the way somebody else might cut them for just that reason.

What technique do you use to memorize the material?

I like to see it on the big screen for the proscenium arch effect. When I've seen everything I want to on a scene, I'll start memorizing it on the KEM. The most dangerous thing I can do is to be in a hurry and say, "Okay, break it down," and then cut the scene glibly, before I really know the material. If you transfer all the material to video, you're not lost, you have it right there. You just punch it up and resee it.

The first picture I had video on was *Reds*. On film you don't have the luxury of having all of the material there, because once you've cut it and broken it down, it's in bits and pieces. It's in rolls that are either ins or outs or, in my case, a million trims, because I've used pieces of so many takes. It's an awful thing when you're cutting a scene and you have to go back through your notes remembering all that material. I start physically working on one beat, and I don't break down the next one until I've had a chance to look at it several times more. The only way you can organize the material is to memorize it.

What determines the rhythm of a scene?

It depends on the kind of story. There are pictures that play looser very well. Other pictures, like *The Breakfast Club* are made up of minutes and pieces, because it's nothing but talking heads. The only way you got any movement in that picture was by the interaction of the characters. In the end you look at it and say, "This has energy because it's moving."

What kind of relationships do editors have with actors?

Have you ever tried to work on a scene where an actor comes in and all they see is that little thing they want? They don't know what it's taken to gracefully get from one thing to another in a performance. This is becoming more fashionable in recent years; it can be very difficult. On *The Hustler*, Paul Newman would come to a screening of the dailies and he would give you wonderful, very specific notes. Robert Rossen was a very sharp guy. He'd sit there and never say too much. One day I was sitting next to Rossen and Paul said, "This take, this take, and this take." After Paul left, I said to Rossen, "You know this is a total contradiction to everything you and I have talked about." He said, "Kid, you got to understand, Newman's not only a good actor, but he's such a lovely guy, he wants Eddie to be a nice guy. He doesn't realize this is a total shit. Ignore it."

What was it like to work with Paul Newman, the director, on Rachel, Rachel?

He's just a very gracious man. He was so concerned about protecting the actors. The first thing he said was, "Rachel has to be in every shot." I said, "Paul, she can't be in every shot, you've got to have cutaways." He said, "I don't like cutaways. I want to be on her, this is all her experience." We sat and did diagrams in a Connecticut restaurant about how you cover scenes. By the second or third day, he suddenly began to say, "Oh, I like that on a long complicated move, but I like this on the other one better." I said, "Okay, you just answered it. If I don't have anything to cut away to, how am I going to get between this take and this take? "Ahh," he goes, "I see what you mean." *Rachel, Rachel* was a labor of love on everybody's part. The crew was very warm and giving and they all adored Newman. He's an intelligent but modest man; therefore, you break your neck for him. The first thing he said to the crew was, "I'm a virgin, so go easy." A crew will do anything for you if someone says, "Hey, I'm not sure if I know what I'm doing."

Do you feel that a director should direct the editor the way he would an actor?

The best ones usually do. Arthur Penn is a very erudite man. He can become almost frighteningly articulate, but he never tells you, he lets you find it. He almost works the way a psychiatrist works with a patient; he'd want to see what you'd come up with. Elia Kazan takes your neurosis and uses it to his advantage. He knows exactly who to shit on and who to send roses to. Possibly, it's very manipulative, but his talent at getting what he wants is incredible. George Roy Hill is an extremely in-command director. A very tall man with an authoritative quality, not pompous, but very specific and very definite. Everything he says is true; then he's perfectly willing to turn around and go exactly the opposite way. He was extremely anxious that I know exactly how he wanted everything, but once in a while he would see a scene and say, "My God, I never thought of that!" and he'd be delighted. Then he gave you more and more rope.

Does the method in which you work on a film change from director to director?

George Roy Hill works on films in bits. Arthur Penn works on films in hunks. Kazan's shooting is very organized. All the material had to be put in continuity and we ran dailies that way. He never wanted me to take my eyes off the screen. Barry Malkin was my apprentice at that point. He devised a great big book with lots of room where I could write without taking my eyes off the screen. It was very funny. Robert Rossen was not a noodler, just the opposite of someone who wants to take it and work it to death. When something really works for George Roy Hill, he'll stop. Sometimes Arthur Penn will go on, but always with a reason.

Slaughterhouse Five *was well suited to editing because of the whole time shifting notion. How were the transitions developed?*

George Roy Hill was extremely meticulous, he plotted every transition. The Dresden part was all shot in Prague first. Then I would prepare clips for Ondricek, the cameraman. When they did the transition scenes, they worked out exactly which frame they wanted to use to bring them into the present with the same kind of framing. So basically you were tied to the beginning and ends of these sequences. You had to start and end up at a certain point to make them work. Out of 20 transitions, maybe eight worked the very way they were shot. They all worked technically and visually, but some just didn't work storywise. In compressing the story and making it play better, some of the transitions worked wonderfully as transitions, but the picture died. That's when we hit upon the idea that the transitions always seemed to work better if I compressed them and it was played off Billy Pilgrim. I took all the ones that didn't work and just made them cut around Billy. Sometimes I would have to throw away wonderful shots. We also found some new ones in the material. Any transition really worked if it was right for the scene, the story, the time, the place, and it propelled you. It made that magic moment work. But if that picture had been approached by someone who was not as careful as George in planning everything, the whole picture might not have worked as well. It was that very planning that gave the picture its visual and storytelling style.

Sidney Lumet is known as a director who shoots very little film. What was the coverage like on Dog Day Afternoon?

Double camera. When Sidney does double camera, it will work better than when somebody else does it because he's so precise. All those scenes outside the bank with Charles Durning, and the one with the mother, were shot with two cameras. Lumet did a tremendous amount of rehearsal, which worked for the intensity of the story. I was able to cut in continuity, which helped tremendously. The phone conversations were covered with two close-ups of Pacino and two shots of Chris Sarandon and that was it. There were two takes on each and we used part of one and part of the other. The camera wasn't always in the same close-up at the same time, but you went totally for performance. They were both looking in the same camera direction but it worked; the angles were different enough.

How do you feel when the director is restricting the editing choices by limiting the coverage?

Sidney does that quite a bit. When it works, I feel great about it. He likes to think of himself as someone who plans it all ahead and knows exactly how it's going to go together. Sidney likes to say, "Cut here, cut here." He always has been kind of a genius mechanically.

You are credited as executive producer on Reds *and were very involved with the production of the interviews of the witnesses. How did that come about?*

In the beginning Warren Beatty had no office. My living room was our office on *Reds*. We finally got to the point where my husband Steve said, "Please stop using the house as an office." So we opened an office on 57th Street. Over the years Warren had gotten in touch with people to interview and the list kept growing. We finally organized a shooting schedule, but the picture had no studio. Warren paid for it. We shot all of the witnesses with a quarter of a million dollars filtered through my account. Thank God I had brains enough to get separate color checks. It drove my accountant crazy. We went around the country and did all of the interviews in a three-week period.

What was the average running length of an interview?

They were all pretty long. Before we went to England we had close to a quarter of a million feet of film. The Henry Miller interview was eleven reels, because Henry Miller loved to talk and Warren loved that interview.

Besides putting the dailies on video, what other techniques did you use to keep track of the enormous coverage you had?

I had to get a lot of the shooting transcribed because no two takes were alike, they didn't have the same dialogue. For the whole Eugene O'Neill area of the film, there were millions of takes. Jack Nicholson would say different things in each one and he was wonderful.

There is a scene when Georgie Jessel sings patriotic songs over Reed and Louise Bryant dressing their Christmas tree. How did that come about?

We didn't have an awful lot of scripted material to cover that scene, and it was a rough transition in terms of story, so the Jessel thing was just logical. That wonderful man from Provincetown sang "You Can't

Come and Play in my Yard," which became part of our theme. When you have a song like that, you are going to use it somewhere. It was sad, sweet, and poignant in terms of that relationship. If you have something that moves you in the cutting room, hopefully it's going to move everybody else. You get terribly tired sitting through things that don't work and most pictures have things that don't work in them. *Reds* and *Bonnie and Clyde* are two of the few pictures that didn't have many things that didn't work. It's exciting to work on a whole picture where you could look at it over and over again and it plays, you get lifted viscerally each time.

The coffee cup scene in Reds, *when Reed and Bryant have their first meeting, is compressed brilliantly in the editing. How did that come about?*

Warren hadn't totally written the dialogue yet for John Reed talking to Louise Bryant. He was suddenly caught shooting the scene, which was the first basic seduction; that's when he grabs her. He wanted to shoot it fast to get the feeling of the pacing, so he started shooting and he would say, "21, 22, 23." Every once in a while, he would turn to the camera and would give you something that was real, and other times he would be giving you numbers. I saw this material and I went ape-shit. I said, "Warren, you're going to be able to see your lips, it's not going to work, you've got to give me some dialogue." He said, "No, we'll put it in later." Later, he covered it with the coffee cups, but he hated the bright blue backdrop that cameraman Vittorio Storaro had, so I wasn't able to use too much toward that angle. The material I could use was limited, but it still had to make sense, it had to play.

So did you discover that playing the pouring of the coffee in the cups was a way of showing that a lot was going on between the two characters?

Of course. Also, I had to get off his face all the time. I began taking pieces of various takes and trying to make it montage as though he were talking. What was fun about the scene was having the freedom to make it play visually; that made it possible to find tracks that work. It was a real puzzle. Every picture has at least one scene that becomes your nemesis. The coffee cup scene was one. It all worked out, but that just was a mind-boggling nightmare in the cutting room.

Alan Heim mentioned that Aram Avakian once said to avoid any film that has people coming in and out of cars too often. Do you try to cut around prosaic actions?

Yes, those are called *gezuntis* and *gezatus*—entrances and exits. It's very boring to see someone walk from one place to another. Nothing is going on, in terms of the dynamics of the scene. Almost all scenes are shot with a beginning, middle, and end. Sometimes you make big cuts to get to the essence of a scene in the most dramatic way. The scene can't just sit there like a *latke*. You may only need so much of it, and all that other stuff can be sliced out, usually the beginning and the end.

Have you ever used an optical technique to solve an editorial problem?

Yes. In *Odds Against Tomorrow* there was a long scene in a very creepy elevator between a black guy running the elevator and Robert Ryan. Bob Wise wanted to go back and do it over because the visual wasn't right. They never got around to reshooting the scene. Having had experience with opticals, I went ahead and had an optical push-in done and never said anything to Bob. When I showed it to him he was just delighted because it was so immeasurably pushed in that it got rid of what was bothering him; it enhanced the scene. In the years when I was at Film Graphics we always laid out our own opticals. You learned to find out what could be done.

Do you feel that there is a difference in the way that male and female editors work?

I think there's a big difference between men and women who enter the editing field. Women of my generation are more used to serving someone else creatively, and not feeling maligned by it as much. It must be very hard for certain men in terms of an ego or a macho thing, when they are constantly having to redo something they feel very strongly about. Some people come on very strong and fight for something that they don't necessarily have a reason to believe in. It becomes a fight of personalities rather than the scene they are discussing.

How do you feel about freelancing?

It's very tough in this business. When you are out of work, you figure you'll never work again. It's a terrible, terrible problem. I don't care how many pictures you do, how good you are, or how hot you are—you always find a reason why you won't get any more work. I still do the same thing. We're all in the same boat.

There is a tremendous pressure on the editor to get a film out on time. When you have a tight schedule, what are some of the techniques you use to keep the editing process moving?

I cut a lot of scenes silent. When you're in a terrible hurry, it's much easier to deal with the picture only than to try to keep the picture and the track in sync. This is not the way you do a long dialogue scene, but believe me, when you are running for a screening, cutting a scene silent and then tracking it can save you a helluva lot of time. One of my favorite scenes in *Bonnie and Clyde* is in the theater where they are playing "We're in the Money," and they've just shot the first man. I had to do that in a tremendous hurry one morning. There wasn't that much dialogue in it. I would cut it and feel every sound. You had to know who was saying what at what time. I would hear it in my ears. I knew where my overlaps were. Having come out of sound editing, I think in terms of sound. I can hear it in relationships. Jerry Greenberg was the perfect assistant to have, also having come out of sound. Jerry was able to look at it and know exactly how I had overlapped it, and how to put it together. He would track it behind me. He would put the dialogue to it. I love to train people who come out of sound because you get that added advantage of someone who thinks silently with their ears.

On *America, America,* I'd put a piece of white tape on the back of the film so that my assistant never missed the splice. It saves countless time because track tape is easier to get off, and if you have a properly set gate on the Moviola, your film will go through. My Universal XL projector was great if I was in a hurry. I was able to run cuts just to make sure they worked without double splicing them and without taking off the white tape. When you get on a roll, your hands can't work as fast as you're trying to cut, so everything you do to save time makes that cut work better.

What are some of the technical rules of editing that directors should be aware of?

I worked with a director who came out of commercials and really had his nose in the air about camera right, camera left. I kept saying, "You can't have two people looking off somewhere when they are supposed to be talking to each other." He said, "That's bullshit, I do it all the time." I said, "Yes, you do it in commercials all the time, because you jump from place to place."

Robert Wise would always plan his axis change. On *Odds Against Tomorrow* he shot a bar scene on one side of the camera. Then he would cut to the bartender and bring the bartender around to the other side of the axis. It was a classic example of how you change your axis. There was always one key shot. When you don't get those shots, and you just have somebody coming in without any reason, then you have a scene where nobody relates to anyone. Nobody is looking anybody else in the eye, and it's totally disorienting. The audience might get thrown out of the scene because it's nonconnective. Film is connective; that's what film is.

How much of a contribution does an editor make on a film?

I've often been given much more credit by certain directors than I thought was really fair. Arthur Penn has probably given me more credit than anybody I know because he's totally confident. The contribution an editor makes on a film has to be part of the work. It is totally a team effort, and the minute the personality takes over, you've lost it. That has nothing to do with the work.

Do you think the kind of rapid cutting used in music videos and commercials is going to change the way feature films are cut?

I worry if we're raising enough people in a generation who are able to sit and look at a scene play out without getting bored if it doesn't change every two seconds. We talk an awful lot about cutting, we talk very little about not lousing something up by cutting just to make it move faster. I'm afraid that's the very thing I helped promulgate, through directors I've worked with who liked that energy. It may come to haunt us, because attention spans are short. In the old days, everything played more slowly and people were more patient. Now people are being hired because they're hot, they're flashy. You get worried, then you see something like *The Fabulous Baker Boys*, and you see it's done by a young director who wrote it, and I get all encouraged again. It's about relationships.

What is the hardest editing concept to learn?

The hardest thing to learn when people are starting out is how to correct what's wrong without hurting what's good. I realized it was a problem when I was able to train assistants by giving them material to cut under ideal circumstances. They had the total umbrella of feeling secure. I was the one responsible; it didn't matter to Arthur Penn who cut as long as it was working.

On *Bonnie and Clyde* Jerry Greenberg did some of the most brilliant cutting. He had weeks and weeks to do a sequence, which was exactly what he needed. He had the freedom. On the first sequence he cut, he got into a big mess and we had to pull it together at the last minute. It didn't happen the second time, because that's part of the learning process. That's a golden opportunity you hope every editor has a chance to do. The one thing good about the Hollywood gang-bang theory of putting on 16 editors and hoping you'll get a movie on time is that it is giving many more starting editors chances to learn with a supervising editor there as a back-up. If you can't pass that on, there's no point. We're all going to get to the point where we can't do it anymore. Who is going to train the people? You have to train them, not so much in terms of how do you make a splice, and do you overlap ahead or behind, but why isn't your scene playing, what's wrong with it. You do what an actor or a director does when they sit down with a scene. What's the scene about and how are we going to say it? The fun thing about editing is that you get to come in at the end. You've got a certain amount of material, then you try to put it together in what seems to be the best way. Sometimes it works and sometimes it doesn't.

8

Tom Rolf

Tom Rolf followed editing as a career path on the good advice of his father, who was a film director.

Rolf was an assistant editor on the television series *Leave It to Beaver* and became an editor on *The Big Valley* and *Burke's Law*.

Tom Rolf's feature career is an expression of his versatility and desire to work in every film genre. His diversity is evident in such films as *Taxi Driver*, *War Games*, *Outrageous Fortune*, *New York, New York* and *Black Rain*. He has collaborated with John Frankenheimer, Michael Cimino, Martin Scorsese, Paul Schrader, Adrian Lyne, John Badham, and Ridley Scott. In 1983 he won an Academy Award as part of the editing team on Philip Kaufman's *The Right Stuff*. In 1990 Rolf was reunited with director Adrian Lyne on the editorially complex *Jacob's Ladder*.

1965	*The Glory Guys*
1967	*Clambake*
1969	*Underground*
1970	*The McKenzie Break*
1971	*The Hunting Party*
1972	*The Honkers*
1973	*The Lolly Madonna War*
1974	*The Last American Hero*
	Visit to a Chief's Son
1975	*The French Connection II*
1976	*Black Sunday*

	Taxi Driver (with Marcia Lucas and Melvin Shapiro)
1977	*New York, New York*
1978	*Blue Collar*
1979	*Hard Core*
	Prophecy
1980	*Heaven's Gate* (with Lisa Fruchtman, Jerry Greenberg, and William Reynolds)
1981	*Ghost Story*
1983	*The Right Stuff* (with Glenn Farr, Lisa Fruchtman, Stephen A. Rotter, and Douglas Stewart)**
	War Games
1984	*Thief of Hearts*
1986	*9 1/2 Weeks* (with Caroline Biggerstaff)
	Quicksilver
1987	*Outrageous Fortune*
	Stakeout (with Michael Ripps)
1988	*The Great Outdoors*
1989	*Black Rain*
1990	*Jacob's Ladder*

**Academy Award for best achievement in film editing.

What is editing?

It's imposing my choice over yours, having the arrogance to say this is better than that. It's being a critic. It's an art form you're interpreting. I'm imposing my taste. It's a matter of choices and keeping it straight in your head. It's like having an enormous picture puzzle—1,000 pieces will make it look perfect but they give you 100,000. It's going through all of the pieces, to try to get the best parts. That's what editing is.

Why did you become a film editor?

I was born in Scandinavia. I came to this country when I was about eight and a half years old. When I got out of the service, I had no idea what I was going to do, so I asked my stepfather, who was a director, "What would be your advice if I wanted to be a director like you?" He said if he had to do it over again, he would try to be a film editor, because the editor gets to see all the good with the bad; everything channels into his room. There can be 5,000 people working on a film but basically it comes down to your hands. I thought that was intriguing and I eventually managed to get a job as an apprentice. Once I attained the job of editor, I didn't want to do anything else no matter what they proposed or offered.

You have worked in a wide range of film styles; is this an objective of yours?

I've made it a real effort to try and get different kinds of pictures. For a while I got turned down for anything that had comedy in it because they said, "Oh, well, he's never done a comedy." Now I've done three comedies in a row and I've got to stop doing that, because they'll say that's all I can do.

You cut two movies for director Martin Scorsese. On Taxi Driver *there were three editors. How did you work together?*

The set-up was the direct result of panic. After the picture was shot in New York, nothing at all had been cut. Marty wanted to take a little vacation and start the editing process after he came back. When he came back the studio said, "We're glad to have you back, you know you have to deliver a print in eight weeks," or some ridiculous time frame. Evidently, he had not been aware that he signed an agreement to deliver the picture on a certain date. Obviously, that meant more than one person had to get involved in putting it together. Everybody grabbed what they could and cut as quickly as they could. It was a homogeneous experience and Marty was appreciative.

What was it like to work with Scorsese?

He's encyclopedic, he knows everything and anything, the lore, the history; he's a real scholar and in many ways a genius. Marty has such a marvelous eye.

Does he know a lot about editing?

Oh yes, he started editing when he was at New York University. When he was doing *Boxcar Bertha*, I'd see him sitting there looking very dejected, staring at the screen, trying to figure out what the hell would make it work. He's so committed, so emotionally involved, that you've got to love him for it. Marty has a special knack, he'll show you a scene and he'll hang on a shot and hang on it and you'll say, "Why am I on this shot so long? Why am I watching this image?" My natural inclination, once the shot registers and you know the action or dialogue, is to get off it, because it's moving pictures. It was Marty who said, "Now wait a minute, we can put another eight or ten feet there." All of a sudden you start reinvesting in the shot, because you realize there must be another reason than what the obvious shows. Sure enough, you find yourself getting into it again and again. He's dead right. He taught me a lesson.

Was there heavy coverage on Taxi Driver?

No, not that bad. It was before the days of the real heavy coverage that you get now. It was rather sparse in certain areas. The whole "You talking to me?" sequence was dictated when I saw the dailies. I said, "I don't know how I'm going to put this together." In my mind there wasn't any coverage when I saw it.

It was all shot from the same angle?

Oh, almost entirely. All you could do was to go in and out. I only saw a lack of coverage, when I saw the dailies. It was in resorting to the only options I had that it ended up being what it is. That sequence never changed from the day it was put into first cut. I was kind of shocked at the lack of coverage because there was very little to go on, and yet the end result was very effective and very powerful. De Niro gives you so much to work with. If anything, he gives you too much, because he tries to give you something different, a little original, in almost every take. So you can't go back to take three, and hope to see approximately what was in take two.

Is cutting a performance like De Niro's very involved?

Yes. It's very difficult to cut a performance that has that degree of choices. The one thing you have to have in a characterization is consistency, and if the consistency varies from one take to another, then you have nowhere to go; you just have to stick with one. If they give you no other coverage except that one line reading of that one take, that's it; that's the total impression the audience is going to get. With De Niro, his performances are so within the character, the character doesn't change. But the movement, the timing, the expressions all change constantly so that, where he'll say on one line of dialogue, "Do you want a cup of cofFEE?" in the next take he'll say, "Do you want a cup of COFfee?" To get from cofFEE to the next line is dictated by what you have available. It's all difficult to put together, it's a real puzzle. The character of Travis Bickle always remained basically the same, but with tremendous variations. The real problem is when you get an actor who changes the character on you right smack from take to take, trying to be a little bit different; then you're really in trouble. I once had this problem with an actor. I had to tell him that I had to take all of his good performances and just throw them away. I said, "You did some great stuff but I couldn't use any of it." He asked why and I told him, he understood and, obviously, he never did it again.

What was the main challenge in cutting New York, New York?

That was another big picture that had a lot of footage. It wasn't so much footage of many takes, just an excessive amount of scenes; it was a long, long movie. We ran a cut one night, we finished about midnight, it was three and a half hours. My reaction was to call Marty a genius because that picture really worked at three and a half hours. It was so original in its art direction and its staging. The studio was adamant; they wouldn't release a picture if it was over two hours. Unfortunately, down at around two hours, it didn't have the connective tissue to make it work. You didn't know the characters, you didn't understand them.

You cut Paul Schrader's first film, Blue Collar. *Do first-time directors require special attention from the editor?*

They want to feel well served by the editor. They have to feel the editor is on their side. It's a pretty shaky circumstance to be a first-time director. They're very vulnerable, and you've got to be careful when you present an idea that is radically different from what the intent was. You have to do it in such a way that they don't feel threatened or subverted.

Is there such thing as an editor's director?

An editor's director is one who anticipates the needs and angles to make every sequence work, and who remembers that such mundane issues as overlapping dialogue are a problem. If directors allow actors to get away with overlapping and do it to a fault, it limits the choices and the way that you can physically cut a film.

What was your role in the editing of Heaven's Gate?

Essentially, the original arrangement was that I cut the body of the film. Bill Reynolds came in to cut the prologue and epilogue. I cut 31 or 32 reels, we ended up with 35 or 36 reels. We knew we had a big problem, because nobody is going to see a 36 reel movie.

How long would that be?

Six or seven hours. It was staggering. I suspected very early on there were enormous problems, but then your paranoia backs in and says, "Hey, maybe I'm wrong and he's right, maybe he's really the genius," and you start doubting yourself a little bit. It was just so overwhelmingly pretentious. I just knew it didn't have a chance. The script didn't measure up to the production, or the money, or the time, and the 1,300,000 feet of print. I put 17 months of my life into that film. You've got to go a little bit wacko after 17 months, especially when you're dealing with the egos that this picture represented, mine included. It was a pretty horrifying experience. In the years that I've been in the business, it was the only bad experience I've had. Others have been difficult, and you have pictures that might not succeed for whatever reason, but that one was just a plain horror story.

Were you still on the film at the point when it was to be released?

By that time, I had been gone from the film for three or four months. The director and I were not communicating at that point. It was not worthwhile to hang around and not be able to contribute anything. If you had a suggestion it was ignored or reversed; so why bother? It was a shame.

Did you have anything to do with the recutting of the film?

The day after the New York opening, I was asked by United Artists if I would be interested in recutting the picture. However, when I found out that the director had also volunteered his effort in recutting, I realized that was a no-win situation and I declined.

In a film like War Games *where the clock starts early for dramatic tension, does it intensify the editing process?*

Only in that the steady feeling of time eroding away has to be constantly referred to. You have to keep that tempo going all the time.

Were the scenes in the war room covered well?

It was well covered. It was an easy set, you always had something you could feature. That was a fun picture to do, it looks more complicated than it is. You just have to keep everybody "alive" all around the room, all the time. It's something you get used to.

In talking to Michael Kahn about working on Fatal Attraction, *which was directed by Adrian Lyne, he said there were a lot of beautiful pieces of film that had to be structured. Did you find this to be true when you worked with Lyne on* 9 1/2 Weeks?

Totally true. Any shot that Adrian Lyne composed as a master would exist only for the particular second for which he composed it. The minute an actor walked into that frame, it no longer resembled what he originally composed.

Was there a lot of construction in the editing?

Very much so, and a lot of destruction, because we had to tear a lot of it apart. The picture had some major problems. It was a very difficult movie to work on. I was not the original editor; the lady who worked on it for a year left to have a child, and Adrian was just at a loss with the movie because it tested very poorly with any kind of preview audience. They hated Mickey Rourke and Kim Basinger because he was a mean son of a bitch and she was a bimbo for staying with him—so who are you going to like? After I saw the movie the first time, I said, "You have to make them more likable, somebody's got to like one or two of these people, or nobody's going to want to go see the movie." By massaging and manipulating it a little, I think we got the characters to be as appealing as they could be without going back and reshooting anything.

How did you go about doing that?

I went through every piece of film available looking for any facial expression on the two principals that could in any way soften their character. I made Mickey Rourke a bit more human by using material taken after the director yelled "Cut," when he would smile in a kind of relief that the scene was over. I would use that smile.

How did you cut the sequences in Black Rain *that are in Japanese?*

I had an apprentice who translated for me. There are many more colors and nuances in Japanese than English, so you shouldn't cut away from certain pronunciations. I tend to cut early on punctuations, where a certain train of thought ends, or you're going to start a new one. With Japanese that doesn't work, because it's all in colors and you just can't cut in the middle. It's fascinating to cut that material.

Many editors have told me that the hardest kind of scene to cut is a dialogue scene between two people. Do you agree?

I disagree. I have an overall formula and philosophy of editing, and that is action, reaction, action, reaction. I hate to start dialogue off-stage and then go to the reaction. I always want to be on-stage and have people react to what they've seen on-stage; it satisfies an audience better. They see the effect of a line of dialogue or a piece of action if you go immediately to a reaction. I tend to overlap quite a bit in my dialogue scenes. The minute a telling word or a question is posed, even within the framework of a sentence, I go for a reaction to see the reactor reacting to the question being posed, how they are trying to formulate the answer in their face or dialogue. I find it much more interesting to be on somebody, trying to figure out what they are going to say at that juncture of the sentence.

Dialogue dictates how a scene should be cut. I find the most difficult thing to edit is reams and reams of film, such as in a courtroom drama where you have twelve jurors, the defense, the prosecution, the family, the witnesses, the judge, the bailiff. You have everybody and you've got to keep them constantly "alive" so that they don't appear out of nowhere. The same for a major eating scene, where you have a lot of people passing food; the milk is never at the same level in the glass.

What is the purpose of an overlap?

Overlapping full lines of dialogue keeps the flow steady in the narrative line. Overlapping the ends of words gives a much smoother editing experience. Sometimes you want it a little rough, abrasive and staccato; you don't want it to be smooth. Some people are almost married to the fact that you go from a long shot, to a medium, to over-the-shoulder, to close-up, and gradually build a scene in a very dramatic fashion. I will go from a big head close-up, to a master shot, to over-the-shoulder, and back to a two shot. I don't necessarily want to match anything; it depends on the kind of movie, on the kind of story you're telling.

Do you feel you have to know all the rules in order to break them? Did you once obey them all?

Sure. I did all the gradual steps to get into the big head close-ups, thinking that was unobtrusive. It was, but it wasn't necessarily very dramatic. On *Black Rain*, which is about a man caught in an alien culture, I desperately tried to make the cuts a little more unbalanced, to go from a big close-up to an over-the-shoulder, because it just makes it a little more jarring, more unsettling. That also carries over into telling the story. I think it's much more dramatic.

Why are films so heavily covered these days?

People are covering more now because they know less. They figure if they get enough time or enough editors to figure it out, somehow they can put it together. That's not making films, that's just shooting a lot of film. To make a film you goddamn well better have a point of view going in.

When you do have that kind of coverage, how does an editor give a point of view to the film?

If you have enough time, you can make it have a point of view by sorting everything out, spending days, weeks, months, even a year or more. You're dictating it on your own, but that's just wasting time and money. I have no respect for people who shoot that amount of film and say, "There's got to be a pony in there somewhere." When you end up on day one, with 20,000 to 30,000 feet of dailies, you've got to say to yourself, "This is going to be disastrous." Twenty thousand feet is two features right there. That's not directing.

What does your first cut on a film look like?

I try to make it as polished as I can, but I'm not one of those editors who likes to pre-mix a lot of music and sound effects, to try and sell what I've done by making it look too polished. That's not the way I was taught, and that's not the way I like to do it. A lot of people do that now; they almost have what looks like a finished product you would put in a theater, just to show to the director and producers. I think there's a danger in putting all that music and extra sound, because you camouflage what might be a very big problem in the story. If it works with the bare bones, it's going to work that much better with all the extra stuff in it. Most people now ask you to do it, and I try to resist, explaining to them that they are faking themselves out of their socks by putting this stuff in at such an early date. If you put music and sound effects to a work print, they start evaluating the movie by listening to those sounds.

How long is a first cut compared to the final cut?

If a first cut is 10 to 15 percent longer than it ends up, that's a nice cushion to work with. You can tighten it up, pace it, and still make it a comfortable running time. When it gets into 30 or 40 percent over, then you're in major, major trouble.

What terms do you like to use at various stages of the editing process? Most editors cringe when they hear the terms "rough cut" or "assembly."

I refuse to be identified with either one of those terms. A rough cut means just slapping something together; an assembly means even less, it means you're going to put all of the masters together. I will tell anybody that asks, "When are we going to have an assembly or rough cut?" that you're not going to have one, you're going to have a first cut, and that's what you're going to get.

Have you ever used a piece of film before a slate?

Oh, sure, I tell my assistants, "Never, ever cut anything out of the dailies before the slate, after the slate, and especially after the director yells cut." Anything and everything has to stay in the dailies. Yes, that happens quite often.

What equipment do you use?

I cut almost exclusively on a Moviola. I keep a KEM in the room for viewing and rewinding. I use the KEM to locate the footage I need at high speed. Then I pull it out, put it on the Moviola, and cut it there. If you use a KEM you don't use a synchronizer, which is the nemesis for me. I can't use a KEM because I can never get back in sync, I'm always sliding two or three frames out of sync. I just find it very ponderous to keep reaching across that wing, grabbing the track and pulling and jerking. And you have all these take-ups, and disengaging this, and engaging that. To me the Moviola is just such a magnificent piece of equipment. It is a far better piece of equipment for me. It's really a shame that the younger editors never learned about it; a Moviola just intimidates the hell out of them. They start saying "Well, it's noisy."

I have equipment in my room that is different than what most people use. Anything I find that makes it easier for me, I buy. I have a different kind of editing chair that gives me enormous lateral movement without wheels. It has an arming mechanism underneath that allows me to scoot sideways and back and forth, so I never roll over my film. It's notorious in cutting rooms that people just roll over their film and rip it. I used to say I had a chair that cut two of my features; wherever the chair would rip it, that's where I would splice it.

Did you have the chair custom-made?

I saw it at a furniture exhibition. It was designed for the New York Stock Exchange, for people who had to go from telephone to FAX machine. It had arms which I knew would interfere with draping film across my body, but I asked if they could make it without arms, a stool version. The guy said, "We can try," and this is what I have. I use British wire split reels, so I can take my cut material and instantly put it on the KEM, on cores and run it. They're just for the convenience. They're better, in my opinion, than the American reels. I have a splicing stand. I'm able to put my butt splicer onto a stand that swings out of the way whenever I don't need it.

Do you think that editing rooms are claustrophobic?

Editing rooms are certainly not very aesthetic; sometimes no windows, institutional green walls, and the asphalt tile on the floor. It's pretty grim and I try to stay away from those. I demand better surroundings. I try to get rooms with windows, carpeting, and a nice place to sit and relax, to have coffee or a drink.

How does an editor learn to listen to the material?

There's a sensitivity gauge somewhere, it depends on what you are sensitive to. If you give a picture like *The Accused* to a woman to cut, you'll find not a different picture, but you will see a different substance or texture to it overall. It's a sensitivity to the editor's life experience and values. It's going to be different.

How intuitive is editing?

It's totally intuitive to me, I cut that way. I'm sometimes sorry that I've done something radically wrong, and I have to go back and correct it, because like a house of cards, once the first choice is wrong, everything else is wrong. You go back and build the old foundation again.

How many years do you think it takes to become a good editor?

I don't know yet. I'm still learning because I'll change my mind tomorrow about something. To learn the mechanics is nothing; to have the confidence to do what you feel is right and just cut, that takes a few years. You go through the stage of "What if I'm wrong?" and that's a big fear for somebody when you're dealing with an audience of millions. It's when you become confident enough to accept who you are, that's how long it takes you to become an editor.

Have you ever made the decision not to cut?

Yes. It's much more important to learn what not to cut. That's the hardest thing for any young editor starting out; it was for me.

Why is that?

You're drawing a salary, man, do something, cut, make edits. You learn that the scene is playing, you don't have to justify your existence by making a cut; it works. It happened more when I was beginning; now I'm much colder about looking at things than I was then.

What is your average schedule?

I try to maintain a very civilized schedule. I'm there by nine and out no later than seven. I hate working nights and I choose not to. I don't mind working a sixth day of the week; I hate the seventh day. I think long hours are very unproductive. Producers are very silly in some of their demands of postproduction crews, in trying to force them to work these outrageous hours and days. I find myself going back after X amount of hours and just tearing everything apart, saying, "I've done something very wrong," and it shows. So I try to maintain a realistic schedule in terms of the people I work with, and certainly myself.

What is the role of the assistant in keeping that schedule realistic?

It's almost all on the assistant. It's all anticipation; he's got to be able to anticipate. You don't have to go tell him, "I need this next." A great assistant knows that and it's just there and provided for you. Believe me, it takes so much off your back. You are so able to go forward when that is being done. I think a good assistant is worth their weight in gold, twice their weight, three times their weight.

Do you try to overcut so everything is there in the cut, and you don't have to find trims?

No, I try to make it as close as possible. If I have to pull stuff from the KEM to get new lines of dialogue, I pull in excess of what I need, and then I go back and refine it all on the Moviola. Sometimes it's going to be a couple of frames over, sometimes a couple of feet over. The feet go in the trim bin, the frames go in a trim book. I'm very careful of my frame trims. If I'm taking two or three frames off of picture and track, I make sure I tape them together. I used to clip them together but they fell apart. Now, I tape them together and then I put another piece of tape across the face of either the picture or track and write the number. I always arrow it to the head. At the end of every week, you come in and take this box of frame trims and give it to one of the apprentices. They sit there and sort the whole thing out. They put them into envelopes. Each scene has its own envelope, so I can say scene 125, key number 2555, boom, it's there inside of seconds. I must say I've never lost a frame. I am really hysterical about that, because when I want to go back and reconstruct something, if I can't find the frame, I go nuts. When you lose material you have to go back and reorder it—then somebody finds it. Somebody forgets you have a second print and now you use part of it, then there's duplicate key numbers. You can just go on and create such big problems for yourself.

Is the organizational system that you use in the cutting room the same from film to film?

It varies only because of different directors. My assistant Willy on *Black Rain* had worked with Ridley Scott before on *Someone to Watch over Me*, and I am grateful he knew what to anticipate. As long as you employ people you trust, they take care of you. So it changes a little bit, no big deal.

How do you personally know when an assistant is ready to cut?

When they really start bugging me. There are some that have a lot of arrogance, which I used to have. You say, "Big deal, I can do that," and then you get in there and start doing it and become humble. When they start asking, "Come on, let me do a scene," I always deal with that. "Take that one," and they say, "You mean the whole scene?" "Well, you want a scene, right?"

When did you learn how to cut scenes?

I was the assistant to Dick Belding, who was one of the editors on *Leave It to Beaver*. I asked him if I could take the trims of a show that had already been on the air and see if I could cut a scene. In those days they would print one master, maybe two, a couple of close-ups, a couple of over-shoulders—the minimal coverage for a half-hour comedy. I would try to take what was left after the show was done and cut scenes. There was no film left. The good stuff, where the close-up should be played, was taken, so I ended up playing it with everything off-stage. In those days it was cutting with scissors and then hot splicing. If you wanted to make a change and go back and put it the way it was, you had to put a black frame in. It was fun. I would show it to Belding the next day, and he would look at it and laugh, but it gave me the confidence to just keep doing it. That was my first cutting experience. It was totally safe. I was not being judged by anyone, my job was not on the line.

In those days did you ever think there were going to be answers to those technological problems?

No, I never really thought about it. You do the best you can, make it as good as you can, and walk out the door.

What personality traits do you think are necessary to be an editor?

You have to have an ego, but you can't have too much. You have to be able to stand up for your taste and your opinion. You've got to be a pretty good diplomat. You can't take things personally. If somebody criticizes an area of the film or a certain cut, you can't take it that you necessarily did something wrong. You just saw it differently than they did. You've got to roll with the punches.

Where do you think the art of film editing is heading?

I can't see it being different than it is now. It has always been a matter of making choices, and there will always be the human choice. If it's an action piece, it will be dictated by one set of reasoning. If it's a matter of philosophy, it will be dictated by another set of reasons. It's just a matter of making choices, and I don't think the electronic wizard has been invented that will make those choices for you. There will always be editing. We are in such a visual age. I imagine film will last more than another few years, and tape is the film of tomorrow. God knows what's after that, mind transference? I mean, who knows? There's still going to be editing. There's still going to be someone saying, "This will be better if you do it that way." If it's mind control, there's going to be somebody editing your mind control. Editing is an ongoing profession.

9

Maury Winetrobe

Maury Winetrobe began his film career as an apprentice music editor for Columbia Pictures, where he advanced to the head of the studio's music editing department.

In the 1960s, when it was difficult for a music editor to make the transition to picture editing, Winetrobe practiced cutting scenes on his own in the early morning hours. After spending a full day in the music department, he would return in the evening, cutting scenes to gain the experience he needed to become a picture editor. That opportunity came with *Funny Girl* in 1968, when director Herbert Ross and supervising editor Robert Swink gave him musical and then nonmusical scenes to cut. As part of the editorial team for *Funny Girl*, he received an Oscar nomination on his first time out as film editor.

In 1980 Winetrobe began a collaboration with director, Harold Becker. Their four films together—*The Black Marble, Taps, Vision Quest*, and *The Boost*—merge the craft of editing with the directorial art.

1968	*Funny Girl* (with supervising editor Robert Swink and William Sands)*
	The Wrecking Crew
1969	*Cactus Flower*
1970	*Getting Straight*
1972	*Last of the Red Hot Lovers*
	T. R. Baskin
1974	*Mame*

1977	*Twilight's Last Gleaming* (with Michael Luciano and William Martin)
	From Noon Till Three
	The Choirboys (supervising editor, with Bill Martin and Irving Rosenblum)
1978	*Ice Castles* (with Melvin Shapiro)
1979	*Ravagers*
	The Frisco Kid (with Irving Rosenblum)
1980	*The Black Marble*
	The Jazz Singer (with supervising editor Frank Urioste)
1981	*Taps*
1985	*Vision Quest*
1986	*The Arm*
1989	*The Boost*

*Academy Award nomination for best achievement in film editing.

How did you get into the film business?

I took journalism in college; I wanted to be a sports reporter. One summer I got a job at Columbia Pictures as an office boy and just fell in love with the whole studio and all of the departments. After school I joined the Navy and after serving my time, I went back to Columbia and got into music editing as an apprentice. I have a musical background, I used to play the fiddle when I was a little kid. From there I moved into being an assistant music editor, then to music editor, and finally to the head of music editing. It was tough to get into film editing, especially if you were from music or sound effects. I went to a couple of friends of mine, Reggie Brown and Tony DeMarco, who were very helpful. I would come in around six o'clock in the morning, get a couple of sequences from them, work until around nine, then I would go down to my department. At night after they had gone, I would go out and get a hamburger, and from about seven to ten I'd sit at their Moviola and hack around with more scenes. Not being an assistant picture editor, that was the only way I could get any experience.

Along came a Columbia picture called *Funny Girl*. I was the head music editor. It was being directed by William Wyler, and Herbert Ross, who was doing all of the musical sequences and was very helpful. He gave me all of the musical sequences to recut. Bob Swink, the supervising editor, was also extremely helpful. He gave me a couple of sequences that were nonmusical to do. The picture was nominated for film editing on my first shot, so I was very excited. After *Funny Girl* I went back to head of music editing. Phil Karlson was going to direct the Matt Helm picture, *The Wrecking Crew*, with Dean Martin. I had been music editor on some of his films. The associate producer was Harold Kress, a fine editor from Metro Goldwyn Mayer. I went up to Harold and said, "Look, I know my experience has just been on *Funny Girl*, but I would sure like the opportunity to cut your picture." He said, "Well, all right, let me talk to Phil Karlson." As luck would have it, they agreed to give me a chance. That was the first picture I cut by myself.

You have cut four films for director Harold Becker. Does he have a good understanding of the editorial process?

Harold had a career as a cinematographer and in England he was rated as one of the best directors of commercials. He understands every facet of filmmaking. He has the best understanding and appreciation of the editorial system of any director I've worked with, the most down to earth, and a real human being. He covers a film very well. He allows his editor much more freedom than a lot of other directors. You can discuss any point you want with him, and if he thinks your point is valid, there is no argument. He may try something another way once in a while, but if it comes back to the way you had it, there's no rancor, no problem. Even six months before the show, I'll be talking with Harold and sometimes he will say, "Hey, read this script, if you have any ideas, let me know."

In Taps, *when the George C. Scott character announces the closing of the academy to the boys, you use a lot of reaction shots to capture the enormity of their feelings. What were you trying to accomplish?*

Some of these boys were just starting in the school, some were graduating, and some were midsemester. We were trying to show how it affected all of them, regardless of their age, and what term they were in. We can see by the reaction shots, all of them were nonplussed. I enjoyed holding back the extreme wide angle of the whole field until a strategic place in his speech, and then dropping back from close-up to an extreme wide angle of the whole regiment.

In the scene where the National Guard drives in on trucks at night to try to end the siege, there are reaction shots of the boys where we see the headlights on their faces. Did the timing of the light patterns become a concern of the editing?

That sequence was a bit of a tough nut to crack, but it was worth the time. What was shot first was the line of trucks. Then the camera turned around and shot the reactions. Sometimes you might catch the light just coming on the person you wanted to cut to, or it might be leaving, so that was a bit of a problem. What you would try and do is match up the reaction with the lights hitting them.

The sound in this film is especially effective and dramatic. Do you get involved in the sound editing?

Oh, yes. I think every editor does or should. As editor you should be involved in every phase of making the picture: the photography, the sound, the music editing, and the dubbing. As the film editor, it's your responsibility and pleasure to be involved in any aspect that you can.

Taps *ends by bringing back the parade sequence with George C. Scott. Is this a reprint of the earlier scene or did you use different material?*

I had a discussion with Harold, we were wondering how to end the picture. We were kind of concerned that the end, where Sean Penn is carrying out Timothy Hutton, was too downbeat. Harold and I were talking about some way that we could possibly reprise the march, the band, and the military feeling. This was a brainchild of ours, and also the music came in very low and very reverbed like it was coming in from left field. We were hoping reprising part of the march would have the audience leave on an upper feeling, rather than seeing this sad scene of the dead body being carried away. I think it helped. It's not an exact replica, we just picked out excerpts.

From the cut sequence?

Yes, and also some material that was eliminated from the march, because it was cut way down. We went back to the trims.

In Vision Quest, *was there a lot of material for the circular wrestling drills in the gym?*

Yes, and unfortunately not all the same tempo. We had to do some intricate jump cutting there or cheats to make it look like it was all gradually getting faster and faster. We did frame cut here and there to make the tempo gradually increase until they all flop.

How were the wrestling matches put together?

All of the wrestling matches were very heavily covered. Peter Berger put the last two wrestling matches together because we were so busy with the other stuff. When Peter left, I went into it because then I had time, but Peter did an excellent job on both of the wrestling matches. I just went through and made some eliminations and inserted some angles we felt would help heighten it.

Twilight's Last Gleaming *made extensive use of split screen work to tell the story. Why did director Robert Aldrich use this technique?*

It did two things. It saved time on the clock and also added to the excitement. Instead of trying to show this is happening, that is happening, they could use the same amount of time showing what was happening in four different places at once. We're showing what is happening at the attack, in the reserves, and with the people who are responding. After they realized how much film they had, they started hiring other editors. I cut most of those multiple screens. My assistant, Ralph Hall, would be in the next room with his six-gang synchronizer full of film. I would be in the other room with my six-gang synchronizer full of film, and we would go room to room saying, "With this footage we'll do this, with this we'll do that," and then ordering the effects and putting them in. Irving Rosenblum did a fine job at that.

Boy, just making it work at times was a chore because you could fill panel one and panel two, but what were we going to do in panel three? Maybe there wasn't enough film on four. You'd have to dig up something from someplace else and hold on to it. It was a lot of trial and error. We would run two projection machines at once to check it. The split screens on that movie were really the biggest chore.

What was the coverage like?

Bob Aldrich always used two cameras on every single shot. They weren't different angles, they were right next to each other. One was for close-ups; the other was for a medium or long shot. So you always had barrels of film. In first cut the picture was about three and a half hours, and it went out about two hours and 20 minutes. The material was enormous.

What did the script tell you in terms of the split screen?

It didn't tell you how to do it. It would say, "Screen one shows this, screen two shows this, screen three shows this," but any correlation between what it said in the script and the film you received was two different things. Bob hated to come into the cutting room. He very rarely came in, but sometimes we would call him and say, "Hey, Bob, we need you, what are you going to do, there isn't film here?" Or "Bob, there is too much film here, what should we show?" Most of the time, we hacked it out ourselves. Considering how intricate everything was, I think Bob controlled the whole project very well.

How did you work with Frank Urioste, the supervising editor, on the Neil Diamond version of The Jazz Singer?

He would take one sequence and I took another. We just traded off, whether it was a musical or dramatic sequence. Frank did a little more than half the picture, and I did the rest of the picture. Frank said to me one day, "Maury, you're the person whose style is closest to mine," which I took as flattering. We both edit very closely, whether it's style or pacing. We defied anybody to find out who cut a certain sequence, because they are so similar. The director mentioned it, too. Once in a while, Frank would give me a sequence and say, "Gee, Maury, I can't see what else I can do, will you take it please?" We'd do that with a musical number once in a while, too. Conversely, if I thought I'd come up against a stone wall, I'd let Frank have a chance on it and see what he could do. Sometimes you're losing something and need a fresh aspect; you're on it too long and somebody fresh can come in and point something out that perhaps you've overlooked.

Is there less pressure when you are working with a supervising editor?

When you're the second editor on a film, something mental affects you, and that's, "Hey, I can just relax and cut." The phone calls came about this or that and Frank Urioste, being the supervising editor, used to get them, unless it was a sequence I had cut. Frank had the main responsibility; all I had to do was cut the film and it was rather relaxed.

What is the technical procedure for cutting a musical sequence?

They prerecord the songs and shoot to a tape with start marks. They do parts of the song from consecutive start marks, starting from the beginning. The music editor gives you a combine of the master, which has on it the vocal and the instrumental, coded with a music number. Instead of matching the dialogue code number, you're matching a music code number. You cut it like most other things; you try and get the best angle where you are in a song. Is it just an out and out performance? What are you trying to say? Is somebody watching the song that you have to play a dramatic scene against? Or how about the crowd reactions? In *The Jazz Singer* the crowd played a very large part in most of the song numbers.

What particular concerns did the musical sequences present on this film?

This was a different kind of music than on *Funny Girl*. What you do when you cut a musical sequence is apply the same basic principles you do when you're cutting a dialogue or action sequence. What is the best way to tell the story? What is the best way to tell the song or what's happening? Neil Diamond blows up with some musicians in the recording session. What leads him to blow up are the problems he's having with his family, who are not happy with him being a singer. So it's still affecting him and he snaps his cap. What was interesting was to try to cut the sequence in such a way that he doesn't blow real hard at the beginning, and that it just builds, builds, builds, and he finally cracks open and leaves.

From one of the films you have cut, can you give an example of a scene that was created in the editing?

There is a scene in *Cactus Flower* that was created by the Moviola. They were in a museum and the producer, Mike Frankovich, told our director, Gene Saks, to shoot three shots of the ceiling. One was real close, one was wide, and one was an extreme wide angle. Gene said to me, "I don't know what they're for. Mike told me to shoot them, do what you can with it." They were great to use to emphasize the sound of the echo in different degrees, cutting from the close-up to the wide shot, to the extreme wide shot, with correlating sound. Simple but effective. A picture is an amalgamation of endeavors.

What are some of the options available to an editor when the coverage on a scene is not adequate?

One that comes to mind is photo effects. We were constricted on *Last of the Red Hot Lovers* by the coverage not being as close as we might have wanted. The sequence with Paula Prentiss and Alan Arkin on the couch smoking pot started out having some coverage, but later there is just a wide angle master. We ordered a 50–50 blow-up so it looked like we moved into a closer two-shot.

Do you feel that most films are too long?

There hasn't been one film that I didn't feel could have gone out at least ten or 15 minutes shorter, including *Cactus Flower*, which previewed at 1 hour and 45 minutes and went out at 1 hour and 43 minutes. I'm not advocating that you cut every sequence shorter. You have to look at the overall picture and see if there is deadwood. If it's holding up the story or what you're trying to say, definitely it has to go. All being human, directors, writers, and editors fall in love with certain sequences they think are vital to the picture overall. Whoever has the last word usually wins.

Can you think of an example where you made a sequence longer so it would be more effective?

We had a sequence in *Cactus Flower* where Ingrid Bergman rushed into the office to accost the dentist, Walter Matthau. She rushed in and out on the master. Thank God we had close-ups, we could build and build, until the line which tops the whole sequence. It would have been completely lost if we played it in the master, but by delaying it, it was quite a payoff when she comes up with the top line.

Have you worked on any of the video editing systems?

No. There is something about picking up the film and running it. Harold Becker and I were recutting something and I said, "You know they're talking about these electronic editing tools now." He said, "I don't think I'd like it. It cuts down the thinking process. I see when you mark the film and bring it over, and you're splicing it, you're thinking. I can tell, because you come up and say something, even before we run. I'm afraid an editor would be so wrapped up in what he's doing electronically that he wouldn't have the time to think. When he takes it out of the Moviola and splices it, he's thinking all the time."

I was born with the Moviola and when I bid farewell, it's going to be with the Moviola.

How does a person know they can edit?

You can be an excellent assistant editor, music editor, or sound editor, but that doesn't make you an excellent film editor. You can have 20 years as an assistant editor, and if they give you a film to cut, you either have it in you or not. You need an operation, you go to see a doctor.

One guy's been practicing five years, and the next guy has been a surgeon for 20 years. The guy that's doing it for five years is an artist, and the guy that's doing it for 20 years is a butcher. How do you know? I won't say it's God-given, but there's a certain amount of dramatic ability that you come with. It's something you can't bring on the way to the party; you come with it, you can't purchase it.

Do you feel a responsibility toward your assistant?

Of course. I do think that you have a responsibility, if you're the editor. You have to take care of your assistant. Conversely, I think the assistant should be very loyal to the editor. I also think you should try to give your assistant some sequences to cut. Start out extremely simple, but that's the only way they'll learn. While you're making changes on one reel and you've got a minor change in another reel, let him do it, let her do it. It's a two-way street. My assistant and I are friends first, editor and assistant, second.

What personality traits do you think are necessary to be an editor?

Perseverance is extremely important. If you have the type of personality that gets hurt easily, you are in trouble, because a lot of times you have to make changes and sometimes they're changes that you don't believe in. It's just like saluting somebody. You're not saluting the person, you're saluting the rank or the flag. So if a director asks for changes or a producer says try this or that, don't blow your cool. Hey, it's film. That's what's so great about film. You can try it a million ways, and put it right back together again. The more easy-going and relaxed you are, the better it is. Don't approach your film like it's going to be a battle, because you've lost already. Say, "Hey, here it is, I'm going to have fun putting this thing together." If you don't enjoy it, you're not going to enjoy doing it. Don't fight the film, don't look at the roll of film on your bench as the enemy. These are your friends, they're toys, they're going to give you enjoyment. You're going to create something out of those little separate rolls.

Where do you think of the profession of film editing is headed?

I think it has nowhere to go but up. More and more people are becoming aware of the editorial process, we're getting more publicity now. You're beginning to see "Edited by" now on advertisements. Many directors are guilty of saying, "I'm editing my film." Well, your editor may show you the film when he gets through editing, then you may want to make some changes, but you didn't edit the film. I feel there have been a lot of directors who have been reluctant to give credit where credit is really due. Sometimes a director will take credit where it's the editor's. Of course, you're going to say the editor wouldn't have the film if the director didn't shoot it, that's true, but I don't think the director would be shooting if somebody didn't write the bloody story. I do think that editors should not, not, not undermine or deride another editor when they're trying to get a job, because that helps nobody. If you want to drag yourself up by your bootstraps, do it on your own boots, don't do it on somebody else's.

We're beginning to make strides, we're going up. A director like Steven Spielberg is aware that Michael Kahn has made a large contribution; he is aware of what help Michael has been to him. Harold Becker is aware of the contribution. There used to be a feeling by the director that the editor was editing the film, but didn't have the same heart, feeling, or the desire because it wasn't his picture. He was just getting paid to do a job. You can't edit a film without having some of your blood, your feeling, your heart and soul in it. If you are editing a film, it *is* your film. Not only do you work with it during the day, you take it home at night—and yes, you may even take it to bed. The whole craft is being recognized for what it really is. We're making strides and whether you edit on the Moviola, KEM, Steenbeck, or electronically, it has to come from the heart. You may press a button or step on a pedal and make it go, but it's in the heart, and I think people are beginning to be aware of that.

10

Jerry Greenberg

In 1963 Jerry Greenberg began his film editing career as Dede Allen's apprentice on *America, America*. After working with Aram Avakian and Carl Lerner, he edited his first feature, *Bye Bye Braverman*, for Sidney Lumet in 1968.

In 1971 Greenberg won an Oscar for cutting *The French Connection*. The film's chase sequence redefined the art of montage in a thrilling display of editing craft.

Jerry Greenberg's career is filled with bravura, editorial set pieces: the museum sequence in *Dressed To Kill*, the Rodeo Collection scene in *Body Double*, and the helicopter battle in *Apocalypse Now*. At the same time, he is capable of great subtlety, serving the story of an intimate relationship film as in *Kramer vs. Kramer*.

Greenberg has collaborated with Arthur Penn, William Friedkin, Francis Ford Coppola, Robert Benton, and Brian DePalma. In 1979 Greenberg was nominated by the Academy for his efforts on *Apocalypse Now* and *Kramer vs. Kramer*.

1968	*Bye Bye Braverman*
	The Subject Was Roses
1970	*The Boys in the Band* (with Carl Lerner)
1971	*They Might Be Giants*
	*The French Connection***
1972	*Come Back Charleston Blue* (with George Bowers)

1973	*The Seven-Ups* (supervising editor, with Stephen A. Rotter)
	Electra Glide in Blue (with Jim Benson and John F. Link)
1974	*The Taking of Pelham One Two Three* (with Bob Lovett)
1975	*The Happy Hooker*
1976	*The Missouri Breaks* (with Dede Allen and Stephen A. Rotter)
1979	*Apocalypse Now* (with supervising editor Richard Marks, Lisa Fruchtman, and Walter Murch)*
	*Kramer vs. Kramer**
1980	*Heaven's Gate* (with Lisa Fruchtman, William Reynolds, and Tom Rolf)
	Dressed to Kill
1982	*Still of the Night*
1983	*Scarface* (with David Ray)
1984	*Body Double* (with Bill Pankow)
1985	*Savage Dawn*
1986	*No Mercy*
	Wise Guys
1987	*The Untouchables* (with Bill Pankow)
1988	*The Accused* (with Nicholas Brown)
1989	*National Lampoon's Christmas Vacation*
1990	*Awakenings* (with Battle Davis)
1991	*For the Boys*

*Academy Award nomination for best achievement in film editing.
**Academy Award for best achievement in film editing.

How did you get your first job in film editing?

I was a failed engineering student and a complete cipher ready to be factored up to one. I was an avid moviegoer, but in my upbringing, the movies or any of the popular arts were made almost verboten. I was interested in the theater and while trying to work as a stage manager, I backed into somebody offering me a job at a sound effects editing service. I needed work. I took it and learned how to be a music and sound effects editor. It was valuable training. Work prints would come into our shop, mostly documentaries, industrials, and training films. There were all these splices in the work print. I was interested in the heads and tails—what was not in the film. How do you arrive at the portion of those shots to put into a film? It took somebody to make those decisions. I knew then I wanted to be a film editor. It became profound. Why did I really want to be an engineer or a doctor or a lawyer, when I knew this was in me? My opportunity came to factor zero up to one, to something I wanted. I didn't realize I would be able to factor it up to infinity, by becoming Dede Allen's apprentice on Elia Kazan's *America, America*. That was truly magic. I won't diminish it by saying it was only a springboard. It was never didactic. She never taught or imposed her own feelings, rather how she worked and thought. It was inspirational and rewarding.

At this time did you find yourself going to the movies more often? Did you start reading books about film?

Thank goodness, I didn't have enough time to do any of those things. Working was more important to me, as it is now. The New York film community was small enough so no matter what you did you were included, and that was a good feeling. Not only was I an apprentice editor but I was also given a ticket to the film community.

After America, America *did you continue to work with Dede Allen?*

Yes, I did a couple of industrial films with Dede. It taught me that there was a whole other film world out there; industrials and documentaries were the big thing here in New York. The documentary film editor was more courtly then. These were people who were the intellectuals of our business. They truly wrote with their splicers and deserved a very high position in editorial firmament.

Was it clear to you at the time that the only reason to be an assistant was to become an editor?

Hallelujah! Yes. It was clear to me and to Dede as well. When I was her assistant I was there by her side all the time. I wanted to be what she was. Dede not only encouraged but inspired me. I never thought about all those other things that I was responsible for. Making lists, putting away trims, all of that was done, but I was preoccupied with seeing what Dede did. Somehow, I could feel vicariously that I was doing it too.

The French Connection *has long been acknowledged as a film that showcased the editor's art. Why was this an editor's movie?*

It was a visual picture and the editor has a greater responsibility to carry it off than in a dialogue film. It used imagery to tell the story and to illuminate the obsessions of the characters by studying how their faces react to a situation. It was not a tight script. The director, William Friedkin, allowed it to develop with actors in the shooting, and later on in the cutting room. It became a tight picture; it has compactness to it.

How much material did you have to work with for the chase scene?

I cut it on a Moviola in a huge room. My assistant, Maury Schell, and I set up a system with barrels. We lined up an aisle of six barrels on each side, twelve altogether. Since a lot of the shots were short, each hung on its own pin. Eventually, we got to cover one side of each barrel, top and bottom row, with one shot apiece [approximately 300 shots]. There was a lot of intercutting, and no way to know from the script where it might work best. Cutting from the car to the train, to reaction shots, to stunts, all of that had to be developed from what Friedkin had shot. We tended to take big bites and make each section as developed as possible. In trying to make it a little more of a contiguous piece, we were able to juxtapose certain elements in time that didn't necessarily have a prior logic in the way it was shot. So we kept everything out, knowing if you wanted to change something you might have to go to a trim or another take. It was nice knowing that everything was close at hand.

Did you first make the sequence long and then shorten it?

Yes, that's basically what editors do. It is always a valid approach to see things at their outer limits before you approach the inner limits. I find the distillation process the most important and exciting one. You control the process yourself. You watch all of the elements approach critical mass.

In an AFI [American Film Institute] seminar, William Friedkin said he shot and cut the chase scene to the Santana song "Black Magic Woman." Is that true?

I got a call a number of years ago from a young woman who wanted a job. When we were about to say goodbye, she said, "By the way, in cutting the chase scene in *The French Connection*, did you cut it to Santana's 'Black Magic Woman'?" I sort of fell over. Maybe Billy Friedkin did shoot and cut it to "Black Magic Woman," but I didn't. I knew nothing about it at the time and I can tell you that I was there; the film never left my hands.

Do you think of the sequence as a classic?

There is no denying that the chase scene is talked about in editing circles. The actual shooting techniques have been done many times over. There are more limitations to what we do in film than opportunities. What we've learned to do best of all is to work within those limitations to alter and explore the infinite qualities within them. That is what differentiates one chase scene from another; the techniques are pretty much the same.

On this year's (1987) Academy Awards show there was a presentation designed to show what the editor does on film. They showed a clip from the chase scene, and underneath they keyed in a counter which kept track of the number of cuts in the clip. Did you get the feeling that the Academy was trying to make the point that a lot of cuts makes for good editing?

That shallowness was what they intended. The fact that you can abstract just a portion and say, "Hey, this is what editing is all about," doesn't tell the whole story.

It's also a shame they neglected to mention the name of the man who had cut the sequence.

They also miscounted by six cuts; that was surprising. I was contacted before the show, and they had already done all of the graphics. I mentioned it and they said, "Should we alter the count? It would be great trouble to do all that." What's funny is the person said, "Are there any secret cuts?" I think the notion of "secret cuts" kind of follows along with their idea of what film editing really is, that things happen without your noticing them. Yet often that's not what we want. We want to make the audience aware of all those cuts, but we want to do it within the framework of some other aspect of the movie. So a "secret cut" is, "Hey, have you done it so well that you even fooled us?" Unwittingly, I must have. What they did was to count cuts on a locked-off camera shot. You see a car veer from a woman with a baby carriage, and it hits a bunch of trash cans. A carton hit the camera and fell over, but I liked that the camera went awry. It became a moving camera, it caught a lot of the trash that went by at the same time. The camera became so shaky and erratic, they thought there were a whole series of jump cuts built into it.

So they misunderstood what a shot unit was.

Precisely. The day after, a film reviewer was commenting about the television coverage of the awards. One of the things he said was wrong was they chose a film that was 16 years old for an example of film editing. I was incensed with the comment, because it was not germane. A film 16 years old that displays the craft of editing is valid. It's valid if it's 40 years old or if it was done yesterday.

On The Seven-Ups *you are credited as supervising film editor and associate producer.*

Also second unit director. Phil D'Antoni, the producer of *Bullitt* and *The French Connection*, knew he would need a good editor and a lot of help in preparing for his first directorial job. I helped him to mentally storyboard the film.

During the preproduction and shooting periods, did you find yourself thinking like an editor?

I tried not to. It's hard when that is all you really have to fall back on. People who have original concepts tend to think in very expansive terms. Editors think in very minimal, small steps. Trying to have some confluence of those two ways of thinking is the ideal. That's why I enjoy working on Brian De Palma's films. He is able to put those two parts together before the film is shot. He's able to relate the concept of a writer and how the finished product might look stylistically. From a theoretical standpoint, that's a blessing. On the other hand, a lot of editors are intimidated by a director's foreknowledge of editing. They think the director is taking away the broader part of an editor's ability to put it all together.

The chase sequence in The Seven-Ups *has a whole different feel than the one in* The French Connection. *Sound is used very effectively as a dramatic device.*

Instead of making an overall sound that blends all of those visual bits of information, there was an attempt to put a frame around it, to edge the sound with the image. It worked on that particular chase scene with the banging up against the guard rail, the muttered words, etc. We've pretty much run the scheme, and I'll believe that until somebody has the audacity to say, "I don't know what you mean by the chase scene in *The French Connection, Bullitt,* or *The Seven-Ups;* I'm going to go ahead and do a chase," and they'll do it ten times as well.

There was a large editorial team on Apocalypse Now. *Did you work on specific sequences or throughout the entire film?*

I worked on specific sequences, because it behooved us to break the film up so we could concentrate on just those sequences. What Francis Coppola often did was take a sequence that was put together by one editor and himself, and run it through another editor for critical evaluation. Sometimes he would come up with another result, slightly altered, sometimes insignificantly so. Sometimes it stayed the same, or sometimes it was just another version he could use or blend. It was an ongoing process of switch and review.

Specifically, what sequences did you cut?

The helicopter battle. I feel a little uncomfortable that one should want to know exactly who did what, when four of us got credit on the picture. It's more important that you know the picture looked like some unified whole; basically, we were one. Francis utilized us like that. He was able to create that in me. I don't lose sight of that. I've always had a great deal of wonderment and awe about that film, still to this day. Nothing is finalized in that film. I still think about it a lot. The Vietnam experience is still very much in our consciousness, so *Apocalypse Now* continues to be the germ of a maelstrom about that period in our history.

The two french toast scenes in Kramer vs. Kramer *communicate very different emotions and are edited in diverse styles. When you use two similar scenes to make contrasting points, what do you say to yourself as an editor?*

In the first scene it's a joust. It's the father who doesn't know how to make the toast, but wants to, and the son who knows how because he's watched his mother do it. So there is the contrast of knowing there is something each of them wants to show the other, but it's not going to work. The reason comes when Dustin Hoffman burns his hand and says, "Goddamn her." The kid knows the "her" he loves so much is the reason why he can't make the toast, because "her" is no longer there. The father and the son are both important in that scene, to show us they need to be together but cannot be. In a very subtle way, the shooting and the editing intimates that. It is the opposite at the end, when they are to be separated and don't want to be, because they have come together and should always be together. *They* make the french toast. To characterize that emotion, you need not fractionalize all of the shooting; you do it in what would pass as one shot that always has the two of them in it. You don't want to keep them separated.

You have cut many films for director Brian De Palma. Does he draw storyboards for his films?

Yes, he does, as primitive as they are. On *Dressed to Kill* he had these 3x5 cards with stick drawings on them running through a great deal of it. It produces material which does a lot of the terrible work an editor has to confront. So you are able to pick it up at a more developed stage in refining a sequence.

Do the storyboards get dropped once the film is shot?

The script gets dropped. The storyboard is just another blueprint that is a viable, valuable part of making a movie. Anybody who follows a storyboard religiously is asking for trouble. For the director, the storyboard is a good indicator of how he is going to organize the shots in a sequence. To an editor it shows how the director wanted that scene to be organized before he shot it. After it's shot, I would only use that storyboard as a starting-off point. You may actually follow that storyboard line for line and it will work, but what if it doesn't? What do you do then?

In the museum sequence in Dressed to Kill, *when Angie Dickinson and the stranger pursue each other, was it necessary for you to understand how the museum was laid out? Is that kind of specific continuity important to you?*

We can play with time, things that happen in real time, happen in half the time and in twice the time. We can go from one location to another. I just want to know, if necessary, where I can violate that geography. The Metropolitan Museum never had that kind of contemporary painting, even though we know it was supposed to take place there. It is the magnificent collection of contemporary American artists in the Philadelphia Fine Arts Museum. So there again, we're telling a lie! So what? She walks out and we see the Metropolitan Museum of Art in New York. The word "cheat" is not a negative word in our business. Cheat is what we do. We earn a lot of money for cheating. We can tell an entire life in two hours.

Is the museum scene one that you are particularly proud of?

Sure, I'm proud of all of my babies. It's visual storytelling where the communication is between the director and the audience. To have the audience deduce what the characters might be thinking without dialogue utilizes the medium to its fullest. The actions and consequences become potentialized by not using dialogue. You get into that visual world of Brian De Palma. I am prejudiced toward that kind of loaded filmmaking. I enjoy those sequences so much that I attempt to prolong them. Given all that wealth of material, I try to make them not seem as though they are happening in real time, to expand them, and make them more dance-like, so they do not have to tumble out as quickly as other expository parts of moviemaking. You can balloon things in the middle. You can allow pauses to say or imply a lot. Often those things do come out at the end, but it gets me into the fun of moviemaking quicker than a dialogue sequence would.

I believe there were some problems with the rating board on Dressed to Kill. *When a film receives an X rating and the filmmakers want an R, do you offer suggestions as to what should be deleted?*

No, I don't. Once you say, "I know what you want," you are just as guilty of being a censor as they are. If there's two feet of one shot that's offensive to a person and a foot and a half of the shot is not as offensive, they must suggest to me what they want me to execute. I really won't do it. My job is to suggest to a director and accomplish what should be done. I'm not a censor.

What was your involvement in the editing of Heaven's Gate?

Bill Pankow and I were hired to put together a self-contained battle sequence that was self-explanatory. You can pretty much say the same thing about an action sequence in any film. You go out and construc them to be action interludes, and they have their own conventions. Bill and I hadn't read a script or seen anything. When I went out and met Michael Cimino for the first time, I was told that I would have absolutely no need to know about anything apart from the battle scene. They were looking to save time. They sent it here to New York. I was to work on one sequence, while the rest of the film was being edited in Los Angeles. Bill Pankow and I enjoyed it very much, yet we had absolutely no idea what it was going into. When we were finished, I took the cut to Los Angeles and we reviewed it. Bill Reynolds and Michael Cimino showed me just a very few of the sequences they were working on. Although they wanted to know my feelings, it was clear I was not there in any editorial capacity.

In the chain-saw scene in Scarface, *we know that the blade is going to enter the man's body, but as that is about to happen you cut to Al Pacino's reaction, as he looks on in horror with blood spurting on him. It's a perfect example of how two shots can produce three. Many people think they have actually seen the blade pierce the skin. Is this what you were trying to accomplish?*

Sure. You don't have to show it happening. The horrible part is that it is happening. The implied violence is often worse, because once you show it, there's a sense of release; the mystery is no longer there. When it's not shown, the capacity of an audience's brain is to imagine a whole panoply of images which will always be worse or more effective than actually seeing it. It doesn't make the cutting off of the arm any more inventive or aesthetic, it only has to do with effectiveness, and that's what we should deal with.

In the beginning of Body Double, *we see Jake coming into his apartment. When he reaches the bedroom, you cut to what he sees: his girlfriend making love to another man. You cut back to Jake for his reaction, then back to what he sees again, the couple on the bed, and then back to Jake for his reaction. How does the editing work to achieve a dramatic emphasis?*

If you take an emotion that is surprising and has an initial velocity, you often want to take the different changes the actor provides, and frame them very quickly. We know those emotions progress very rapidly: the shock, disappointment, and then anger. If it were happening in real time, the audience could not understand why you were staying on one thing to read the transitions from all of these emotions in the actor's face, but given the editor's understanding that time can be played with, you can contrast each part of that emotion with what he is seeing or experiencing. Even if it's the same image again and again, when you go back to that subject, you will probably feel the alteration in that emotion a lot more than if you had stayed on it. Bill Pankow cut the sequence and did that very well. He was able to section out all of those elements of the same reaction, so it said to an audience, these are all of the things that are going on in this guy's mind. We know that by contrasting it with what he is actually seeing, cutting away from him so that we can come back and stress the change, you will get a better idea of it.

Later in the film, Jake is on the terrace looking out to the other homes in the neighborhood. In reality, there are two subjective views of what he can see. One is looking through the telescope, at various focal lengths, at the woman dancing, and the other is what he sees with his naked eye, which is a long shot of the woman. At one point Jake looks up from the telescope, and instead of the point of view long shot, we see a medium close-up of the house. What was the reason for this choice?

You are trying to be as economical as you can, so you pay attention not only to the reality of a situation, but you also abandon that reality for the sake of other elements. You want to enhance the ability of the camera to see as we see, and to imply what we want to see closer, in our mind's eye. I violated the verisimilitude of the scene many times. If there is a logic and it's apparent to an audience, they buy the tricks. They will accept it as what the character is actually doing.

How did the slow motion material in the baby carriage scene in The Untouchables *affect the editing of the sequence?*

It gave me a wedge to get inside the action. It gave you a chance to take one step back and look into an action sequence that ordinarily might happen too quickly for you to see everything.

The audience has to see the baby carriage a number of times to maintain the drama of the situation. Do you start by showing it a lot and then eliminating it? How do you know when we need to see the baby again?

How long do you keep an action going? How long does it really take? How much more time can you add to that action by intercutting other things that themselves are happening in their own time? You consider all of that from the very beginning, and you mix the parallel elements to see how you can stretch it. Once you look at it all together, maybe A is too much, but B and C aren't. It's because there is too much of A that B and C seem like too much, so if I take a little bit of A away, does that mean I have to take a little bit of B or C away? So you start knitting the fabric, doing the alterations. It becomes a little more complex and that's the fun of it.

I understand Brian De Palma covers his scenes well. In this film the scenes are played in singles or with very few shots. Was this a conscious decision from the beginning.

Anamorphic lenses do that. When you are shooting in CinemaScope, it's hard to think in terms of conventional coverage; you have to think in broader terms.

Bill Pankow shares credit with you on The Untouchables. *How does this co-editor situation work? Are you both approached to cut a film or do you suggest that you work with someone?*

It can be either way. At one time, schedules were never quite as severe as they are right now. Now there is a likelihood you will be told there will be more than one editor, and if you are lucky you will be put in an advise-and-consent capacity as to who the other editor will be. Producers are never reluctant to say, "Look, we'd like to hire you and we've already hired this person."

When you work with a co-editor, do you work in the same space or do you work independently?

All solitary workers such as editors need their solitary spaces. Often, because of financial or space considerations, people have been thrown together, but I think it is necessary that co-editors have their own separat² spaces.

When you are cutting a film, are you thinking about whether it's going to be successful at the box office?

I don't have to know that a film is going to be successful. That's not the reason I am working on a picture. My effectiveness on any project is to fulfill the promise the picture has up to the point we start editing.

How much of an impact can an editor have on the structure of a film?

It's like somebody doing a patchwork quilt or a mosaic. You have all these little pieces of tile. How does the mosaic artist go about creating— abstract, realistic? That is the way you have to do it, a tile at a time. Directors might say, "Make this shot the same length as the next shot," because for them the altered pieces of film information take a back seat to the length of time they are on the screen. What they fail to realize is the editor has a built-in clock that doesn't quite meter out the way the director would want. You have to pay attention to rhythms or tempi you can impose. These are the ones that only the material can tell you; they are a good part of the editor's arsenal.

Looking at the body of your work, attention to pace seems a prime concern. Is it?

For me it's a policy that the film never flags, so we don't become disengaged. Films and stories have their high and low points. We learn to appreciate that the low points enhance the high points. The editor should always be aware if the low points are going to sag so much that the audience has no chance to continue along the way. Pacing has a lot to do with the entire project. You have to step back and make a broad determination about what is absolutely necessary. In making the film as economical as possible without destroying the essence of the film, we often cut out too much because we fail to see anything other than pacing or tempo. I'm always acutely aware and cautious of doing that. Part of what we editors do is to understand everything that has preceded us, the other crafts. People are putting their faith in what we do to preserve what they have already done. Films are a series of details— details within details. It is important that we pay attention to all those other details: story, character development, what the cinematographer wants to see, what the actor is trying to do beyond what he or she is asked to do. All of these things should command the attention of a good editor, and I believe that they do. The perception of the way we see movies now is that everything is moving at such a rapid rate. If you can cram something good into a shorter space of time, it makes that particular project better.

The music video syndrome, movies like Flashdance.

That's a good example. I don't know if it is just a trend, or if we should look at it as a danger. Films tend to have their own specific gravity. We don't know what it is in the writing stage or shooting stage. If any stage is going to tell us, it is the editing stage. A film does have an optimum length, not by it being exactly an hour and 45 minutes, but that every element is dealt with as far as linear time goes. So in the cumulative time you have spent, none of it is wasted. You listen to the material. If the film means to be two hours and 15 minutes, that's the way the film should be. If you have to take out 15 minutes because of the way the contract reads, then you have minimalized the quality of the film and you have touched upon the cynical part of our industry.

Do you think that editing is an intuitive process?

It's really not intuition; it's somebody telling you something, only they're not shouting it at you. You have to listen to actors, directors, cinematographers, and art directors. If I didn't listen to something, I'd have to be able to edit myself. That's the most exciting part because I've integrated myself into the process. I don't sit outside of it and make judgments. The down side is, through some insecurity, I always believe that in the material which has not been used is the real scene. I always compare what I have constructed to what I know is in bits and pieces outside of it. Have I gotten the best material? You never know, because in combination things tend to change.

After you complete your first cut, what tells you when you must edit yourself?

Seeing the movie for the first time, you usually become distraught and desperate about it. The entire piece, which played so well as you read the script, now is suddenly the worst thing and you are responsible for it. You saw all of the bits and pieces, you looked at all of the scenes. All together it should be okay and it isn't, so you've done something wrong. Once getting over that, you understand something wrong turns into the thing which now has to be molded. It takes another kind of thinking. As long as you can try to grasp it in one piece and make it right, you've just gone on to the most gratifying step of all.

Have you been involved in cutting music videos?

Yes, Brian De Palma's video of Bruce Springsteen's "Dancing in the Dark" was edited by Bill Pankow and I supervised it. I think it ranks above most because there were some very mundane film editing principles incorporated into it. Brian, Bill, and I insisted on them. It was shot and edited as a story. It never got as flamboyant as it could have using all the video gizmos.

Do you think video is going to merge with film editing in feature filmmaking?

Yes, I've always thought that. I root on technology to make my job easier. I don't want films which ordinarily take six months to edit to take six weeks, but conventional film editing can be made more interactive with our thinking process. I've been rooting on video to be able to do that.

How do you feel about supervising assistants and apprentices?

I'm not too good at being a supervisor. What I like to do is to edit film. I can't break up the creative part of me and say, "The other part of me is to watch over the assistant and apprentice." I like everybody to work up to me. The reason they are there is not to put away trims. Nothing I do is sacrosanct. If everything is going well within the hierarchical structure, the assistant editor will want to know what I do, and the apprentice will want to know what the assistant does, and eventually what the editor is doing. They are there as editors, not as handmaidens. The fact that their jobs require a certain amount of housekeeping is the nature of the beast, but it shouldn't stop their curiosity and desire to know how to edit film. I insist upon it. It puts more weight on them, because they do all of that housekeeping work, but they also have to help me create. I find it's necessary to have somebody I can share that creative part with in the cutting room. So the assistant fulfilling that is extremely important.

Do you feel you are continuing the tradition of the apprenticeship system that you were trained under?

It certainly was the inspirational part of my existence working for Dede Allen and others as well. I think they all should be stated: Carl Lerner, Aram Avakian. These people became the mentors and tutors because of their zeal and love of what they did. That's not anything you can teach; it has to be there. I would like to think I'm imparting that to other people who come through my cutting room, but I don't think I'm ever quite aware of it. Nor do I think I do it as well as Dede, Carl, and Aram could do it. Their generation's expectations about what they wished to impart created a kind of chemistry that can never be gotten again. There can be a different kind of chemistry with subsequent generations, but it never can be the same, because times do change and you have to leave it to the historians to objectively see the difference.

I can't judge that, I'm still too much a part of it, but for me in those days it was such a sublimely happy time, that it created the muzzle velocity to do what I do. I hope to see that in younger people today, but I don't see that right now. Things tend to be a little more held back. I see a lot of cynicism creeping into the business. Certainly, the commercial aspects of the business have always existed; we're all prey to those things. Still there was this wonderful dedication and intellectual and political aspects, even though you were working on some dumb exploitation film. The chemistry which was created between the subordinate and the tutor in the cutting room was a very happy and electric time for those of us who were lucky enough to be a part of it.

11

Lou Lombardo

Lou Lombardo started in the film business as a cameraman but launched his career as a feature editor with two of the most influential American directors of the 1970s: Sam Peckinpah and Robert Altman.

Lombardo expanded the boundaries of our perception of time and space on *The Wild Bunch*, with a supercharged montage style that rearranged the notion of real time within a scene. He defied many of film editing's traditional principles and helped to shape Peckinpah's dynamic directorial style.

His freewheeling approach to the structure of *Brewster McCloud* and *McCabe and Mrs. Miller* explored new methods of telling a film story and served Robert Altman's iconoclastic vision.

After pursuing a directing career for six years, Lombardo returned to film editing in 1987 on Norman Jewison's *Moonstruck*, which he followed with work on *January Man* and *In Country*. In 1989 he co-edited the John Hughes hit *Uncle Buck* with his son Tony Lombardo.

1969	*The Wild Bunch*
	The Ballad of Cable Hogue (with Frank Santillo)
1970	*Brewster McCloud*
1971	*McCabe and Mrs. Miller*
	The Red Sun
1972	*Ace Eli and Roger of the Skies*
1973	*Thieves Like Us*

	The Long Goodbye
1974	*California Split*
1975	*The Black Bird*
1976	*All the President's Men* (with Robert L. Wolfe)
1977	*The Late Show*
1978	*The Changeling*
	Cheech and Chong's Up in Smoke
1985	*Just One of the Guys*
1987	*Stewardess School*
	Moonstruck
1989	*January Man*
	Uncle Buck (with Tony Lombardo and Peck Prior)
	In Country (with Antony Gibbs)
1990	*Defenseless*
1991	*Other People's Money*

How did you become a film editor?

I was Robert Altman's cameraman on industrials and training films in Kansas City. I came out here to Los Angeles with him and he couldn't get a connection. I went knocking on doors. I finally got into Republic Pictures as a loader in the camera department, then I became an assistant cameraman. I always wanted to direct. One day we were out on a ranch shooting a Western, and I was running across furrows carrying a Mitchell on my shoulder. I thought, I'm never going to get there from here. So I switched over to editorial with Revue. Naturally, I had to start out as an apprentice. I cut my salary in half by switching over, because I was already an assistant cameraman. At that time there was a rule that you had to be in the guild for eight years before you could cut, so I put in my eight years. For six of those eight years I was cutting this and that but never getting any credit for it. When my eight years were up, Altman was going to do a CBS pilot and asked me if I would do it. I was legally able to do it. Walter Grauman at Fox saw it and he gave me a shot at a TV series he was going to produce. That was a big thing. I never expected to go beyond the pilot; I thought I would have to go back to assisting.

How did you get to be Sam Peckinpah's editor on The Wild Bunch?

I was doing camera work on the weekends and word came down that Sam Peckinpah was looking for an assistant cameraman, so I went out as an assistant. He was doing *Noon Wine* for television with Jason Robards, Olivia De Havilland, and Per Oscarsson. It was mainly a tape show. Most of what I shot was film of Oscarsson running through the woods. Sam liked me and asked me what I did, so I said, "I'm cutting at Fox." About a year later he called me and said, "I've got this picture called *The Wild Bunch,* maybe you could do it. What do you have that you could send over that you're proud of?" On the *Felony Squad* TV series I had a shoot-out where I had to manufacture slow motion, because they didn't shoot slow motion in television. You got one take and that was it. Joe Don Baker came out with a gun and was being shot by all these police. I printed every frame three times and created slow motion. I intercut him being shot, falling, this guy shooting, that guy running, Baker falling. Sam and Phil Feldman, the producer, saw it and said, "You've got the job—and as a matter of fact, we'll use that kind of thing."

Peckinpah was known to talk in a very obtuse fashion. There is a story that on Cross of Iron *he walked up to James Coburn after a take and said, "It's too Western," and the film was about World War II. How did you communicate with him?*

Sam knew how to articulate his feelings. He may have done it in his own fashion, but you got the message. I mean, he used to grunt and I knew what he meant. You get to be in tune with a guy; if he starts to squirm, you know he's not pleased.

How did you visualize the whole choreography of the opening gun battle in The Wild Bunch? *Were there storyboards or master shots that gave you information?*

No, there weren't any storyboards and there were very few masters. Having done gunfights in police shows on television for a few years, you know how you're going to build a battle. I told Sam that my concept in that street fight was to involve the audience. I wanted them to think they were in the middle of an explosion that went off around them. You sketch it out. The point is, everybody in the world is shooting at these guys and hitting everybody else except them—and they're shooting back. The street fight was 21 minutes long when I first cut it; that is three reels. It went on and on. I went the standard route, I had everything making sense. Then we started taking it down and meshing it. You let the film take you there. It went out at four and a half minutes.

How did you cut it down?

I used a piece of everything I had in the 21-minute version. Instead of 20 feet long, the shots became shorter.

What was the coverage like on the gunfight?

Peckinpah had six cameras going at different speeds on the street fight, but he gave me a one-sided fight. I had people being hit with nobody shooting at them except in wide shots. I didn't have coverage of the men on the roof shooting at the Wild Bunch down below. Peckinpah was concerned with the main characters, as he should be, so I directed the second-unit material of Robert Ryan and the men on the roof shooting down at the Bunch.

Did you discuss the camera positions with him?

No. I just told him I was going to get the guys on the roof shooting at the guys down below, and I covered myself well.

When someone is shot in The Wild Bunch, *it seems as if they are falling endlessly and suspended in time. How was this accomplished in the editing?*

It's a ballet. I may start a guy falling off a roof and then go to three other people being hit. In real time he would have already fallen, but I'll come back and hold him in the air for a while, continuing to fall off the roof, in an eight-frame cut. Just before he hits the ground, I may go to the other guy that got shot landing on a ledge. I found myself speeding up some angles that Sam had shot because they were too slow. We had to speed them up to get the rhythms right.

Would that also be done optically?

Yes, you would drop every other frame; that would speed it up a bit. It was good action but it was too slow. I adjusted it if I didn't like it. If I had a shot and I thought it would work better if it were normal, I'd make it normal by dropping every other frame or every third frame, whatever brought it to the speed I wanted it to be. I was intercutting different speeds. A guy might be riding in slow motion, but he's hit normal. It snaps him and I let him fall in slow motion. I might let him land normal. Intercutting with different speeds was very effective.

That film was done by the seat of our pants. It was my first feature. I came out of television. In television you learn to deal with a lot of film and to make a lot of decisions very fast.

The sequence where the bridge is blown up as the Bunch is crossing is an amazing piece of editing.

I used a trick in there that I learned from the editor Bud Small when I was an apprentice. He taught me the use of clear frames. If you put a couple of clear frames ahead of an explosion, it really gives it some balls. You can use it for a guy taking a flash photo, if the director didn't flash the person whose picture is being taken. You can put this frame of clear in and it gives you that illusion. We had six cameras on the bridge and I just put two frames of clear in between every camera. It made it look like it was exploding to hell and gone. It blew up again and again and again. If you look at it closely, you'll see frames of clear in between each angle.

How did you lay that scene out?

It was pretty obvious. Sam shot the guys as they rode on the bridge, which was wired. You had three elements: the guys on the bridge, the guys riding away, and the dynamite wick. You kept pyramiding it; the cuts kept getting smaller until finally it blew up.

How many frames was the shortest cut of the fuse?

I don't know, it's all feeling with me. I never count frames, it's what I felt at the time. If it wound up to be four frames, because I know four frames is eye retention, it was an accident. I never thought about it. It's just what I felt. I'm sure you can pattern it by going from 16 frames to 11 to eight to six to four frames, but I never counted them. I go just by feel. You run it, you feel it, and you mark it. With me, it's all touch and feel. It is all emotion with me. If it demands lots of cuts, then that's what I do, or if the emotion is there in one set-up, I'll let that play. The film talks to you, it tells you.

You broke a lot of rules in The Wild Bunch. *One is that the film is shot in CinemaScope, and at that time rapid cutting just wasn't done on a wide-screen format picture.*

You cut it the same way you would cut 16mm. I don't care if it's Scope. I never used that corrective bubble on the Moviola; it got in my way so finally I ripped it off. So the figures were a little bit elongated. I don't have to have them the right size to know what the hell they are doing, or to get the emotion out of it. I cut *The Wild Bunch* with everybody looking long and thin, but I didn't care for one moment whether the aperture was 1.85:1 or if it was CinemaScope. It didn't matter to me.

The other rule that you broke was to cut into the slow motion shots. Many editors believe that a shot has a natural beginning and ending that shouldn't be violated.

I did everything that nobody wanted to do. That's not the way you're supposed to do it; well, just do it anyway.

Didn't The Wild Bunch *set a record for the amount of cuts for a color feature?*

Yes, 3,642 cuts. I'll never forget that figure and I'm sure it still holds the record. That was the 2 hour and 14 minute version. The first cut was 5 hours and it was all gold. It was a tough picture to cut down, because everything we cut out was really good stuff.

In the last scene we see the members of the Bunch superimposed over the sky. They are laughing after they have been killed. How did that come about?

I said to Sam, "Let's bring them back." Throughout the whole movie their philosophy had been they screw up, get angry at each other, and then they laugh it off. I said, "Now they really screwed up as bad as you can screw up—let's have them laugh it off." So at the very end I brought them back superimposed in the sky and they were all laughing. It tore your heart out.

Do you think your contributions as an editor had an impact on the style of Peckinpah's films? Do you think if you had cut Straw Dogs *it would be a much different picture?*

I can't say whether it would have been much different or not, but it would have been different. Sam, for being the tough son of a bitch that he was, also was a pussycat, and he loved moments. There were a lot of moments in *Straw Dogs*, but that was Sam, "Give me more, let them look longer." I used to get those moments out. You've already made your impression—get out.

How did you become Robert Altman's editor?

Bob had called me to do *M*A*S*H* when I had already committed to Peckinpah to do *The Ballad of Cable Hogue*. After *M*A*S*H*, Bob's editor, Danny Greene, wasn't available so Bob called me to do *Brewster McCloud*.

What was Robert Altman like to work with during the editing process?

Bob always gave me my head so I enjoyed working with him. I wouldn't see him in the cutting room until the polished first cut. He never bothered me while I was cutting. When I got it to where I liked it, then he would sit down and look at it. Then in re-editing, if he had something he wanted to do, he would be very precise in articulating it. It made my job easy.

The editing of Brewster McCloud *was very innovative, especially in the way the story was structured with intercutting. Can you give an example of a scene that was transformed by the editing process?*

We had two sequences that were dull. After Brewster is in bed with Shelley Duvall, he goes and tells the Angel, played by Sally Kellerman. That destroys him as a pure virgin birdperson. That didn't work, so I said to Bob, "Let me flashfoward." "What do you mean flashforward? I've heard of flashback." I said, "While he's in bed and Shelley is saying, 'Are you going to tell anyone?' let's show him telling Sally. Then we'll keep coming back, posing questions and going ahead, to see the ramifications of what's happened." I didn't sit down and think it out, it just came to me when Bob was saying, "What the hell are we going to do?" Suddenly I said, "Let's do that."

Rene Auberjonois plays a bird lecturer whose comments indirectly relate to the main plot of the film. How did that concept come about?

That was an afterthought that Altman had. Originally *Brewster McCloud* was about a guy who dreamt about flying. That's all he thought about and he would murder people to further his ambition. It was a serious piece; they were going to use Bobby Blake because the guy had big arms. All of a sudden Altman changed it around to a comedy. Who the hell would believe that Bud Cort could strangle anybody? After the picture was shot, Bob wrote all the stuff for Rene. It was referring to the characters and we integrated it into the picture.

At times you used it as voice-over. Was all of it shot on camera?

Yes, all of it was on camera.

At one point you leave him for quite a while to have the story develop without him.

Yes, right, you didn't want to overkill with that stuff, because it was an afterthought. We didn't want it to look like we had gone through the film and just stuck it in here and there.

Did you cut with two tracks, one for the voice-over and one for the dialogue?

No, I was cutting on a Moviola so I couldn't do that. I knew what the other track was going to be, so later on we built units and mixed it. But I had to know what was going to be there, because I had to time it out so it would fit. I could only have one track and I had no facilities to do any mixing in Houston, Texas. Today with the KEM, I have more freedom to build those tracks simultaneously and play them back.

The structure of the film is so snakelike. Did you work on it scene by scene or in sections at a time? Did you begin at the beginning or did you pick a point where you wanted to begin?

Bob likes to shoot in continuity, but on that picture he didn't. I would cut whatever sequence was complete. I don't have to start at the beginning. The director has to be sure that his people are in the right place with their deliveries and their acting, but for me it's no problem. I can hook the back to the front. I smooth it out as I go through it, so that it progresses the story properly.

I love the scene where Jennifer Salt and Brewster make love without touching. Did you cut that in continuity or did you work with her material first and then start to intercut him?

Oh no, I don't cut that way. I do it with feeling. When you've had enough of her, you better go to him and get him doing something.

So you integrated it right away.

I have to, otherwise I might just as well take the slates off of her, let her jump up and down, and then put him in. That never works. I've got to go back and forth. I've got to cut it when I'm feeling it. The other way is too mechanical, it's numbers; this cut is a foot and a half long, so his should be a foot and a half long so it matches and their rhythms are the same. I don't do it that way. That scene stayed in first cut. That happened quite a bit with Bob. He knows what he's shooting. With Peckinpah he would put six cameras up and point them everywhere and say, "Figure it out."

McCable and Mrs. Miller *was a breakthrough film in its use of sound. Was the overlapping dialogue recorded and mixed directly onto the production tracks during the shooting or was it accomplished in postproduction?*

Bob wanted to do it all on the set, which was a mistake because you lose control and get feedback between mikes. The master mike is reading the close-up mikes, and they're phasing. It's a tough thing to do and we couldn't straighten it out on *McCabe*. Altman never liked to loop. He's changed his mind about that somewhat now, but he was adamant. He wouldn't loop it, and I had a lot of overlaps and crap that I couldn't get rid of; it was married on the set. I had to replace it if I wanted to get rid of it and he wouldn't let me replace anything. His concept was, you walk into a room, you hear all of these conversations, and tune in and out listening to the one you want. What Bob forgot, or wouldn't accept, is that you are a human being. A machine can't do that, you hear it all. You can't single out and shut that down. That's what you do on a mixing stage. You can build 50 dialogue tracks, have the whole room alive, and bring this down and that up. On *McCabe* we really could have achieved what he wanted if we had control. I know you say you don't have the spontaneity, but believe me, you can create the spontaneity.

Are there problems in cutting a multi-track film?

On *California Split* we used an eight-track system. I had three sound heads on the Moviola and was reading the background, the foreground, and the main characters. I found myself cutting badly, because I would let it go until somebody in the background had finished a sentence, when I should have cut earlier. Finally, I shut it all off and played one track. The dialogue guys went crazy because I cut where I wanted to cut. I was cutting in the middle of words and they had a terrible time straightening that out.

In McCabe and Mrs. Miller *did you have the Leonard Cohen score while you were cutting?*

No, not at all.

Were you cutting to scratch music?

Nothing. Altman had this terrific idea. He had a fiddle player sitting around in the bar and that was going to be his score throughout the whole movie. The fiddle player would start playing once some climactic thing had happened, and he would relieve it with the fiddle which segued into the next part. It was great and that's the way we cut the picture. When we got the whole picture cut, Altman's son brought me an album of Leonard Cohen songs and I put them in. It was not especially written for the movie, but it fell right in. The lyrics depicted the characters. Altman saw it and said, "This is our score." I said, "What about the violin? This guy's rhythm is so slow that he's taking my rhythm and making it that slow, plodding, Leonard Cohen pacing." I didn't change the cuts, but the picture was now in his rhythm. Take that music out and that's a different movie. Altman was adamant about it, so we got stuck with it. I had a pretty good clipping movie happening and it made it plodding. It was Leonard Cohen's energy, it wasn't mine or Altman's.

Do the textures in the photography in a film like McCabe and Mrs. Miller *give you a feel for the editing rhythms?*

No. I've had cameramen come to me and say, "Can't you stay on the master where I did that lighting thing?" I say, "I didn't notice it." I don't look for that. It would really screw it up if you became involved or interested in that; then you're looking at the wrong thing. If it's working for the scene, that's one thing, but if it doesn't mean anything for the scene I don't use it. A lot of cameramen have gotten upset with me,

"Couldn't you have used that other take where I did this?" I say, "Yes, but the guy was terrible in that take. Sure, the moon shaft was better, but the acting was shit."

You left editing for about six years to pursue a directing career. After that did you find it difficult to get a job as an editor?

If I ever write a book about Hollywood, the title's going to be *What Has He Done Lately?* because that's all they wanted to know. So I really needed a comeback picture. Norman Jewison had asked me to do a couple of pictures in the past which I couldn't do, so when I heard he was going to do a picture with Cher I called him up and said, "I'm available and I would love to do your movie." He hired me to do *Moonstruck*, which was my comeback picture. Otherwise I'd still be trying to convince these guys I didn't forget how to edit. It was real strange because when I was cutting, the phone was always ringing off the wall, and then nothing. So God bless Norman, he didn't care what these guys thought. He knew I could cut, he'd seen the work, so it was no problem.

The music in Moonstruck *was very important in setting up the mood of the film. How much input did you have into it?*

When I was cutting *Moonstruck*, Norman wanted to open the picture with opera music. I was cutting one day and Dean Martin was singing on the radio, "When the moon hits your eye . . ." I said, "That's the song for this picture," and I put it in. It shows the audience it's a comedy. The other way, with Puccini over the titles, they'll think it's some high-brow movie. The picture was shot to open up just with Cher going around collecting money. I took moon shots from other parts of the movie and put them up there for the credits. I put them all up there to play under this song and to denote that everybody is going to be working under the moon's magic and doing crazy things.

How is Norman Jewison in the editing room?

He's great. Unlike Altman, Norman shoots the script. He does all the work on the script and then he shoots it. He has a lot of good ideas and he knows when he's wrong.

You did a wonderful job in compressing and montaging the material in the scene where Cher goes to the hairdresser.

That was shot straight. Norman just shot the whole procedure. I said, "Let's take all this dialogue and just wrap it around the room, off of her. Let's cut to her doing this and that and you just hear all these people. I just kept the dialogue going solid, eight things happening at once, and it worked for her transformation—there she was.

Before you go off to do your first cut, do you have a detailed discussion with the director about what you are trying to accomplish?

No. I mean, that's why they hired me. I'm a better film editor than the director is. I respect and appreciate his position; he should do that with me, give me my shot, then let's play with it. Whoever hires me has got me for 24 hours a day, because I never stop thinking about the picture. I might be home eating dinner and I say to myself, "Goddamn, that's it, that's what will work!" I'm thinking about it and I've solved a problem. There's a lot of spontaneity involved, too. There might be a problem area and I may be running the machine and suddenly there it is, it comes to me, this is the way to do this and it will be perfect. Nobody involved could see it, not even me, but suddenly it's so simple. Many times simplicity is the key to everything. The film tells you when it needs to be jazzed up, but for the most part, simplicity is the key.

How involved do you get in the sound editing process?

I get involved as far as seeing that it's covered. I try to inspire the guys to get creative. They can help you a lot if they start thinking, and not just do the things that you see, that are obvious. Give me something off-stage that makes the scene more interesting, like a distant train whistle blowing, or a coyote howl through a night scene. Get creative with it.

Do you think of the editor as a moviemaker?

Oh, you bet. It's the most important job outside of writing and directing. You take everyone's endeavor and make it work. You put that in the wrong hands and it doesn't work. I don't care how good these people are, it really doesn't work. Everything depends on the guy sitting in the editing chair.

How much impact can an editor have on the success of a film?

In my opinion, he can make it or break it.

Do you feel that current audiences demand a fast-paced film?

Audiences are educated by television and the television guys take a lot of chances, because they have to tell a story in a certain amount of time; they can't dilly-dally. You've got to do some real futuristic type of editing. I mean no old-fashioned bullshit, you don't have time to linger. That's what the audience is used to.

How do you feel about the new video and laser disc editing technologies?

I think an editor must learn how to operate all the new equipment, but the machine has nothing to do with it. Just to be able to operate a machine doesn't make you an editor. A lot of people put a lot of importance on that: "Look, he can work that machine, he's really something." I don't give a damn if he can work the machine, can he cut the film? Can he make a scene make sense? Equipment will change but talent is going to be the same.

What is the role of the editor on a film?

A movie should have a beginning, an end, and somebody in the middle to cheer for it, and that's what a film editor is. You've got to be behind a film 1,000 percent. Otherwise you're cheating yourself and the people you're working with.

12

Evan Lottman

In 1956, after attending the University of Southern California Film School, Evan Lottman returned to New York and became an apprentice editor on Lionel Rogosin's documentary *On the Bowery*, which was edited by the legendary New York editor Carl Lerner. After completing the film, Lottman took a job in a commercial house, where he learned the technical craft of film editing by working on hundreds of television commercials.

In 1961, Lottman made the transition to features, when Dede Allen asked him to cut the pool-playing montages for *The Hustler*. Since then, Evan Lottman has become an established New York feature editor. He has edited a wide range of films, including *Honeysuckle Rose*, *The Protector*, and *The Muppets Take Manhattan*. Major releases among his credits are *The Exorcist*, *Sophie's Choice*, and *Presumed Innocent*. Evan Lottman has helped to train feature editors Craig McKay and Trudy Ship, both of whom were his assistants. He has worked with directors Paul Newman and William Friedkin and has had continuing collaborations with Jerry Schatzberg and Alan Pakula. In 1973 he was nominated for an Academy Award for *The Exorcist*.

1970	*Puzzle of a Downfall Child*
1971	*The Panic in Needle Park*
1972	*The Effect of Gamma Rays on Man in the Moon Marigolds*
1973	*Scarecrow*

	The Exorcist* (with Norman Gay, Jordan Leondopoulos, and Bud Smith)
1976	Dandy, the All American Girl
1978	On the Yard
1979	The Seduction of Joe Tynan
1980	Honeysuckle Rose (with Aram Avakian, Norman Gay and Marc Laub)
1981	Terror Eyes
	Rollover
1982	Sophie's Choice
1984	The Muppets Take Manhattan
1985	The Protector
1986	Maximum Overdrive
1987	Orphans
1989	See You in the Morning
	Forced March
1990	Presumed Innocent

*Academy Award nomination for best achievement in film editing.

How did you get into the film business?

I was trained as a cinematographer in the Army Signal Corps. I decided to go to USC cinema school on the G.I. Bill. In California it seemed possible to get into the editing side of the business more than anything else. I took an editing course and saw the possibilities, but it was a lot of theory, and what I really wanted was the technical background. I was very impatient to get on with my career, so I quit. I came back to New York and still wanted to become a cameraman, but an opportunity opened in a cutting room. My first job was as an apprentice to a very famous New York film editor, Carl Lerner. I had never heard of Carl Lerner and had no idea I was working for such a great personage. The film was a theatrical documentary called *On the Bowery*. When it was finished, Carl liked me enough to get me a job in a commercial house as an apprentice. That was the only steady job I've had—ever. I was there for two years and then became an assistant editor.

Commercials are terrific for learning technique. Every commercial is a miniature movie. Everything is there: preproduction, actors, dailies, sound, the composer, the mix, opticals, the answer print, all accomplished in a week or so. I must have worked on hundreds of commercials, but documentaries were the big hot ticket then in New York.

Anybody who was anybody in editing was in documentaries, and editors were given a lot of creative freedom. I decided I wanted to get into documentaries and be a freelancer. I became Lora Hays's assistant for two years. She was working at ABC doing public affairs documentary films.

How did you make that difficult leap from assistant to editor?

It's an awful time because it's so easy to get work as an assistant; you're so good at what you do. But nobody will hire you as an editor; they keep calling you for jobs as an assistant. So there is a point when you have to say, "Stop, I'm an editor. I'm not going to accept any job that isn't an editing job." That's a lean, hard time, and the better known you are as an assistant, the harder it is to make the jump.

As an editor, what personality traits do you look for in hiring an assistant?

Someone who is hard-working, loyal, and has a sense of humor. I cherish people like Craig McKay and Trudy Ship, not just because they were good assistants, but because I like them and respond to them as people.

How did you get into feature film editing?

After doing the series *Winston Churchill* for ABC, Dede Allen called me to do the pool game montages for *The Hustler*. I edited five montages to be used throughout the film, but they only used two of them. The director, Robert Rossen, went into Ames pool hall and shot pool games for two weeks. They ended up with a roomful of film of the pool games, just very loosely organized with no particular editing idea in mind. I started after the photography was completed. I didn't know anything about pool. I remember going to a pool hall to try and learn about it. I had a chart of all of the balls in black and white photography so I could see what color corresponded to the grey scale, because when they called the balls you had to identify them in black and white. I'm not sure that Rossen had any great idea for the montages at the moment; Dede didn't, and I certainly didn't. The script merely said "Montage." Rossen said, "It's a 36-hour pool game. Boil it down to a minute and make a montage out of it." So I started doing it with a lot of quick cuts. I showed it to him and he said, "No, no, no, no. I want a montage, a montage!" I didn't really think he meant the old Slavko Vorkapich stuff, because I thought that was so old-fashioned, but that's what he really wanted. I found out later that he did such montages in most of his movies. In fact, in *All the King's Men*, Slavko Vorkapich himself did the montages.

Right, newspaper headlines, the leaves of the calendar falling ...

... the wheel of a train, you name it. He kept saying, "A montage! Don't you know what a montage is?" Finally, I began to understand that he really *did* mean superimposed images of the games, but I decided to make the images interact dramatically with each other, revealing the actual progress of the match as it went along. Paul Newman would make a shot and superimposed over it in real time were the people watching. They would respond to that shot. I had three supered images visible at once.

What was the editorial challenge in cutting Scarecrow?

There was a lot of footage, it was very improvisational. What we were doing on the movie more than anything else was compressing it, cutting it down in size. We would drop scenes completely and compress some scenes dramatically. For the hitchhiking scene at the beginning of the movie, Jerry Schatzberg shot thousands of feet. It went on and on. In the script it took about a minute or two with the opening credits on it. The first cut was about ten minutes, almost a whole reel.

The scene in the cafe where Al Pacino and Gene Hackman are discussing going into business together is played in a long take without cuts. How did that come about?

I show that scene frequently to students as an example of when not to overedit. It's a brilliant scene, whose action is carried by a virtuoso improvisational performance. Each take was slightly different, but to use more than one or to cut away would have marred the dramatic impact of the scene and the integrity of the performances.

There were four editors on The Exorcist. *How did you work together?*

Basically, Jordan Leondopoulos was going to do the beginning of the picture, Norman Gay was going to edit the middle, and I was to work on the end. Bud Smith, who had previously worked with Billy Friedkin in documentaries, came to New York just to do a rough cut of the opening Iraq sequence, and then went back to California. At that point he took over the postproduction details, work hirings, etc. After Bud left, the Iraq prologue became part of the movie that we all worked on and shaped into a final cut.

Did Warner Brothers have any input into the editing of The Exorcist?

Billy was so protective and secretive about the movie that, as far as I knew, nobody from Warner Brothers saw it at all during the time that I was on the picture.

While you were working on the film did you ever think it would become such a megahit?

I have a terrible record of predicting whether a movie I edit will be a success. I worked on *The Exorcist* and had no idea that it would be successful. I thought that this was a pretty good, well-made, slick, scary, horror movie and that it was going to have a respectable little run, but Friedkin sensed that it would be enormously successful even when Warner Brothers apparently did not. They wanted to open it as an art film.

Was Friedkin knowledgeable about editing?

Yes, I was very impressed with Billy as a director and I learned a lot. I remember having a discussion with him about a particular scene that had what I thought was some important exposition in it. In the middle of the exorcism, Max von Sydow goes out and takes a pill because he has a heart condition. Jason Miller enters and they both sit down together on the stairs and there's a long conversation in which Jason Miller says, "Why her? Why did the devil possess her?" I thought this was a very important question. In fact, I felt that the logic of the picture depended on it. People were going to ask that question, "Why was this little girl picked?" But Billy demanded its removal. I really felt deeply that the scene should stay, and he felt equally deeply that it should go. He felt you couldn't stop the action, you had to keep moving, the hell with talk and questions, nobody cares. Let them ask the question later when they go home, but we've got to drive the action here. I feel now that Billy was right and I was wrong. In fact, I can't remember ever meeting anybody who saw the film, who wondered about the unanswered question, or who didn't feel that the action at the end was relentless and powerful. I edited the scene when Ellen Burstyn is knocked to the floor and the dresser comes toward her. I showed Billy my cut and he looked at it and said to just cut everything in half. At first I resisted, but he told me you didn't have to have 20 frames of this, it could be five frames—flash cuts. I was always very concerned with linear things, the clarity, and logic of cutting. Billy loosened me up.

In the exorcism scene Jason Miller says to the devil, "Come on to me," and he becomes possessed without the angle changing. How was that effect done?

Billy threw that to me as a challenge to make that work and I believe I did. I made a jump cut with a quick dissolve to soften the change of image. Everybody seems to remember the scene where Linda Blair turns her head completely around, 360 degrees. That was done simply by matching a live action shot of Linda beginning to turn her head, to a perfectly made lifelike dummy, expertly positioned to make the matched cut possible.

Did the film go through structural changes during the editing?

Only at the end of the movie. Billy rarely screened the picture. He didn't want to lose his objectivity by seeing it too many times. He would have the three editors screen the picture, and follow it with a discussion of how we felt about the cut. One result of these sessions was that we three editors totally reconstructed the end of the movie, eliminating the final scene with Lee J. Cobb, the kindly old detective, asking the priest to go to a movie with him. Almost as a challenge from Billy, we moved the final scenes around to end with the priest looking down the fatal stairway, and up to the boarded up window in the house. We three editors totally reconstructed the end of the movie. It had never happened to me before and hasn't happened since. We totally remade the ending of the movie.

In the suicide scene in Rollover *you seem to hold on the shot of the car's exhaust coming out of the pipe for three or four beats longer than we expect. It brings a different feeling to it. Do you have an inner clock that tells you how long to play a shot like that?*

Absolutely, it's all inner clock and a lot of experience. We held on the shot of the carbon monoxide slowly chugging out because its very simplicity made it intense and horrible.

In order to get the proper timing on a shot like this, is there a lot of trial and error?

Sometimes, although with experience you can feel the timing and pacing of a shot, frequently, before you cut it.

On Honeysuckle Rose, *which musical sequences did you cut and was it difficult dealing with all of the music tracks?*

I edited the whole last concert. The end of the film has a lot of the music from the concert laid over the drunken bus ride, Willie Nelson and Slim Pickens's race to get back to the concert in time. There's a lot of overlapping and montaging of material. The script said, "They get on the bus, drive back, and have a conversation." Intercutting it with the concert was something that came about in the editing. We had a room where we had set up a KEM flatbed for pre-mixing, it was inter-locked with a Nagra tape recorder. It was each editor's responsibility to pre-mix every time he did a cut. I had to prepare the work track, the dialogue track, the overlapping concert music, and go in and pre-mix. It was a very cumbersome, expensive arrangement. Of course, every time you made a three-frame change, you'd have to remix again.

You have cut many films for director Alan Pakula. Would you consider him an editor's director?

He's an editor's director insofar as he's a director who respects the editing process and the editor, and loves to work in a collaborative way. We sit together at the KEM, talking about the film and about how to convey his ideas through the editing process. He has strong convictions about the way he wants the movie to be. As an editor, I always respond to directors like that. You join in his vision of the film and trust him because you know the work will improve the film ultimately. I can't say this about all directors.

Were there any problems in adapting the novel Sophie's Choice *to the screen?*

From the point of view of film editing, the first cut was very, very long. There were long, partially improvisational scenes of Sophie speaking about her past life that were too long and top-heavy, and required a lot of judicious compression. The main difficulty and challenge in cutting the picture had to do with the wealth of material. It was hard to make choices, but I think the result was worth the effort.

Was the "We became best of friends" montage at the beginning of the film written into the script?

No. Alan directed improvisational scenes which he knew he would use later in montages when he felt they were needed to illustrate the love that all three of the characters had for each other. We felt that Nathan had to be made more charming and generally sympathetic, as a counterbalance to the scenes in which the horrible side of his personality became predominant.

Did you use only that improvisational material or did you take footage that was intended for other parts of the film?

The material of the three characters sitting on the roof of the house was shot for the montage, but there were other scenes that were previously lifted out of the movie that were included. For instance, there was a scene of Stingo discovering that his money was stolen from his room. This part of the story was dropped from the cut, but we incorporated some leftover shots of Stingo writing in his room, Sophie seen on the porch through his window, etc., into the montage.

Did Meryl Streep's performance emerge right away from the dailies?

Yes. *Sophie's Choice* was shot largely in continuity. That helped the ensemble acting technique. It was wonderful for Alan to be able to deal with a small number of actors in a closely set dramatic situation and work in continuity. The hard part of the editing was preserving those performances—going for the gold.

In the scene where Sophie is talking about her past, you're going from the close-up to the flashback material and back. What tells you when you have to come back to her?

Instinct. The feeling of the scene. The sense of dramatic timing.

That is a gorgeous close-up.

We searched a long time for that frame. It was the image we used at the end of the movie.

How did you work with the Polish language scenes? Did you cut with translations?

Actually, I had three translations: Polish as Polish, Polish written out phonetically in English, and the English translation. The same for the scenes in German. I cut it very painstakingly, carefully going over line for line with my assistant, Trudy Ship. We didn't want to chop anything in midsentence, or lose the natural speech cadences. Finally, in order to screen the work print properly, we made the English subtitles printed on a black and white slop print.

Trudy Ship was an associate editor on this film. Did she cut scenes?

Yes, she did. She started as my assistant. I did the first cut. When the crew went to Yugoslavia to film the European material, we stayed in New York, and Trudy became the associate editor. She did a wonderful job cutting some very big scenes, including the climactic scene in the Auschwitz railroad station at the end.

It's a remarkable scene. When her daughter realizes that she's being sacrificed, her scream is played over a shot of Sophie with her mouth open, bringing the child's terror into the mother's mouth. Did that develop in the cutting of that scene?

Yes, it had a lot to do with the performance. There it was; Meryl did that and you use and manipulate the performance as effectively as possible.

The Protector *was a pure action movie. Do you have any principles for cutting action scenes?*

I have very strong feelings about it. The cutting should be logical, the point of view must be maintained at all times. The danger in cutting an action sequence is losing or confusing the audience.

The sound work is very important in action scenes. Did you do more of the sound editing yourself than usual?

I try to do my own rough sound editing on the work track, where a reasonably good track exists. The helicopter scenes had a lot of original sound. I wanted the machine guns to hit at certain points, so I cut them in myself. Later on, the sound editors try to follow the original work of the picture editor, and then add to or enhance it as necessary.

What were some of the technical challenges presented by working with the Muppets on The Muppets Take Manhattan?

One of the technical problems in doing a Muppet movie is that the stages are built four feet above the floor, so that the actors can work underneath, holding the Muppet characters over their heads, viewing the performances on small, individual video screens with earphones. After shooting one side of the set, the whole stage would have to be rerigged, floors rearranged, to shoot the reverse angles. The waiting period between the dailies for one half of the coverage and the final reverse angles caused a lot of nervousness, impatience, and anxiety in the cutting room, but because the picture was so carefully storyboarded beforehand, things generally went rather smoothly.

Could you describe your typical editing procedure from the time dailies come in?

At the beginning, I try to be on the set as much as possible, acquainting myself with the crew, showing the flag, so to speak, of the editing department. When the film starts piling up in the pipeline and when I feel there is enough for me to fruitfully spend a full day cutting my first scene, I start working. Then I pretty much stick to the cutting room all day. There are times when a director may want me on the set, or he may want me to cut one scene quickly because of some technical or acting problem. Being present on location enables me to do that. When the shooting is finished, I've usually got anywhere between one week or two weeks to present my first cut. I try to make it as smooth and seamless as possible, occasionally even pre-mixing some sections, putting in some sound effects or music where I feel it might help. Considering the effort spent on the first assembly, I think the term "rough cut" is a little harsh.

What equipment do you use?

I cut on two Moviolas. One is a cutter Moviola without arms, and the other one has arms. I like to have a high-speed KEM flatbed for viewing and to make minor changes. I don't cut on the flatbed. I find it a slower, more cumbersome machine to work on. Because I use the Moviola, I use the bench and work everything through a synchronizer. I don't actually mark frames until I'm in dead sync in a synchronizer. Recently, I've started using an Acmade Edit-All—a British editing machine which is really a motorized synchronizer with a small picture head. It enables me to eliminate one of the Moviolas.

How do you find the pace of a film?

The whole picture has a rhythm. When you screen a first cut, you see the film in a different context, reflectively and quietly, so you can think about it. You see it all together, as a whole dramatic piece, and you're not concentrating on any one problem. Screening gives you an objective reading of the whole film. You can evaluate the pace of the movie. Is this part too slow? Does it take too long to get into the story? Every movie has a point at which it should really begin. There should be a point in the beginning of a movie when there is a major piece of action, excitement, or a development that happens right off the bat and draws you into the story. As an editor, you have to judge if it's taking too long to get there.

What is the hardest kind of scene to cut?

The hardest kind of editing is the most subtle. Like the final scene in *Sophie's Choice*, where Sophie and Stingo are sitting in the hotel room and she tells Stingo about the arrival in Auschwitz. I think it's some of my best work in the movie. I'm not sure that people would recognize it as well-edited, but I think it is well-paced and deals with the subtleties of the performances and the emotions.

Do you think an editor's work can ever reconceptualize material in a way that has a directorial impact on the film?

Only when the picture is in trouble and it isn't working to begin with. Then desperate measures are in order. But it's hard for a film to take off on a direction all its own, once it arrives in the cutting room. You can point it and shape it, but it's hard to create what isn't there in the first place.

Do you think you have a style as an editor?

Generally, editing is invisible. The director and the material dictate the style. If I lean in any direction, it would be that I do tend to be linear, logical, and generally as communicative as possible in my editing. I couldn't edit one of those MTV jobs if they hung me by my thumbs.

Why do you think that film critics so rarely mention editing in their reviews?

Because it's invisible. Seeing the finished product can not tell you the value of the editing. You don't know whether the material was great and the editor screwed it up, or if it was poor material and he made a wonderful movie out of it. You don't know whether moments in the movie were created in the editing room or whether they were part of the director's original conception. But if the picture works, the editing works, and nobody's going to call special attention to it.

How has your work method changed over the years?

I've become less concerned with technique and more with content. I think that's the normal process of growing experience. The technique serves the meaning; it doesn't dominate it.

What advice do you give to people who ask how to become a film editor?

I'm going to sound like Horatio Alger, but it's really a lot of stick-to-itiveness, making the rounds, banging on doors, and being reasonably aggressive. Don't be a pain in the butt, but don't fade into the woodwork, either. It's like anything else that you really want to do. If you are motivated, determined, lucky, and you hang in there, you're going to do it.

13

Alan Heim

Bronx-born Alan Heim studied at the City College of New York Film Institute in New York during the late 1950s and worked at the Army Pictorial Center in Queens, New York, where he learned sound editing.

Heim began his feature film career as a sound editor and worked for Sidney Lumet on *The Sea Gull*, *The Group*, *The Pawnbroker*, and *Bye Bye Braverman*. While sound editing on *The Producers*, Heim made the move to picture editing, when he was asked to finish the film, edited by Ralph Rosenblum.

In 1972 Heim edited the television special *Liza with a Z* for director Bob Fosse. This began a collaboration which produced three daring feature films: *Lenny*, *All that Jazz*, and *Star 80*. Fosse and Heim shared an artistic vision that brought a new kind of filmic language to contemporary editing. They developed a mosaic of imagery most dramatically seen in *All that Jazz*, for which Heim won the Academy Award in 1979. This interview was conducted shortly before Fosse's untimely death in 1987.

Heim worked on *Hair* and *Valmont* for Milos Forman. His reunion in 1976 with Sidney Lumet on *Network* earned him an Oscar nomination.

1970	*The Twelve Chairs*
1971	*Doc*
1973	*Godspell*
1974	*Lenny*
1976	*Network**

1979	*Hair* (with Lynzee Klingman, super- vising editor, and Stanley Warnow)
	All That Jazz**
1981	*The Fan*
	So Fine
1983	*Star 80*
1985	*Beer*
	Goodbye, New York
1988	*She's Having a Baby*
	Funny Farm
1989	*Valmont* (with Nena Danevic)
1990	*Quick Change*
1991	*Billy Bathgate*

*Academy Award nomination for best achievement in film editing.

**Academy Award for best achievement in film editing.

How did you become interested in filmmaking?

The first job I was ever paid for was at 13 as a projectionist for the Police Athletic League. I wanted to be a still photographer. I went to City College here in New York, dropped out, and went back to school, this time studying at the Film Institute. It was middle to late 1950s. Hans Richter, the experimental filmmaker, was in charge. The people who taught there were serious filmmakers: Sidney Myers, Manny Kirschei-mer, and Roger Tilton, who taught the editing class I had to take at night because there were so few students. A lot of the students remained in the business. Larry Cohen and Ulu Grosbard were in my class.

How did you become an editor?

George Stoney took over the Film Institute. He liked my work and introduced me to people who got me a job at an editing company on weekends. After I got out of school I went into the Army Pictorial Center in Queens, where I worked with a civilian who taught me how to edit music. I was beginning to work as a sound editor. I've never been a musician but I was able to make music fit a particular sequence by cutting it; that has served me in good stead. I worked on films for Sidney Lumet as a sound effects editor. It was a valuable training ground. I worked on *The Sea Gull, The Group, The Pawnbroker,* and *Bye Bye Braverman,* which was edited by Jerry Greenberg, who had been my assistant on sound jobs before that. In those days Sidney was so eager to look at things together, he rarely allowed you to polish. He stood over the editor's back and told him exactly where to make the cut. I learned an enormous amount, but was not being allowed to contribute. I found it a little stultifying, and I really didn't want to do that anymore.

Was there ever a specific moment when you understood what film editing was about?

When I was doing sound editing, Aram Avakian was working down the hall. He said, "Look at this." It was a cut between two waist shot close-ups of actors, and I said, "What's so wonderful about the cut?" I had no idea what he was talking about. He said, "Look at the way the actor's hand moves and takes your eye across the screen." Suddenly, how to edit became clear to me. It was like a vision, almost like a religious experience. What I try to do now is to move to what is comfortable in the frame. I know people think some of my work is jarring, but not in my eyes. As staccato as many of my films may be, the one thing I go for is fluidity, a flow between the cuts.

How did you make the leap to picture editing?

I had done some sound work on *The Producers*. The editor, Ralph Rosenblum, left the film. I had known the producer from my sound work on *The Eleanor Roosevelt Story*. They were looking for another editor. There were a few scenes to be done and the main titles to be worked on. I suggested that I take over the film and he said that Ralph had suggested the same thing. There is one scene in *The Producers* which never got any laughs and Mel Brooks said, "Would you redo the scene? It just doesn't work." I was a little terrified, I hadn't cut picture since college, apart from a little documentary work, and I really didn't want to be in the room with him. He's a very high-energy guy; he tumults a lot. It's the scene where they go to sign Kenny Mars at his apartment. It was all done in a master shot in front of a mantlepiece with a big portrait of Hitler on top of it. My theory at the time, which has since gotten more sophisticated, is that nobody is going to laugh at a scene that has a big picture of Hitler in the middle of it! It also had a lot to do with the timing of the actors. On stage, actors can feel and play the audience. They can speed things up or slow things down, but here it was done in a very long master shot and there wasn't enough visual interest.

I'm a great believer in a long shot when it works, but when it's not working, you have to start moving things around. When I looked at the trims and the outs, I discovered there were an enormous number of close-ups which were very, very funny. There is a wonderful close-up where Kenny Mars sticks his hand up and does an imitation of Churchill with the Churchill "V" right in front of his enormous face. It's beautifully framed and he says, "Churchill, he was no dancer. Hitler, now there was a dancer. Hitler could paint an entire apartment in one afternoon, two coats." He held out his hand for the two coats. Mel had used none of this. As I started cutting the scene, I found that within six or eight frames of my marks, there was a splice where the film had been reconstituted; it was clear that Ralph Rosenblum had already cut the scene this way and Mel hated it. So I put it together the way it felt comfortable to me. We had a sneak preview at the Baronet Theater and the audience laughed so hard through that sequence that I was thrilled to be in a theater and to actually feel a response from an audience. That's when I decided I wanted to stay in picture editing, because clearly, the director had some material he didn't know what to do with, and I had taken it and made it funny. The editor has another way of looking at the material. It's always important to be able to look at something differently.

You became the principal editor on the next film that Mel Brooks directed, The Twelve Chairs. *What was that experience like?*

I ended up in Yugoslavia for four months. They don't code film in Yugoslavia. I got there two weeks after they had begun shooting, and I started getting out from under an enormous amount of film that nobody had touched. I flew down to Dubrovnik to show Mel a half-hour of cut scenes, which should have ended up about ten minutes in the picture. For a first cut, you put together everything the director has shot, unless it is truly horrendous. This was just very verbose. I felt pretty good about the cut. I knew just where it had to be changed, but I didn't know what else to do with it, short of taking out enormous amounts of dialogue. We screened the film; there was Anne Bancroft, the assistant director, and the associate producer. Anne had begun to leave immediately, she sort of backed out of the room. Mel began by saying, "It's remarkable how close you are to my original concept." From there to what seemed like 45 minutes later, it was pure excoriation. He just lit into me about touching his material and daring to change what he had in mind. That's an interesting problem, because as an editor, you're the last obstacle between the director and his pure vision. Often you have to change the director's concept to make something work, and even though the thing works, the director will resent you for it. This happened with Mel and Ralph Rosenblum and happened to Mel and me, although we eventually ended up working well together.

How did your association with Bob Fosse begin?

I had done the television show *Liza with a Z*. That was the year that Fosse had won the Oscar for *Cabaret*, the Emmy for *Liza with a Z*, and the Tony for *Pippin*. I discovered in Fosse a really kindred spirit. The whole freedom of editing that I got from Bob fits into my own psyche. We've worked very closely together. I do very little cutting during the shooting. Bob likes to be involved. He spends a full day in the cutting room. We'll discuss a scene and then I'll cut the scene. Bob will be next door or out with some people, and then come back to look at it. We work on a musical number in basically the same way. I'll know exactly what section will be used, where and how. A lot of what I've got, I've got from Fosse. He's referred to me as a collaborator and I think it's a great honor. He's not on my back; we're working together to try and make the movie good. He respects the editor's contribution.

Was the basic structure of Lenny *in the script?*

The script was thrilling for an editor, you could just see the transitions. The basic structure was there, but neither of us were happy until we suddenly began to really fragment the script. In the cutting room we developed this technique for fragmenting things drastically. A lot of people found fault with this, they felt they couldn't follow the routines. But you've got to do what is best for the movie; you can't really hold it back. If the audience really sticks with it they'll follow and understand what's happening. If they don't, then maybe we shouldn't have made the film in the first place. A lot of people said the same thing about *Liza with a Z*—they never got a chance to see the dance numbers. In a Fosse production the dance numbers are not so much about full-bodied dancers moving on the screen, but about movement in a frame. It is a little like silent film cutting. The juxtapositions are what tell the story; the flow of the images is what propels it forward.

As we started cutting *Lenny*, we realized that the story had always been intended to have a comic sequence and a flashback or flashforward, something relating to that comic sequence. In the routine where he's talking about lesbians, we intercut the scene with Lenny watching his wife and the other woman. We discovered if we took the rhythm of his comic routines and found natural places to open them up, it gave them more of a bite. By structuring the film that way, it just made everything come wildly alive. Suddenly, these little one-sentence, two-sentence comments were making very astringent comments on his life, rather than having a neat capsule comedy routine and then a sequence dealing with that comedy routine. By merging them, we thought we had made something much more pointed. Once we found that, it was really marvelous. I didn't want to go home. We would stay till eight or nine at night finding the best moments, just knocking out sequences. E. L. Doctorow once said, "There is real time and there is screen time and there is Fosse time."

One of the nightclub scenes is shot in a single long take that plays for about six minutes without cutting. Why was this decision made? Had the scene been covered in any other way?

We were shooting in Florida, it was hot and humid. None of us knew at the time that black and white film has a tendency to develop static, so we barely had coverage, but we could have done the scene with cuts. We looked at the scene and two things played; Dustin Hoffman was marvelous in the long shot, and it was also the quality that he was almost under a microscope. He was like a bug on a stage. You became part of that audience watching it. We were aware that people were going to jump on us for fragmenting this film. Dustin was real good and we felt he deserved a scene that wasn't cut up, manipulated emotionally in the cutting room.

What was the most difficult problem to solve in Lenny's *structure?*

The big problem became the ending. We had to show the film to the producer, David Picker, on a Thursday and it was now Wednesday. From the time Lenny was dragged out of jail, to the dead body shots, was just not working. It was a lot of material, about two reels. There was a sequence of him saying goodbye to his daughter. There was a really marvelous sequence shot from the back of the room, where he was calling his wife. He's walking around stoned eating peanut butter. Fosse, myself, and the people working with me, went out to dinner about twelve o'clock at night. We had been kicking this around all through dinner. We got back at one in the morning. In the elevator I turned to Bob and said, "Why don't we just kill the son of a bitch? Why don't we just cut to him dead." Bob lit up, I lit up, and we did it. We just took out two reels, cut about 20 minutes, and went right to him lying on the bathroom floor and it worked. I was as surprised as anybody else. By that time it was two o'clock in the morning. We were all exhausted, we had to show it to David Picker in the morning, and we just left it that way. We had an ending and it was thrilling.

Endings are very hard in movies. Beginnings are tough, but the audience will give you ten minutes or so. Everyone thinks a scripted film has an ending and it's wonderful. It doesn't work that way. It's murder to put an ending on a film and make it seem comfortable. Either it's very predictable or it seems to come out of nowhere. You want to get a balance there, weighing one scene against the other, making the audience either comfortable or uncomfortable. By just killing him we surprised them, we did something else. I think it was a very important movie, if movies can be important. The things that we did structurally have become part of film use.

You crossed paths again with Sidney Lumet in 1976 as the film editor on Network. *Can you describe that experience?*

Dede Allen, who had cut *Serpico* and *Dog Day Afternoon* for Lumet, was not available to cut *Network*. Paddy Chayefsky called me. I was very nervous that Sidney was going to try and tell me how to cut the movie, but he had no time. Six days after we finished shooting it, we saw it in a theater. My fears about him making me do things were not justified. I learned things from Sidney that have been very valuable to me. I learned to read performances and make quick decisions. When you edit, there is very little that you can't fiddle with if you want to afterwards. The important thing to do is to look at something as a whole and then polish it.

I understand that Lumet does not give an editor a lot of coverage. Does he only shoot what he thinks he will need?

Sidney never shoots a lot of material. He will often do one take, maybe two. He will print one take, and it will sometimes be take one. Usually when Sidney knows he's going to use a close-up, he'll only shoot that amount of film. He shoots what he needs. Sidney has a real gut feeling for what's right. As an editor, where you run into trouble is when you run a shot in a sequence, and you don't have the reaction shots. It's a wonderful way to shoot if you don't get crazy. In *Network* we needed a shot of Faye Dunaway and there just wasn't one where she was doing the right thing. I used a little piece of film I found that was before the slate that was just enough.

Did Network *go through many changes during the editing process?*

We took out a whole bunch of transitional scenes that Paddy Chayefsky wanted to shoot. Sidney knew that they would go, people getting into cars, stuff that was totally unnecessary. Aram Avakian once told Barry Malkin, "You've got to be careful of any film that has a lot of people getting in and out of cars and going through doors." I'm a great believer in cutting that out; that's boring stuff. There's no real reason any more. The audience knows how to go from place to place. It was a little long; we shortened a couple of scenes, dropped a character. Lee Richardson was in the film originally. He was superb. Now all you see is his back. We flipped two scenes. William Holden and Faye Dunaway go up to Long Island, the famous scene where she's giving statistics while they are under the covers making love. That used to be followed by the scene where he and his wife, Beatrice Straight, confront each other and she kicks him out of the apartment. It never worked. The reason it didn't work was very clear to me. Faye Dunaway was so unpleasant, so terrible, and his wife was so strong, that it became ludicrous, why he'd be leaving this wonderful woman. I suggested flipping the scenes. We really argued. Sidney didn't want to take the time to see the scenes rearranged and instead they wanted to drop the scene with Beatrice Straight entirely. I jumped up and down and insisted that we keep it in and move it, and they would not do it. Sidney I couldn't brook. I worked on Paddy. The producer, Howard Gottfried, also wouldn't listen to me. Dan Melnick flew in from California. We showed him the film and he loved it. Dan said, "The one thing that is bothering me is that scene with his wife. Why don't you turn those two scenes around?" Monday morning I get a call from Howard Gottfried who says, "Listen, Dan has this great idea, why don't you turn the two scenes around?" I said, "Howard, I have been saying that for weeks and you wouldn't even look at it." He said, "It doesn't matter where it came from," and he's right. I didn't care either. We changed the two scenes around and went into sound editing and we were finished with it.

Stanley Kauffmann in reviewing *Network* said a brilliant thing about the editing which was something like, "The audience was always where they wanted to be, even if they didn't know it at the time." That's a fascinating concept, because it's true. I always try and show the audience what's interesting on the screen. I try to make them go where I want them to go. Now, they are a bit captive, because once I make the cut and it gets into my answer print, it's not going to change. But if it's right, it works for the movie.

There has been so much talk about All That Jazz *being autobiographical. Did Bob Fosse see the film that way?*

Bob didn't like the idea of people saying that he was Joe Gideon. In fact when we started, he and I were having a tough time together, because I would refer to a sequence by saying, "Here, where you . . . " Well, he would say, "It's not me!" He would get really angry about it. At one point I wanted to quit. I really felt insulted and hurt. It took a couple of weeks before he calmed down and I found enough of a way to diffuse the situation. It was very tense.

Was the time-shifting structure of the film in the original script?

It was in the script. The overall structure was similar to what you see in the film. Bob wrote it with Bob Aurthur. He took a lot of the techniques that we had worked out in the cutting room for *Lenny* and wrote them into the script. When we tried to change certain things, we found it a little harder to be as free with the material.

How were the "It's showtime" montages created?

Each one was different and the choices were made in the cutting room. There was a particularly interesting one that was not planned at all, which intercut him coughing with his daughter leaving him in the rehearsal hall studio. It was the only one that was intercut and not played as a little chunk by itself. There were giant close-ups of him squeezing his eyes and taking the pills. The enormous violence of the coughing was something that just seemed right for that place in the movie.

What was your involvement in editing Hair?

Lynzee Klingman, the supervising editor, asked me if I wanted to do one sequence, the draft board scene. She and Stanley Warnow both did a different version of it with the director, Milos Forman. It didn't work. It was ugly, it seemed racist, it was just wrong. They were trying to put too much political comment into the film, too much love for the period. The draft board scene was a real old-fashioned, big, flashy, show-business number and the fun of it was lacking in the piece. I put it back together in dailies form, and found the flash they had been skipping. We cut it from scratch with that in mind. This was not a political piece. We didn't have to push the story forward; it was just a production number. I treated it that way and it worked.

The Fan *was the director's first film. What was that experience like?*

Ed Bianchi had done commercials. The first day's material went painfully slow and after the dailies I said, "You really have to pick up the pace. It's going to be very hard to make the film play at this pace." He missed the point of what I was saying and took it badly. After that the crew came and they applauded the dailies. I decided I would do as I usually do, which is to take the material as given. If I really needed something I would ask for it. Clearly, he did not want to listen to me. I had some contributions to make which would have helped. Later, when I put the film together, I showed quite a bit of it to Ed and he was really appalled. He saw exactly what was wrong. He said, "Why were all those people applauding? You were the only guy telling me negative things. I wanted to hear positive things."

What was it like to work with John Hughes on She's Having a Baby?

He's a good editor. Once you start putting the film together, he's very self-critical and willing to lose material that he shot at great length. I rarely had to argue with him if I suggested dropping a scene. He suggested dropping a couple of longer scenes that weren't bad, but looked strange for the character.

Is there such a thing as an editor's director?

Fosse is an editor's director because I think his sense of imagery is so enormous that the stories often can be told without words. The way we put together scenes tells a story within itself, just the way his dance sequences use parts of bodies, little cuts and things. If you know where to look, they are showing you a different dance, a screen dance. The pictures tell a story. Most directors have a sense of editing, but Bob is an editor's director. He's also an actor's director, and a cameraman's director—a film director.

Have you cut music videos?

Only once. I did a video for Cyndi Lauper, *True Colors*. Pat Birch was the director. Cyndi and Pat wanted a story there. I find the problem with most music videos is that they are very fragmented—and for me to say that is something. When I try to cut a sequence I like strong visuals, but I'm not so sure that putting them on top of each other really does anything to the dramatic flow of a piece. I look for more than just the sheer visual impact. I wouldn't use fancy dissolves unless I had a real dramatic reason for it. A Fosse dance number still follows the lines of the music and the dance. A lot of the stuff in videos seems to me to be arbitrary, but that may be because I am getting on in years.

What equipment do you use?

I do most of my editing on an upright Moviola. For the most part I don't like editing tables. I do a lot of my editing on a synchronizer and rewinder by hand. Basically, I'll know what takes we are using from the dailies screening. I make my marks and overlaps and rough out a lot of things on the synchronizer without looking at the film again. I used to cut whole reels without looking at them after screening. At the end of the day, I would have my assistant put the material together, look at it all fresh, make a few adjustments for mechanical reasons, and leave it for a while. I did that on *Network* because there was so little coverage. Since then, it's been harder and harder to do. Now there's a lot more cutting, the material is more complex, it's hard if you get a lot of coverage. You have to start going from day to day, because you're constantly handling big chunks of film, looking for excellent moments.

I've used the Steenbeck and KEM as well. With Fosse I work with a KEM almost exclusively. It is difficult to work with because of its size, the sheer bulk of it, but the image is big and it threads very easily. It is nice not to have to worry about the film ripping and catching in the Moviola, which it often does. Also, the director and others can sit down and look at a screening in a comfortable way without all crunching around and pushing each other aside to look at the tiny Moviola screen. I keep a Moviola around, too. Most of the editors I've known here in New York feel there is something about working on the Moviola; very few work on tables. In California they do more work on the tables except for the real old-timers.

Does your logging and coding system vary with the demands of the film?

No, not really. I'll do whatever my assistant feels comfortable doing. There are different ways of coding. In California you can code every take individually and you have your own coding machine. Usually the apprentice is working on it. You can code every take and indicate the scene and take number, so when you look at it you don't need a code book. What we do here in New York, for the most part, is code 1,000 feet of film with a letter prefix and a four-digit number, so you can look it up in the code book. It's really just the mechanics. I don't mind the process. There are directors who really hate the time you have to take to look up things in a code book. I find it valuable to just step back for a moment and think about the film while somebody is looking for the film that I'm missing.

Do you ever use charts?

What I like to do is to put the scenes on index cards with the scene number and a small description, and pin them up on the wall in reel order. Then you have in front of you the entire layout of the picture. As you begin to rearrange and pull things out, you put the cards into other positions. You keep the outs and the lifted scenes in a box so you can find them very quickly. You have an immediate reference as to what is out of the picture by number. You know 738 is going to be moved and it's not on the wall; you look in the box and see what state it was in when it was moved.

I understand that many assistants are using a computer to log material.

Bud Molin showed me a system he used on a Carl Reiner comedy that he was thrilled with. For instance, if you wanted to know any scene involving dogs, you would just type in "dog" on the computer, and all the scenes involving dogs would come out. I would have found it very valuable on the train sequence in *She's Having a Baby*. A lot of material was shot without a system and no logging before I got on the picture. They would call me and say, "What did the conductor wear in the summer?" I had to go through all this material because I had no indication of what was summer and what was winter. Had I gone through it once and typed in the descriptions, it would have saved me a lot of unnecessary screenings. So I'm tempted to start getting involved with the computer for the log book, at least.

How much do you think production people know about what goes on in the cutting room?

There are a lot of people who really have no idea of what editing is. I worked on a film once and when they got the bill from the sound effects editor for the purchase of sound effects they said, "We don't have this on our budget." Now this was a man who had produced films before. I said, "How are we supposed to get the sound effects that we need?" He said, "Can't they just supply them?" Yes, you can make a flat deal with the sound effects guy, but you'll be paying for the sound effects in a different way. So there's a certain ignorance of the movie-making process which is shocking.

How do you work with your editing crew? Do you consider yourself to be a good supervisor?

I like being in a cutting room. Most of the editors I know do. That reflects on the way I work with my assistants and apprentices. I really like to push people to help me out and they learn a lot, so I'm considered a good guy to work for. I arrange the time so that there is a minimum amount of overtime for everybody. I like to work with one assistant and two apprentices or two assistants and one apprentice, depending on the bulk of the movie. There was a lot of film on *All That Jazz*. I had two assistants. I promoted one of them at some point, and I had a couple of apprentices all the time. The idea is to try and keep up. I generally have a lot of trims when I cut; somebody has to put them back into the filing system. I don't use an assistant the way a lot of people do. I like to be able to delegate work to my assistant, editing a scene under supervision. I don't have my assistant standing next to me handing me film very often. I like to have my assistant around making things easy for me, but I like to do the physical part of the film. I like to make the cuts and put film in barrels myself. If something is real complex, I'll have my assistant working with me. I'll give them trims and they will put them in barrels, because I tend to put them on the wrong pins if I'm working very quickly. You get involved with the making of the movie and you just want to get on with it.

What is the atmosphere like when you have the director working with you in the cutting room?

The editor, the assistant, and the apprentice have been together for, say, three months. You've been sitting there looking at this material and occasionally muttering under your breath, being unhappy about it in some way, and suddenly, here's the perpetrator. You've got certain loyalty and the director is now an outsider. You get to the point where the editor has to make the director feel comfortable in the cutting room.

You have effectively used intercutting in many of the films you have edited. What are your prime concerns in using this technique?

Crosscutting has been going on since the silent days. It's a way of building tension. The tensions have to be equal, not in the sense that they are equal in time; they have to have equal weight. They have to build in certain ways. It might get shorter on one side, and stay longer on the other. That's one of the delicacies of editing that I always find intriguing.

How do you feel about cutting material shot with a zoom lens?

I never much liked zooms. Sometimes it just takes too damn long. It has to be timed out just so by the director, because often you do get locked into it. To cut into a zoom shot is very hard.

Do montage sequences, like the one in Star 80 *where Paul takes Dorothy's sister to a carnival, give the editor more freedom than tightly scripted scenes?*

It's another way of looking at the material. It's the freedom of a documentary. It's not scripted. You have four minutes of carousel horse, the roller coaster, five minutes of the whip. It becomes a question of how to make the sequence visually interesting, because in this period of video, it's very rare that you show something new to people, maybe a heart operation like in *All That Jazz*, but even that is on the news now. The audience is so hip. You have to try and make it visually interesting for the sequence, so you push it. You take a look at the material and you make it work. You can do anything you want, but you really have to do it within the structure of the story. What I try to do is to keep a visual line flowing, to keep you going up and down and across the screen in interesting ways so that the audience doesn't notice they're swinging around in that way.

Do you get involved in the lab work?

People consider that the expertise of the cameraman is in the lighting, color, the look. The expertise of the editor is in cutting the picture. This compartmentalization really shouldn't occur. In reality they overlap a great deal. The editor and the director are the two people who spend the most time on a movie. They should have the greatest overview of the film to make all of the parts come together in a fluent whole. The editor should be involved in the lab work. It's a frustrating procedure but I do like to get involved in the timing. I've done it on a few occasions. At the same time I would turn to the cameraman, because it really is his expertise and it is his vision, too. I wouldn't dream of just walking away and not doing the job; it's significant to the final look of the movie.

I go in and check theaters before the film opens up. I go with the engineers from the studio trying to get the sound working right for the picture.

What are the differences between cutting movies made for television and theatrical films?

In television there's more exposition. In a good movie you trust the audience.

Have you ever sacrificed technical quality in favor of a take that contained a better performance?

On *She's Having a Baby* there's a long scene involving the two main characters in bed. There were three takes. In the third take, a mistake had been made at the lab; it was all very hot, quite washed out. There was no shadow detail to speak of, and that was the take where there was a really good performance. The other two takes really were terrible. The cameraman said, "That take can't be used, it's technically bad." I made the decision when I saw the dailies to go with that take, and it's the take I did use. I didn't close myself off. I looked at the other two takes. If I used one line of the better take, I couldn't have used any of the other material because the difference of the lighting would have been noticeable, so I had to go with one take or the other. It's one of those things where nobody in the audience is going to know. We timed the scene down. You'll never get the shadows, it will be darker and the other scene will be a little lighter, but you go for the performance. You can't worry about the technical nuances. I used the one that was poorly lit. So? It's a good scene.

Do you think that there are any specific personality traits necessary to be an editor?

You are sitting there juxtaposing yourself between the director and what was shot, which often doesn't quite match. There are skills that I have in dealing with people that I never knew I had when I was younger. There are ways of getting your view across without challenging the original concept of the film. The whole process is a compromise and you have to be willing and able to get other people to compromise. That often leads to some tensions, and you'll lose a lot of the fights. To me, a lot of directors have a real obsession and sometimes I just find it can be very wearing. I can work on a film and be tremendously intense about it, but after all is said and done, it's the director's movie. At some point you have to be willing to give up and let the director do what he wants to do, even if you feel it's not right. You just have to be able to walk away from something that you care about a lot.

You have a wonderful collection of old editing and film equipment. Why is it important to you?

I've always been intrigued with mechanical processes and the fact that there are so many ways to do a simple thing, such as splicing a piece of film. In the early days of film, people used film without sprockets. You'd cut by eye and with a scissor. I've got some splicers that are so enormous and bulky; they do such simple things, it's almost like a Rube Goldberg device. I have items from the 1950s and 1960s, when splicing tape first came out, with arms that reach around and mechanical sprocket devices that always broke. I learned how to splice on one of those. I keep them around on occasion in my cutting room, it gives me a sense of solidity and security. The old film equipment was really a more honest kind of thing; you whacked away at the film with it, you cut it, you spliced it. I'm intrigued by that.

Do you think that video-editing systems are going to take over feature film-making in the future?

They are eventually going to take over theatrical films. It's certainly taking over most of television editing. There really seems to be a lot of interest in making video-editing systems that would be applicable to feature films. When they started, they would ask Jerry Greenberg and people like me what was needed. There is no reason why it shouldn't be as useful a tool as any other device for screening material. They're certainly neat, you don't have to cut film. I think that's what I miss about it, the fact that you don't cut film, run it through your hands. You push buttons. I suspect that had I started in this business, having been in the position to push buttons, I probably wouldn't have stuck with it.

14

Richard Halsey

Richard Halsey graduated from Hollywood High School and began his film apprenticeship in the Warner Brothers editorial department. Moving on to 20th Century–Fox, he worked his way up to editor and honed his skills editing television's Peyton Place, a landmark show that became the model for prime-time soap operas.

Since becoming a feature film editor in 1972, Halsey has remained fiercely independent. He built and maintains a complete postproduction facility in his Los Angeles home. Halsey strives to work on films that offer diverse editorial challenges and demands a one-to-one relationship with his directors.

Richard Halsey has had a fruitful collaboration with writer-director Paul Mazursky on *Harry and Tonto; Next Stop, Greenwich Village; Moscow on the Hudson;* and *Down and Out in Beverly Hills.*

The recipient of an Academy Award for editing *Rocky*, Halsey worked with Paul Schrader on *American Gigolo* and cut *Beaches* for Garry Marshall. His recent work includes such projects as Julian Temple's *Earth Girls Are Easy* and John Patrick Shanley's *Joe Versus the Volcano.*

1972	*Pay Day*
1973	*Pat Garrett and Billy the Kid* (with David Berlatsky, Garth Craven, Tony de Zarraga, Robert L. Wolfe, and Roger Spottiswoode)
1974	*Harry and Tonto*
1975	*W. W. and the Dixie Dance Kings*

1976	*Next Stop, Greenwich Village*
	Rocky (with Scott Conrad)**
1977	*Fire Sale*
1978	*Thank God It's Friday*
1979	*Boulevard Nights*
1980	*American Gigolo*
	Tribute
1982	*The Amateur*
	That Championship Season
1984	*Moscow on the Hudson*
	Dreamscape
1986	*Down and Out in Beverly Hills*
1987	*Dragnet*
	Mannequin
1988	*Beaches*
1989	*Earth Girls Are Easy*
1990	*Joe Versus the Volcano*
	Edward Scissorhands
1991	*Article 99*

**Academy Award for best achievement in film editing.

How did you get your start in the film business?
I went to Hollywood High School. John Philip Law, Yvette Mimieux, Mike Farrell, and Sally Kellerman were all in my class. In college I was a theater arts major. I got a job as a messenger boy at Warner Brothers during summer vacation. This was in the late 1950s. It was like old-time Hollywood, which was not going to be there much longer. Mervyn LeRoy was directing a movie on the Western street. Then television came in and that was it. So at least I got to witness that; it was really something special. I didn't go back to school. I was interested in camera and editing, but if you weren't the son of a cameraman, forget it. In those days it was even hard to become an assistant editor. It took me a long time; eventually, I got in the editorial department of Warner Brothers. Getting in the union was difficult, advancement was difficult, everything was difficult at that time. I was drafted into the military. When I got out of the Army I got a job as an apprentice editor at 20th Century–Fox. Three months later I became an assistant editor on *Peyton Place*. I assisted George Nicholson, an editor who had tons of experience. He

edited sound and music on *Dragnet*. He taught me the ABCs of editing. Two and a half years later I became a film editor on *Peyton Place*.

How do you decide what directors you want to work with?

I do research on my directors before I work with them. Even an unknown director doing his first film has a film history. I get a feeling right away, before I ever meet the person, just from the kind of films they've done. I analyze what it's going to be like; then I make the conscious decision of whether I want to work with this person. I always think in terms of tempo and beat, the rhythm of a script, the rhythm of a film. That's what I talk about before we start. I tend to like to work with directors who haven't been around a lot. I like directors who set up the camera for a specific reason; they're not just putting the camera somewhere and finding out what happens. They're always planning where it's going to be from shot to shot. I prefer to work with directors who don't go out and shoot thousands of feet of film with A, B, and C cameras. Certain directors shoot so much film you have to have five editors. I avoid those kinds of directors.

How do you work with a director?

I deal with them all differently. Generally, I have found that honesty is the best policy, but sometimes one has to be more reserved, depending on the personality of the director and the kind of role I am going to play on the picture. I may dominate and lead, or I may sit back and interpret the director. I try to approach every new job like it's my first picture. Sometimes directors are very opinionated, they seem to know exactly what they want. I am about to work on *Joe Versus the Volcano* with John Patrick Shanley, who is a first-time director. This man has got it together. For his presentation he played music as he read the script, and brought out his own personal drawings for all the special effects shots. You knew this man had a vision. Shanley was extremely specific, much like other directors I have worked with—Paul Mazursky and Paul Schrader. A good director never says, "You should trim this or you should do that." A director talks in terms of the content, what he's trying to achieve. Don't tell me to cut from this shot to that shot. I've had those kind of directors, that's not the way to talk to me.

So you are at your best with a director who has a vision.

I prefer working with a director who has a vision and is open to creative input. Writer-directors always have the strongest point of view; they are the most free with their film. They have the freedom to let an editor interpret their vision. They take your good ideas and help you when you're off. I've found them to be the best editors. They get to the point and are less reluctant to hold on to material that is extraneous.

You have had a long relationship with the director Paul Mazursky. What is it like to work with him?

I would say he's the finest filmmaker I've worked with. I've always admired his work. He was a personal friend before I worked with him. Paul is a lover of life, a student of film, an actor, a mimic, a comedian; he's an undiscovered musical talent. He's a good writer and a good filmmaker. He's a really good storyteller. He gives me total freedom and total control.

How did the opening of Down and Out in Beverly Hills, *which establishes Nick Nolte as a homeless man in Beverly Hills, develop during the editing process?*

The music for the opening was preconceived with Debussy, simple piano. When we screened a first cut of the scene it wasn't working. There were scenes with him talking to the dog. I recut the opening and took out the dialogue so it was all visual. I took out the Debussy and put in the Talking Heads' *Stop Making Sense.* Mazursky didn't know whether to have a heart attack or to jump out of his seat. It took him a couple more screenings and he just flipped for it. I felt we needed to contrast the downness of this bum. The piano music made you feel very emotional towards him. When you contrasted it with the Talking Heads it lifted you way up.

There is a lot of camera movement in American Gigolo. *How did that affect the editing?*

The director, Paul Schrader, had this concept of fluidity. I cut a scene with him right away after the first day's shooting. I said, "Paul, we're going to have difficulty with some of this material, I think you ought to cut down the camera work a bit. You're getting a little too carried away. If it's at all mistimed, it starts creating problems." He started to simplify it and still maintained the same style he wanted to achieve. Directors should take advantage of editors to enhance their style.

Were the fight scenes in Rocky *choreographed?*

They were choreographed, but the director missed some of the moments Sylvester Stallone wanted. When he got hit, the mouthpiece was supposed to fly out of his mouth. It was storyboarded and shot with five cameras, but it wasn't isolated enough, it was not choreographed in the camera. Some of it was missed by shooting multiple-camera. So we had to search and find.

How do you know what a fight scene is going to look like before you begin editing?

I don't think you do. You know what you're trying to achieve. It's a slower editorial process. It's editing and re-editing. I would always look at the master shot, which was very seldom used, to see what happens when and where in the choreography. Your master tells you the structure. I was not a big fight fan and neither was the director, John Avildsen, which worked to our advantage because we wanted to make it more like a ballet, more abstract, with more emotion and feeling.

How did you cut the climactic scene at the end of the film when Rocky fights Apollo Creed?

There was so much film on the fight sequence, 80,000 or 100,000 feet, that I brought in Scott Conrad, who had assisted me on my first picture, to cut it. He was roughing it out for ten weeks. They set up five cameras and let them roll. I was the guy behind the KEM with a fresh point of view getting a rhythm for the fight. One of the editing problems in that sequence was we didn't have enough people in the crowd. So a lot of the times during the fight you'd see empty seats. That created a particular challenge. We bought stock shots from a Muhammad Ali film called *The Fighters* and popped them in. We even took the sound of the large arena off the optical track. I came up with the concept for the chant of the crowd. It was like the beginning of group Foley. We did it on the scoring stage. We got 50 people chanting, "Rock-key, Rock-key, Rock-key." Bill Conti orchestrated the crowd like a conductor. We staggered them rhythmically to give it a big sound. We previewed the picture at USC before we had finished cutting the ending. It brought the house down and the film wasn't even finished.

When you were working on Rocky *did you have any sense of how popular it would become?*

I had just finished working with John Avildsen on *W. W. and the Dixie Dance Kings*. He sent me the script for *Rocky*. I had recently seen *The Lords of Flatbush* with Stallone. I read *Rocky* right here in my den. After reading the script I said to myself, "This is a great script. If we do our jobs right, this script will be nominated for an Academy Award and I will be nominated for editing." That was my exact prediction and I wish I had listened to myself even more. I wish I had said, "Richard, you should get an agent and negotiate for half a point of this picture."

You were right, Rocky *did go on to win the Academy Award for best editing. How did you work with director Julian Temple on* Earth Girls Are Easy?

I went to meet him at Musso's. I liked this guy so much. We just talked a little back and forth and he said, "Richard, I want to do it." That's what I respond to! Somebody who is not afraid to say, "I want to do this with you and I'm going to stick with you." It's like a marriage. I told Julian, "I am going to give you the greatest gift a film editor can give a director. I'm going to teach you how to edit your own films." Julian was a complete neophyte in the cutting room, he was afraid of the equipment. By the time *Earth Girls Are Easy* was finished, he was editing side by side with me. The film was complicated. In order to get through all that material, he could be going through rolls and picking pieces as I was cutting. Julian was marking and doing pulls. I taught him how to splice. He even cut his finger a couple of times and I said, "Ahh, that's it, you're getting into it now, Julian." He had such an understanding and a respect for the editor. I respected him because he learned how to do that.

How does an editor learn to listen to the material?

The material cries out to me emotionally, I just react to it. It's creating a tempo and a technical viewpoint using complementary shots and angles that best serve the purpose and the energy of the scene. I may not go for a radical edit on the scene right off the bat, I don't work it to death. I take an initial response. I leave it and put other scenes around it, knowing I haven't solved that scene, but trying to structure it with what I consider to be the key elements. On *Beaches*, the director, Garry Marshall, made a shot which was a close-up of Bette Midler driving a car. When I saw this shot I said, "That's the key shot for the movie." It was a shot you could cut off of, always getting her point of view, her reflectiveness and emotion—being inside her head. As it was written, you lost the fact that this movie was told in flashback. With that shot placed several times throughout the show, you're always playing from her point of view in the flashback. I liked the simplicity of it, much as Bob Fosse and Alan Heim used the close-up of Roy Scheider in front of the mirror in *All that Jazz*. I'm always looking for key shots in the dailies. Even though there's hours of material, I'll just pick four or five key shots and cut the scene together and see how it plays. Then if need be, I'll go in and edit it some more, but if it works with those four or five key shots, that's it. Just because they shoot all this material doesn't mean you have to use it.

How close is your first cut to the finished film?

On the first four or five films I did in my career, my first cuts were more like finished films. I attribute it to the scripts being better or more controlled. Now filmmakers are either rushing you or the scripts are overly long. I consider myself a get-to-the-point editor, but even after throwing out scenes, I have first cuts that are 2 hours and 40 minutes long.

What do they look like?

You find lulls and material that's not moving the story forward. On the first cut of *Beaches*, there were a couple of scenes I never put in. One scene was never even cut together. I discussed it with the director and he said, "Fine." We knew the film was going to be a mess, but we had to get it together the way it was written once, look at it and try to get a feeling from it. *Beaches* finished shooting on a Thursday. I ran the first cut at 8:30 in the morning on Friday and videotaped it. The director took it home. We conferred over the weekend. I came in on Monday and cut about ten minutes out of the movie. Then we looked at it and rearranged it.

Have you ever made a decision not to cut?

I make that decision every time I cut. I've found myself overcutting. I always think, "How can I tell the story in the least number of shots?" When there is a lot of material you have to think like a shot maker, like a director.

Film editing can be very mathematical. Are you quicker to say, "I need a frame here or there," or rather, "I need a beat here or there?"

I never say frames, I always say a beat. I'll look at the mark once. I have a tendency not to cut as tight as I should and then I end up squeezing it.

Is that because you don't like to keep asking for trims?

Yes, it's a gradual process of elimination. It's a lot easier to cut out than to put back. I try to cut as tight as I can, but I don't like to add stuff back.

What are your sound tracks like while you're cutting?

I used to spend hours filling my tracks; now I'm very conscious of sound. If it's not perfect I don't want to hear it, I just eliminate it. I cut a clean dialogue track, then I build my backgrounds on the stage. I always work with a minimum of three tracks. I do my own temp mixes on the KEM with my own equipment.

What equipment do you use to do your own temp mixes?

There's an actual physical record and erase head on the KEM. I have an eight-track Tascam mixer, a pre-amp, and an amplifier. It goes through a Telex, which is a little box that synchronizes everything. I always screen with two tracks and mix to 35mm right on the KEM and the quality is amazingly good for combining dialogue and effects, even certain types of music. I've been working that way for as long as I can remember.

Where do you get the music that you use for temp scores?

I have an extensive library here in my own editing room and it grows and grows. It's huge now. It's gone from records to CDs. I never use library music. I can just go to Tower Records.

How do you work with sound effects editors?

I make a list of every sound effect as I go, trying to be specific about what I want to hear, and they do the rest. I will talk with the sound editor and try to save him time and work by telling him what to cover and what not to cover. If they bring in every effect, I just weed them out.

Do you think that sound crews are getting too big and that there is too much sound going on in most films?

In pictures where I'm in control of the sound and the budget, I keep the budgets down. It's incredible to me what they spend on sound on some of these movies. I go for simplicity of sound.

What do you perceive as the editor's responsibility at a mix?

I either run the mix or I don't. If I don't run the mix, I'm not there all the time. I'm there for the playback and for the creative discussion afterwards.

Who runs the mix if you don't?

The producer or director. I don't have the patience to sit hour after hour; my ears get burned out. I feel I have created all the concepts for the mix before the mix starts.

In your pre-mixes?

Yes, the kind of music, and where it starts and stops. All the concepts are down. Generally, I like a simplified sound even in a complex form. I don't like to be hearing too many things at once. On *Earth Girls Are Easy*, when the music is on, that's it.

How important is your working environment to you?

I like creating and working in my own environment. That's why I have my own studio and my own equipment. It gives me the freedom to work the way I want to work.

How do you train your assistants to cut?

I have a specific way I like to train assistants. First of all, I involve the assistant. I talk a lot about my feelings and emotions towards the material. I'll talk through what my ideas are and the basic structure. I give them a rough framework. When they start cutting, they assemble scenes where I have marked every single cut point. I block it out and they go and cut while I cut another scene on my own. Then I refine it with them. Eventually, I mark less and less. I talk the scene through. I'll still mark a little bit so they don't forget which line reading I wanted, or I say, "It's this one, but check the others." Pretty soon I just discuss it with them and I'm not marking anymore. I'm just running the dailies with them and we get a shorthand. They know what I mean and they're doing it on their own.

Do you ever go back to the outtakes after cutting a scene?

After I've cut the scene, I quickly go through all the outs. I don't like to leave the best reading in the roll.

Is that an editor's nightmare, that you might leave something good in the outs?

Not since I've been on the KEM. That's the real benefit of KEM editing—I know the material.

Do you feel that you don't know it as well on a Moviola?

I can't remember which is the best reading. The machine is making so much noise. I can't high speed back and forth to compare readings as quickly, putting it in and then taking it out and putting the other one in. It doesn't work as well for me; it's not as easy.

How is your editing room organized?

Organization is the most important word in the cutting room. I have a very simple system. The assistants sync up the dailies in KEM order before we see them on the screen, so the KEM rolls are built by the time the dailies are done with the masters and the angles checkerboarded. Then they are coded by scene. I have my own coding machine. Whenever I do my pulls I keep all my KEM rolls in sync. I pull everything straight across and then I assemble on the synchronizer. I straight cut everything, then I go back through and put my cutaways in. All picture is always filed back and the only things left over are overlaps or unusable track. All the leftover material gets wound up in a blue box for that sequence. You have a blue box for every major scene in the movie. You can look at the rack and say, "I've got ten boxes on the such-and-such scene." I know how long it's going to take me to cut that scene by the amount of boxes. All of the film that's been cut is on one rack and all of the film that hasn't been cut is on another rack, so in the morning, I always know what I'm doing today. If there's a lift, it goes in that same blue box. If I have alternate line readings, I write "save" on it and that goes in the blue box. That way I don't have to go into the KEM roll and wind down 600 feet. I Just go into the blue box and pop out the other one. I have been using this system for every film.

Assistants love me, I'm not one of those editors who has 95,000 pieces of film all over the place. I cut picture and track always in frame. I always cut track in frame just like I cut picture, so I'm always in sync and there are never sprockets left over. I never have to order reprints. Everything is coded in order and catalogued. I don't care if it's a sound effect or music. I always want to be able to find that piece of film. I have a music rack; I have an effects rack. In addition to the code number, everything is labeled.

How do you feel about working with other editors on a film?

I prefer the one-on-one. It's getting increasingly difficult in Hollywood to do that; they want to put on different editors. I avoid it. I've always tried to share that with my assistants. I like my assistants to cut.

Do you ever have the fear that you won't work again?

No, I don't have that fear at all. There's always work. My fear is pacing myself properly and maintaining a high level in my work and choices. I'm looking for variety.

Do you try to find projects that break new ground?

I look for projects that are attempting to break new ground. Sometimes I am looking for projects that don't break new ground because I want to rest. I have to pace my creativity because I work a lot. After *Earth Girls Are Easy*, which was a very taxing film because of the special effects, I went on to edit *Beaches*. *Beaches* was also demanding because there was a lot of film and many musical numbers, but it was much more traditional storytelling.

Do you think that film editors will help to discover new ways to tell a story in the future?

I love the storytelling aspects of film. Once you understand the basics of master shot, two-shot, over-the-shoulders, close-ups, points of view, reverse masters, subjective camera work, then you have the freedom to create a new form, a new style of creating and telling a story. There are so many ways of telling stories. There are many new ways out there that still haven't been explored. It's such a wonderful craft.

15

Michael Kahn

In the 1950s, Brooklyn-born Michael Kahn worked as a messenger for a New York advertising agency. He moved to the West Coast and became an assistant editor at Bing Crosby Productions. Kahn began his editing career on the television series *Hogan's Heroes* and honed his craft cutting over 140 episodes in five years.

In 1977 he was asked by Steven Spielberg to edit *Close Encounters of the Third Kind*. Michael Kahn has cut nine films for Spielberg, serving the director's moviemaking genius and always displaying the kinetic excitement of the editing art.

Kahn is best known for his contribution on Hollywood blockbusters *Close Encounters of the Third Kind*, *Raiders of the Lost Ark*, and *Fatal Attraction*, but he consistently balances his career with small films like *Table for Five*, *Ice Castles*, and *Eyes of Laura Mars*.

Michael Kahn won an Oscar for *Raiders of the Lost Ark* and was nominated for *Close Encounters of the Third Kind*. In 1987 he was nominated for an Academy Award twice in one year for his editing efforts on *Fatal Attraction* and *Empire of the Sun*.

1972	*Rage*
	Trouble Man
1975	*The Devil's Rain*
1976	*The Return of a Man Called Horse*
1977	*Close Encounters of the Third Kind**
1978	*Ice Castles*

	The Eyes of Laura Mars
1979	1941
1980	Used Cars
1981	Raiders of the Lost Ark**
1982	Poltergeist
1983	Table for Five
	Twilight Zone—The Movie (Steven Spielberg segment, "Kick The Can")
1984	Indiana Jones and the Temple of Doom
	Falling in Love
1985	The Goonies
	The Color Purple
1986	Wisdom
1987	Fatal Attraction (with Peter Berger)*
	Empire of the Sun*
1988	Arthur on the Rocks
1989	Indiana Jones and the Last Crusade
	Always
1990	Arachnophobia
1991	Hook

*Academy Award nomination for best achievement in film editing.
**Academy Award for best achievement in film editing.

How did you get your first job in the film business?

I was in New York and answered an ad in the paper. I became a messenger for an ad agency which had a TV department. My job was to run the projector and to file commercials. The head of the commercials department liked me. He said, "We're going out to the coast to make commercials, why don't you come out as my assistant?" They had the Pepsi, Toni, and Philip Morris accounts which sponsored the Lucy show and other shows by Desilu. They got me a job as a secretary to the chief of the editorial department at Desilu. I knew nothing about editing, I didn't even know what it was. But at one point the fellow who ran the department said, "Look, we're slowing down, I'm going to have to put you in the editing department; do you want to get into the union?" I said, "I'm not interested in getting into the editors' union." He said, "It's the best thing for you." So he took me by the scrub of the neck

and threw me into the union. I became an assistant film editor. I was
lucky to work for some wonderful editors who let me watch what they
did. Some of these editors were so wonderful they were intimidating.
I was so impressed with how they took these pieces and made it all
happen. I'd say, "I'll never be able to articulate to directors as well as
they do." I tried to be a great assistant, because I never thought I'd be
an editor. Then I assisted a wonderful human being, Danny Nathan, at
Bing Crosby Productions—a wonderful editor. He said, "Look, you
ought to be an editor one of these days, you want to grow." I said, "I'll
never be able to edit, it's not in me." He gave me a scene to edit and
said, "Do it nights and weekends, but just do it." He pushed me into
editing all kinds of scenes. One day I did a scene for him; it was a hard
scene but he taught me how to do it. It came out quite good. We ran it
for the producer and director, who said, "You did a great job on that
scene, Danny." Danny turned around and said, "No, my assistant did
it." Danny Nathan opened me up and gave me the confidence I didn't
have. He died a year or two later.

How did you become a full editor?

Bing Crosby Productions had the pilot for *Hogan's Heroes* and an assistant I knew was going to be the editor. He said, "Mike, if you come
with me as an assistant on the first five shows, I'll make you an editor
on the sixth." Lo and behold, as of the sixth show of *Hogan's Heroes*, I
started editing. My first director was Gene Reynolds, who became an
important director and producer on the television series *M*A*S*H*. I
didn't know I could edit. I didn't know what I was doing; I was just
joining film together. One day, there was a review for the new season
of *Hogan's Heroes* and they mentioned the film editor, Michael Kahn.
Reviewers don't mention TV editors. It said, "Michael Kahn's rhythmic
editing." I went to the producer and said, "Gee, is my editing rhythmic?"
He said, "Well, yeah, don't you know that?"

I worked with good directors and bad directors, different styles of
directing, and after a while I learned to put film together. By the third
year I started feeling I had control over the film. It takes years to get
the feel. A lot of people say the film tells you what to do, but after the
third year, I started telling the film what to do. I started changing the
structure, maneuvering the film. There are things an editor injects into
a film: structure, pace, symmetry, the little gaps in between cuts. All of
this is a rhythm. I did about 140 episodes of *Hogan's Heroes* in five or
six years and I learned how to edit film. I learned the craft. The best
editors in the world today cut television. The deadlines are there and
it's got to work and you learn how to cheat the film. I had to cut all
kinds of film. When you've cut television for a couple of years and you
get into features, you can put anything together. When I went with

Spielberg, he shot a lot of footage and if I didn't have that experience it would have been difficult. I applaud the television editor. They're really doing it.

You have cut many films for Steven Spielberg. What is it like to work with him?

I was already an experienced editor when Steven selected me to work on *Close Encounters*. It was really the highlight of my life. Steven is absolutely brilliant. I've been with him for a long time now and he has a great facility to know when something works. When he is given options, he always picks the right one. He wants input and he wants it to happen; the man is incredible.

I understand Spielberg likes to work with storyboards. Do you get involved with them?

Steven does storyboards with an art director. A storyboard is not for me, it's for the people on the set—the art director, the cameraman, and for Steven. I don't need it because you can't cut a show from storyboards. Steve and I will examine the film on the KEM and decide which takes or pieces of takes we want to use and he and I will collaborate. We'll put the scene together without storyboards.

As you were cutting Close Encounters, *were you working with the special effects material?*

No. They'd shoot the background, whether in 70mm or in VistaVision, that's eight perf, and they would give me a 35mm reduction from the print that would be coded in a certain way. I would use that in the body of the show. They don't want to start making the effect until they see what the length is, because it costs so much per frame. For the *Raiders* films we got animatics, drawings they would shoot, from Industrial Light and Magic. For example, in the mine car sequence in *Indiana Jones and the Temple of Doom*, I took the animatics and cut them in with the live material to see how they played. When we got it structured the way we wanted, they went ahead and made the effect. You have to have the backgrounds or something to put in, or else you don't know how it's going to work. In the first *Raiders*, the great truck chase was blocked out. A second unit director shot a lot of the wider shots. I had to do the whole scene, structure it all out, and put in pieces of leader where the principals would go. You had to have all of the special effects and second unit put in, so you could shoot the principals correctly.

The editing in the mother ship concert sequence at the end of Close Encounters *is a powerful example of how an editor uses reaction shots dramatically. How do you work with reaction material?*

Every editor has the same decision to make, whether it's that scene or ten people sitting around a table like we had in *The Color Purple*. There are cause-and-effect relationships and one cut should be as a natural consequence of another, that leads to another. They're invisible cuts.

One cut calls for another. That's not done from knowledge; reactions are done from feeling. If reactions aren't true, it hurts the reality of the scene. An audience senses when something is not true.

What do you need to know from a director beyond what's inherent in the material?

I like to know his point of view of the scene. You just can't sit down and put it together; you need a point of view. I like to know if he has any preferences as far as take selections of performances and how he wants to deal with scene transitions. I have to be on his wavelength because he shoots with something in his mind's eye, and maybe I can embellish it, make it better. He's the man I work for. A director makes or breaks a film. This man does everything on the film and I'm one of those spokes on a wheel, but I've got to know where he's at. You're building, taking pieces of film, digging out the values and structuring it. A lot of directors tell you exactly what they want, but it's not what they say, it's what they feel. I try to get into what I think they feel and then I build the scenes. Some directors shoot pieces, they don't shoot scenes. In *Fatal Attraction*, there were a lot of lovely pieces, the action scenes, the love scenes. You have to take them and structure them, give it order, form, symmetry, and make it work with the overall view. Sometimes you have a lot of little scenes that work but the totality doesn't work. So you've got to always think about the whole.

What do you consider an effective method for working with directors?

Some directors don't want to see any footage, so when they see a first cut they have to go back, run, and study every take. Then you've got to play with it for six months getting it in shape. I want to streamline the editing operation. I want to get it out, and I want to get it the best it can be. The way to do that is to strike while it's hot, get it back to the director a day or two after the scene is shot. I may join two or three scenes together or we may change the order. Most of the refining is done before the director and I look at the first cut. A lot of editors like to leave it long and then work it down, but I like to get the scenes to where I feel they should be, so the director is not sitting there looking at cuts saying, "That cut doesn't work, you shouldn't have been on that angle." I like to get that out of the way, that's just a time waster. I refine it with the director so it knits together.

Do you work the same way with all directors?

For some directors you have to change your personality. They demand something from you besides your work. They want a certain kind of personality. If you're going to be a right arm to a director, you've got to assume that role. I've gotten along with all of my directors because I have the ability to change myself. Like anything in life, the guy who succeeds is the one who has the ability to adapt, to make it happen. I'll do anything to get it done.

The skating sequences in Ice Castles *are intricately choreographed. How did you approach the editing in these sequences?*

My daughter was a competitive ice skater. I used to take her to school figures at four o'clock in the morning. We lived on that ice rink. If there's anything I know, it's ice skating. That's not intuitive; I lived it. I was even a judge for a while. During *Ice Castles*, I had to be available for Spielberg's next picture, which was also with Columbia. So instead of sitting around, Columbia wanted me to do something. All of this ice-skating footage was sitting on a shelf, thousands of feet of it. Donald Wrye, the director, came in and said, "Would you see if you could put this stuff together?" I cut all of the ice skating.

Was the scene where the Lynn Holly Johnson character has a skating accident difficult to cut?

That was tricky because it's very difficult to make action matches when you cut in and out of slow motion. You don't want to let it sit there forever. There was enough variance in angles so we were able to accomplish it.

When you first began cutting that sequence, did you overarticulate it and then start to pare it down?

I'm one of the few guys who doesn't do that, I go for it. I tell the director before I start, "If you want me to be innovative, give me the chance to make mistakes and maybe we can do something interesting." I study the dailies on the KEM. I don't start editing until I have a point of view, then I go for it. The director is the boss. I'm not going to go against that, but they want to see what you can do, so I go for the jugular. I have to take the chance, or else what am I doing here? I want to know that I have a 90 percent chance of being right. In baseball, if a player bats .300 in a season, he's been wrong or made a mistake 70 percent of the time, and yet he's a superstar. Look at the film editor. We don't bat .300; we bat .700, .800, .900. You can play safe and leave it all in, and you sit with the director and say, "Let's trim here, let's trim there," but why not give the director a challenge? That's what's nice about film editing: there are a lot of little discoveries you make along the trip, and you put them in. If I find an interesting wrinkle, something different that might work, I say, "If I do it the way the director wants, he'll never see this interesting little wrinkle." I'm not doing my job unless I'm giving him the options. That's the key to this business.

Poltergeist *is a film which really takes its time at the beginning to develop all of the characters. Was a concern of the editing to root the characters firmly before the action began?*

Yes. With everything that was happening to the characters, you had to know them pretty well to care what happens to them. If you don't care for the people, then you may not be afraid for them. If you go right for the action and don't set up the relationship, you don't have a picture.

If you set it up properly and care for these people, you know an audience will sit still for it.

Fatal Attraction *was enormously successful at the box office. I understand that it went through some substantial changes in editing.*

We had an entirely different ending. Audiences liked the picture but, according to market research, when Anne Archer says, "If you come near my husband again, I'll kill you," they wanted to see a confrontation between these two women. Adrian Lyne went out and shot a new ending. It cost them a million four. It was hard to cut that new ending because I didn't believe in it, the director didn't believe in it, and Glenn Close didn't believe in it. When we saw what it did to an audience, everybody believed in it!

What was the original ending?

Michael Douglas comes home after the big knife fight with Glenn Close. He goes to the police and says, "Get this lady out of my hair." He goes home and rakes leaves with his wife. The cops come and tell him the Glenn Close character was killed with a butcher knife. He flashes back and remembers he put the knife down. They say, "We're going to take you in, because your fingerprints are on the knife." He tells his wife, "Go up to my office right away, look up the number of my attorney in the phone book and get me out." They drive off. Anne Archer starts looking for the phone number and finds the tape that Glenn Close left. She plays the tape, and hears, "If you don't stay with me, I'll kill myself." She runs out and grabs the kid, "Come on, we're going to free Daddy." As she's running down the steps we dissolve to Glenn Close in a long shot sitting cross-legged in a bathroom. We're slowly dollying in and playing *Madame Butterfly*. She takes the knife, slits her throat, and falls out of frame and that's the end of it. It was great! We all loved it. I was cutting *Empire of the Sun* and I came back and had this film for the new ending thrust upon us. Peter Berger was also on another show; we had to do this ending. Mentally, it was so tough because I was into *Empire*, and on weekends and nights I had to try and put this ending together with Peter.

What is interesting about your career is that you have done some very big pictures and then you'll turn around and do a small picture like Falling in Love *or* Table for Five.

Yes, it's a deliberate choice. Many times, if I'm not doing a big film with Steven, I try to do a small film to get back to the real world, real people. I'm much more viable and sensitive for Steven and everybody else if I'm in the real world. I don't want to be an elitist editor. I don't want to be the one that does the quote unquote big pictures. I want to do the small pictures too. I want to relate to people and other directors, so I do small pictures.

Is there such a thing as an editor's director?

Yes. Steven Spielberg is an editor's director. So is Adrian Lyne. The early directors like George Cukor shot a nice frame and stayed on great actors. They said, "Action," they would go, and then say, "Cut." The editor takes the scissor and cuts the slates off, but the director has locked himself in and it better be good. Today, people are not going to sit there and languish over a hunk of film, even in a drama. They want energy, something that's going to motivate them. A good angle change will do that; you need pieces. That's why the editor today is more important than he was years ago, because we have more footage to work with. I hope all of the directors I work with are editor's directors by the end of the shoot, because I'm always suggesting other pieces that hopefully will make it better. It may be good, but if we can make it better by picking up pieces here and there, let's do it. After a director is through directing on the set, why shouldn't he come into the editing room and still direct? If you have enough angles and film coverage, you're not limiting options; you're increasing them. So the director can come into the editing room and still change things. You've got to have coverage for that. Any director who gets enough coverage to protect himself is an editor's director.

What are your work habits like?

My methodology is always the same. The Moviola is always where it is now. Everything is the way you see it here in every single editing room wherever I go around the world. I'm very strict and self-disciplined. I get up four or five every morning. I find my great energy is in the morning. I can't wait to get in here to see how it's going to come out. Normally, I'm through with my work at noon time. In the afternoon I'll look at the film, make some adjustments or changes. I always try to keep up my work routine; I don't like to deviate.

Are you intuitive or intellectual in your approach to a scene?

I do it from my heart, intuitively. There's not an editor in town that edits with his mouth. They may talk good but they edit with their heart. You can go to school to learn how to splice, but not to learn when it plays. I take a lot of time looking at films. I look at bad films to see if I could make them better. Why didn't that show work? What would I have done?

The term "cheat" is often used by editors. What does it mean to you?

Suppose the director shot two masters and you've got to join them or else the scene doesn't work. There is always a way to cheat it so it will work. You've got to discover that way. If I run a scene and it matches from cut to cut, you say that looks great. If I ran some of those matches slowly and went from one to the other, it had no right to work because they didn't match. On one side of the cut a character is in one position, and on the other side of the cut he's in another position. It works because it takes one or two frames for the eye to adjust, and if it's cut the proper way, the eye won't catch it. You can cheat, you can get from one scene to another.

Do you ever get input from actors?

No, never. Actors usually don't come into the editing room. If somebody wants to come in and asks me directly, I'll say, "Absolutely, if you get the director's okay." This is not only my room; it's the director's room too. Legally, he has all the right of first cut, previews and everything else. I wouldn't think of showing the film to anybody, even the producer, without getting the director's okay.

Have you ever made the decision not to cut a scene that had coverage?

Once I had a five-minute scene with a lot of coverage, maybe 15,000 feet. I studied the film for a day or so and made the great editing decision not to cut. The master played, I didn't want to cut it. I cut the slates off and I put it in. So editing doesn't mean you have to make cuts, because it's what's best for the film. I decided not to cut.

Do you think you can judge editing without seeing the material that the editor worked with?

Sometimes. You can't tell what was on either side of a splice, because it's in the trims. If I look at a master in someone's film, I don't know if there was coverage, but if you see coverage, you know there's other coverage. What you can judge is the degree of difficulty. If you see a scene with 150 cuts in it, you know he had a lot of choices and it was fairly difficult. If you see 300 cuts, the editor certainly made at least 300 decisions. If you see a scene with two or three cuts in masters, it is not the same degree of difficulty as the other.

Do you think that editors go through stages in their career?

It took me three or four years to really get into what I was doing. When you get the mechanics out of the way, you get into the film. I'm less intimidated now, less uptight about getting the next job. We have people in the business who are 75 years old, great editors: Ralph Winters, Bill Reynolds, Fred Berger. These men are my role models. They are part of the history of this business. Whoever thought I would be sitting here today? I never would have dreamt it. It's like a miracle. If you work hard and get some luck, dreams come true in Hollywood.

16

Richard Marks

Richard Marks began in feature films as Dede Allen's assistant on *Alice's Restaurant*. On *Little Big Man* he was promoted to associate editor, which marked the beginning of his career as a feature film editor.

In 1977 Marks became supervising editor on the most difficult project of his career, *Apocalypse Now*, which demanded nearly three years of constant attention and won him an Academy Award nomination for editing.

His relationship with director James L. Brooks yielded Oscar nominations for *Terms of Endearment* and *Broadcast News*. In addition to editing *Say Anything*, which Brooks produced, Marks was also the film's co-producer. In 1989 he became a key member of Warren Beatty's creative team on the comic-book blockbuster *Dick Tracy*.

1972	*Parades*
1973	*Bang the Drum Slowly*
	Serpico (with Dede Allen)
1974	*The Godfather, Part II* (with Barry Malkin and Peter Zinner)
1975	*Lies My Father Told Me*
1976	*The Last Tycoon*
1979	*Apocalypse Now* (supervising editor, with Lisa Fruchtman, Jerry Greenberg, and Walter Murch)*
1981	*The Hand*
	Pennies from Heaven

1982	*Max Dugan Returns*
1983	*Terms of Endearment**
1984	*The Adventures of Buckaroo Banzai:*
	Across the 8th Dimension
1985	*St. Elmo's Fire*
1986	*Pretty in Pink*
	Jumping Jack Flash
1987	*Broadcast News**
1989	*Say Anything*
1990	*Dick Tracy*
1991	*One Good Cop*

*Academy Award nomination for best achievement in film editing.

Dede Allen has been significant in your development as an editor. How did you first become her assistant?

I got an offer to be a sound apprentice on *Rachel, Rachel*. Dede Allen was the editor and Alan Heim was the supervising sound editor. I said, "If Dede's doing it, I'll wash floors!" While I was on the job, the woman who was Dede's assistant decided not to continue on and the kid who worked as her apprentice thought he could move faster if he went to an editorial company. So she had no assistant for her next film, *Alice's Restaurant*. I put my bid in for the job. Dede checked me out from top to bottom; she called everybody I ever worked for. I was sweating, boy, I wanted that job bad. Finally, she said yes. I was in seventh heaven. It was an exciting time. I never worked so hard in my life. We were on that film for nine months. At the end I added up my overtime, divided by 40 hours, and figured out that I had worked an additional four months within that nine-month period.

At what point did you begin to cut scenes under her supervision?

A month into the shooting of *Little Big Man*, Dede had to go on location in Montana. She said, "Would you like to cut a sequence while I'm away?" I said, "Great, I would love to." She said, "I'll give you a little sequence." It turned out to be about 30,000 feet of dailies. We screened it together and Dede went away. I must have worked night and day, seven days a week, for the two or three weeks she was gone. I decided this was my chance. If I didn't cut the scene, my career was down the tubes. I went nuts, here I was with all of this film. I struggled with the material everything took ten times longer than I thought it should. As an assistant, you don't become dextrous at the mechanical skills of cutting. Everyone's mind works faster than their hands do. Dede came back and said, "Show me the scene whenever you're ready." I was terrified. I felt, "I've blown this." When I showed her the scene she was great, I will never forget her for that moment. That's the kind of situation where you can destroy someone or build their confidence. She looked at the cut and said, "Congratulations, you did a great job. I have a few suggestions, maybe we should sit down and talk about it." She was so constructive even about the parts she didn't like. You never felt like you had done something wrong, just like this was a collaboration and she was going to help you find the right way to do it. I recut it under her tutelage. Her attitude was always so supportive, never negative. Dede is one of the greatest teachers I've ever known. One day she said to me, "I really need a second editor on *Little Big Man*. Would you like to do it?" This was the start of my feature editing career. I can't tell you what an opportunity it was.

How would you define what an editor does on a film?

When you shoot scenes you tend to shoot beginnings, middles, and ends. One of the prime functions of an editor in sizing down a film is to make scenes flow into one another. When you distill scenes, you tend to lose pieces of beginnings, of ends, and sometimes hunks out of the middle. Distillation is really what we do, because something may work well on paper, but when you use it full blown on film it may be saying the same thing six times. In the cutting of a scene, a great moment or a wonderful look by an actor can replace a line or two of dialogue. Cutting a film is an ongoing process where you really try to distill the essence of the idea behind the script. I can take a first cut of anything I've done, look at it two weeks later and say, "Why in the hell did I cut that so long?" Yet I know when I'm doing a first cut, I'm incapable of cutting it shorter because I have to play those moments out just so I can say, "Oh my God, I'm killing that moment by playing it too long." The real fun is when you start to take the big monster and shave it. The first cut is like roughing out a piece of marble, you're roughing out vague shapes. The rest of the course of the film is doing all the fine work, changing subtleties in performance, juggling scenes, making the dramatics play. It's a wonderful building process.

Do you think a dramatic dialogue scene between two people is harder to cut than an action scene?

Yes, because with an action sequence you're cutting on movement. It always gives you justification to cut and create its own rhythms. There's an internal rhythm to a movement. The axiom of action cutting is, never complete an action. Always leave it incomplete so it keeps the forward momentum of the sequence. In dramatic cutting you have to create your own rhythms—how long you stay on a character, how much of a beat you give a character before you cut to someone else, who you play on camera, and who you play off camera. Yet you must try and remain faithful to the internal rhythms of an actor's performance.

Are scenes with a large group of characters more complex than a scene with two characters?

Sure. The greater the number of characters, the more complex your job is to keep all those characters "alive." A lot has to do with the way it's covered. If you have five people in a room having a conversation and it's all single close-ups, you'll have a hard time maintaining all of those characters without making the editing look frenetic.

You have cut two films for Francis Ford Coppola that have very complex editing structures. In The Godfather, Part II, *the story of how the young Vito Corleone became the Godfather is intercut with the story of how his son Michael took over the family after the Don's death. How much did editing contribute to this structure?*

The structure of interweaving the old and present story was written into the script. It was this contrast and juxtaposition that was the underpinning of the film. It always existed, but not necessarily in the exact way that it appears on film. One of our most difficult problems was finding where to go back and forth, because the pace of the two stories was different. The old story was legato and lyrical and the new story was more frenetic. When you put those two together, it kept lurching you in and out of the film. So ultimately, a lot of the old story was lost because it just couldn't exist comfortably with the new story. We were constantly experimenting. We'd try a transition dozens of ways, in different places using different material. The transitions are very lyrical and that really came out of the editing process. Because of the constant cutting back and forth in time, the editing calls attention to itself. The editing structure is implicitly important to the story, so the editing took on a bigger role.

Does Coppola rely on the editing process to structure his films?

He works that way. He shoots long. He shoots beginnings, middles, and ends. He loves the editing process and he relies very heavily on shaping the film in the editing process.

Does he spend a lot of time in the cutting room while you work?

No. He reviews: talking, trying things, coming in and looking at it, talking again, trying other things. Occasionally, he would sit and work on sequences but he didn't live in the cutting room and I think that's a healthier way to work for everyone concerned. It is important for the director to maintain perspective.

What were your duties as supervising editor on Apocalypse Now?

Besides cutting, I took on the logistics of organizing everything, as I tend to do. I think my organizational skills are what garnered me the supervising editor credit plus the fact that I stayed on all throughout the whole process. That film was a logistical nightmare. We had, at one point, over 60 people working on it. To mix the film we built a six-track stereo mixing studio from scratch in an empty storefront in San Francisco near our cutting rooms.

Why was that done rather than using an established facility?

Francis's philosophy is, why rent things when the same money can go into buying them? *Apocalypse* took months and months to mix. Rather than paying hundreds of dollars an hour to a recording studio, it seemed to pay to build a recording studio of our own.

The use of video in the making of Apocalypse Now *was very much ahead of its time. What kind of system did you use and how was it employed?*

There wasn't equipment available to accomplish certain things on video, so we hired electronic freaks to design equipment. It was jury-rigged, it was primitive. I mean "frame-accurate" was not an operative phrase, but it worked. It was a good system. We bought an old telecine chain and all of the dailies were put on videotape. We taped the cut of a scene and then we reconstructed all the trims and outs, so we had a videotaped record of everything that was shot on the film. The system helped us to design the big, multiple-image optical sections. It was a great tool. To try and do that first on film would have been financially prohibitive. It paid for the system to be able to narrow it down on tape and then to interpret it on to film. Francis would often use the system to quickly juggle scenes and structure. We did so much juggling on that film.

How did you feel about having the other editors on the team work on scenes after you cut them?

It's the only way to work on a multiple-editor film because it creates a homogeneous style.

How long was the first cut of the film?

The first cut was seven and a half hours long. It was all these action scenes packed together without a lot of transitions; they were played out full.

What process was used to determine the final cut?

There was no preconceived process. The process evolved from the film itself. We often likened the process of cutting that film to the process of the Martin Sheen character going up river in Conrad's *Heart of Darkness*, the novel on which the script was loosely based. As an editorial crew we were going into our own heart of darkness.

It was a very difficult film, shot under very difficult circumstances. A lot of the script was rewritten as they were shooting. There was a mass of material that had a general idea behind it, but it didn't have all the connective tissue to hold it together. We had a million feet of print. The process of making that film was one of finding and defining that connective tissue. Francis's original conception was that the scene at the beginning of the film, where Martin Sheen was briefed about Kurtz and his mission, was supposed to provide the information and the connective ideas that would unfold as he went on his journey up river. One of the problems was there wasn't sufficient information in this scene to accomplish that. We therefore had to use both voice-over and visual dossier material as the connective tissue and the means of entering the thoughts of the Martin Sheen character.

Why was the ending so difficult to find?

Apocalypse was the quintessential difficult ending, mostly because the Brando material was shot in such a strange way. It was just endless improvisation, with Brando covered with overlapping cameras. I think a certain part of that shows in the final work—it's truly pieced together. I don't think there was ever a clear-cut answer. Not that Francis didn't write an ending; he wrote them, but they weren't necessarily the ones that were filmed, and the ones that were filmed were changed a thousand times in the cutting room.

This film seems to have made a long-lasting impact on all the editors who worked on it.

Yes, it did for all of us. As an editor you can't work on a project for two years and ten months, without it being a major force in your life. I sometimes think the only thing that kept me going on *Apocalypse Now* was that I knew I had to finish it. I could never walk away from a film, and God knows we were all tempted one time or another. It was hard to live with the problems of it, but I always knew it was going to be an important film. I'll probably never duplicate the experience I had on that film and I don't think I would ever want to.

You often used tight close-ups in Terms of Endearment. *Why is that?*

That was the nature of the film. It's an intimate story. It's a performance movie and I'm very performance-oriented. I tend to play close-ups a lot. Close-ups help draw me into a film. I don't see how you can avoid close-ups when you're dealing with the subtleties of emotion. It was important to draw the audience into the emotion of the film.

Traditionally, in a telephone scene, the voice coming through the receiver is filtered to give the effect of it coming out of the phone. This film had many phone scenes where the voices weren't filtered. Why is that?

You don't cut phone conversations the way you normally cut a dialogue scene; you don't overlap dialogue in the same way. You wouldn't want pieces of words hanging over a cut to another location. So the tendency is to cut it in a "Mickey Mouse" way. There were so many phone conversations, they were the emotional backbone of the film. To treat them like telephone scenes was going to really inhibit the way I felt the scene should be cut. So when I was doing the first cut, I made a conscious decision to cut these scenes as I would any other. In my mind, I just imagined that the two people were in the same room. When I first started doing our temp dubs, the standard practice was to filter the off-camera phone voices. This seemed to destroy the intimacy of the scene. So I decided not to filter them and we all got used to hearing it that way. When we got to the final dub, the director, Jim Brooks, and I decided to eliminate the filtering. I love what it represents. It makes us deal with the emotions of the scenes rather than the reality of changing locations. I've been doing it on all the films I've done since then.

How was video editing used on Broadcast News?

Video editing was used specifically for the pieces that were on television monitors in the background.

How did you work on that material?

I had spent a number of months researching various stock footage places to find it. The news stories in the film were constructed as news stories. I edited some of them in Washington, D.C., where we shot the film. I hired a video news editor to do the physical video editing and our consultant was an actual news producer who was the model for the Holly Hunter character in the film. It was one of the most frustrating things in my life to sit there and tell the video editor what I wanted. The lag time between saying what you want, and someone else translating you, is horrible. I would work on these stories at night and on weekends after I finished the rest of my day; it was very complex. We shot and edited the scene where the Bill Hurt character does a videotape interview of a woman who's been raped. There's a piece in the beginning of the film about a Japanese domino tournament. That was a pre-existing two-hour film made in Japan that I condensed down to about 20 seconds to make a news piece out of it.

Were you involved in getting the video material up on the monitors during the shooting of the film?

I was very involved in hiring the people who physically set up the system. They helped build the control room that we shot in and did all the video playback material. We did a lot of careful research in hiring them, and I was around most of the time to make sure we got what we had planned. I created a library of material so that we could fill dozens and dozens of monitors depending on what we wanted. You want roll bars, we have roll bars here. You want a station ID, we have a station ID here. You want commercials, we have commercials. You want news footage of a fire, we have that here. News footage of a flood, we have on this tape. Within minutes we could set up any sort of visual imagery that we wanted in the control room.

It's amazing how much more editors do than people think they do.

Yes, it's true. A lot of it just depends on the individual. I like to stick my nose into things and I enjoy exploring areas that I've never worked in before. That's always fun for me.

In addition to cutting Say Anything *you also co-produced it. How did that affect your work as editor?*

It was a different experience. As an editor, you are always clearing things and asking permission to do things from the producer. I got to ask myself the questions and give myself the answers. There was also a fiscal responsibility; you can't complain to a producer when you need more money for something. It gave me a certain independence I hadn't enjoyed before. As editor I did the same thing I normally do, which is to take over the back end of the film, but I had more involvement on decisions that went into the production.

The films that you have worked on for James Brooks have especially large editorial staffs, particularly the sound crews. Does this have anything to do with the way he works, or is it just part of the existing trend toward big postproduction staffs?

It's a combination of the sign of the times and a particular way that Jim works. Cutting a film with Jim is an ongoing process that never really ends until you bail out because you don't have any more time. Once you've started the sound process, the more changes you make, the more complicated the sound changes are. For me to make a picture change once the film is locked is really simple, but how that amplifies when you give it to the sound crew is enormous. What takes me ten minutes could take them three days just to sort out all the tracks. So if you make changes and preview, and then make more changes late in this stage, you tend to have large sound crews to accommodate it. It all depends on when a director is willing to lock the film and let it go. If you want to keep the process going, you have to be prepared to pay the financial consequences.

Do you ever have the actual score to work with early on in the editing process?

No. Composers are hired for a certain period of time. I work on a film anywhere from six months to a year or more and a composer's block of time usually is about a ten-week increment. It would be incredibly costly to engage the composer in full-time composition that early. There have been occasions when the composer has been decided upon early and he'll come and look at rough cuts of the film. If he has some thematic ideas, he might pick something out on a piano or synthesizer and give us temp tracks to work with. A lot of composers like working that way, because one of the banes of the composer's life is coming into a film when an editor has put a temp score into it. Everyone gets so used to the temp score that when the composer brings in new music, everyone is saying, "Gee, that isn't as good. The temp score worked better there."

Then the composer is in the situation of having to write something that sounds like the temp score.

Right, which curtails their creative freedom. It would be like my coming in after another editor already cut the film and having someone say, "I'd like you to recut it, but keep it somewhat the same."

How do you see your role as an editor at a mix?

I'm a control freak. I believe my area of responsibility goes from reading the script before we start shooting and giving my thoughts on what I anticipate as problems, all the way through checking the release prints that go into the theaters. I am involved in the entire process; if I can't be involved in that process I don't want to do the film. It's important to me, it's all one. To just absent yourself from the sound process is like walking away from the film. It's such an integral part of the process that I don't think it should ever be separated out.

When you are about to work with a producer or director you haven't worked with before, how can you make sure they understand that's the way you want to work?

I presume, just as I do homework on the people I work for, that they do homework on me before they ask me to do their film. Therefore, we come into the situation with a certain given. I don't lay down ground rules and I try to remain as flexible as possible in terms of the way I work.

How do you select your projects?

When you first start out cutting, you grab whatever jobs you're offered because they're hard to come by. If you get lucky, as I did, and develop somewhat of a reputation, you get offered a goodly number of films. Then your process of selection has to do not only with the project itself, but with the people involved in the project. A good script can be ruined by bad people and a bad script can be made better by good people. As an editor, you spend a long time locked up with someone in a room, and ultimately, you want to know that you can get along. It's not like shooting a film. We're not gone in eight or 12 weeks; we're there for a long haul. It's a marriage. Sometimes you make a bad guess and it's a rotten marriage and sometimes it's a glorious one. Generally, it's a combination of the two. As most marriages are, they're tough. You have to make this marriage work under the worst possible circumstances—under extreme pressure.

What personality traits do you feel film editors have in common?

All editors have a compulsive need to solve problems and to build things. There are personality elements that attract editors to film editing. My own private little speculation is that one has to be a completely anal-compulsive human being to do it well. It takes someone who enjoys the process of manipulation. There's a real personal charge I get out of sitting there manipulating events, characters, and emotions. You also have to like to work alone.

Everyone says that the hardest thing to do is to make the leap to editor. How do you know when you're ready to take on that responsibility?

Dede Allen recommended me for an Alan Pakula film. I went to see Alan, I didn't know what I was doing. I was a kid, 24 years old. I read the script, I talked to him and, based on Dede's recommendation, he offered me the film. I went home and thought about it. I had a long talk with my wife about what I should do. I was terrified of saying no, because I felt I was blowing an opportunity out of the water, but I think I was more terrified that I really didn't feel confident enough in myself to take on the responsibilities of a big film. I felt if I blew it, I'd have a hard time getting a second chance, so I decided to pass on it. I told Dede and she said, "I respect your decision." I could have kicked myself for not doing it, because the film was *Klute*, but I never really regretted the decision. It was the best move I ever made, because psychologically I wasn't ready for it. Most of what we do has to do with our own sense of ourselves, and if you don't have confidence in yourself, you're going to blow it. It is always more important to make the time to find confidence in yourself.

17

Tina Hirsch

Tina Hirsch was introduced to film production when she observed the making of Brian DePalma's *Greetings*. Intrigued be the editing process, she became an assistant editor on Robert Downey's *Putney Swope* and DePalma's *Hi Mom*. She established herself in independent films by editing her first feature, *Cornucopia Sexualis or Does Size Really Count?*, co-written by and starring Paul Bartel.

The job as Thelma Schoonmaker's assistant on *Woodstock* gave Hirsch the opportunity to work on the West Coast where she eventually settled and began to work as an editor.

In 1973 she cut *Macon County Line*, a box office sleeper that helped to launch a new era in B movies. Tina then joined the long list of Hollywood notables to work for the king of the B movie, Roger Corman. She cut several films for New World Pictures including *Eat My Dust*, *Big Bad Man*, and Paul Bartel's cult classic *Death Race 2000*.

In 1984 Tina Hirsch edited the box office smash *Gremlins* for another Corman alumnus, director Joe Dante, and worked with him on *Explorers* and his episode in *Twilight Zone, The Movie*.

1972	*Cornucopia Sexualis or Does Size Really Count?*
1973	*Macon County Line*
1974	*Big Bad Mama*
1975	*Death Race 2000*
1976	*Eat My Dust*

1977	*Assault on Paradise*
1978	*The Driver* (with Robert K. Lambert)
1979	*More American Graffiti*
1980	*Xanadu* (with Dennis Virkler)
1981	*Heartbeeps*
1982	*Independence Day* (with Dennis Virkler)
1983	*Twilight Zone—The Movie* (Joe Dante segment, "It's A Good Life")
1984	*Gremlins*
1985	*Explorers*
1991	*Delirious* (with Bill Gordean)

How did you become interested in film editing?

When I got out of college I went to work as an assistant to a fashion photographer. One day someone came into our studio to shoot a pilot. We went to see dailies on a double-headed Moviola. I thought, "Gee, this is so much more exciting than still photography." In 1968 I started going out with my future husband, who produced *Greetings*, a film that Brian DePalma directed. I watched them make it. I was really intrigued by the whole process. My husband's brother, Paul Hirsch, was working at a trailer company as an assistant editor and I thought I should go over there to volunteer my services and learn. I had to argue with the owner of the business for half an hour. I kept saying, "I don't want any money, I'll do whatever you want, I'll get coffee. I just want to hang around and learn." Finally, I convinced him to let me work there. I had been there about two weeks working with a trailer editor, when the Bob Downey movie *Putney Swope* moved in; Bud Smith was the editor. I thought, "Boy, I'm going to learn a lot more in there than I'm learning in here." So I said, "Thank you very much," to the trailer editor, and I went next door and learned something about features.

How did you become an assistant editor?

Paul Hirsch was given the job of editing *Hi Mom*, the sequel to *Greetings*, and he hired me as an assistant. That's when I learned an important lesson about the editing room: when to keep your mouth shut. Paul and Brian DePalma were working on a scene. They were moving some pieces of film around and I was standing behind them putting trims away. Then they ran the rearranged scene and I said, "You can't do that, the characters are talking about something that hasn't happened yet." Paul and Brian both slowly turned their heads around, didn't say anything and then turned back to the Moviola. I realized right away that I had done something wrong. When you're working, you don't want some half-pint interrupting you. What they were doing was a very private thing and I wasn't sensitive to it because they were my friends and it was my first job in a cutting room. I was fired that night. My next job worked out a lot better. I was Thelma Schoonmaker's first assistant on *Woodstock*. I was in charge of all the documentary footage. I had to make sure that everything was in sync and figure out systems for coding. It was incredibly challenging and convinced me more than ever that I wanted to work in film.

What was the first feature you cut as editor and what was the experience like?

The first feature I cut was *Cornucopia Sexualis or Does Size Really Count* that my husband had directed. Paul Bartel co-wrote it with him and starred in it. We had shot it in 16mm. I had no idea of how to cut a dramatic movie. I had only worked on documentaries and industrials. I assembled all of the masters together and then I started cutting in coverage.

How did you come to work for Roger Corman?

After I did *Macon County Line*, one of the guys on the crew who was close to the Cormans recommended me to Julie Corman, who called me in for something. She said, "We're paying $250 a week." I said, "That's what I made as an assistant editor." She said, "I guess you don't need the job." I said, "I guess I don't," and walked out of the office. I thought about it the next day and I said, "You idiot! You just turned down a film! How could you do that! You just messed up your whole life!" A week later she called me back and said, "I've got another film here, *Big Bad Mama*, $350 a week. Do you want it or not?" I said, "Well, I'd like to read the script and meet the director." She said, "God, you're picky." I read the script, met the director, and decided to do the picture, and that's how I started working at New World.

Did working for Roger Corman live up to its legendary reputation?

It certainly did. It was great. Of course, there's no money. You have to save up your money so you can afford to work for him, but it's really worth it in many ways. The reason he turns out so many really good people is because he is willing to take a chance. He gave me a chance. I can't think of a studio in town that I would rather work for. He's the most knowledgeable studio person I've ever met, and I don't think I would offend anybody by saying that. I cut three films and directed *Munchies* for him, and I never really disagreed with him on anything. I certainly can't say that about the decisions that are usually handed down at most studios.

What are the schedules like on a Corman film?

The schedules can really be horrendous. When I realize the amount of time I was given to work on the segment of *Twilight Zone—The Movie*, I know why it looks so good. I had the time to use nail clippers instead of paper shears. I really got to go in and finesse things. The limitations at Corman's New Horizons are really impossible. I just got a call the other day from a guy who said, "Roger is telling us we can't have apprentices anymore." I said, "I hate to say this to you, but we didn't have them in the old days." He said, "How in the hell did you get dailies out on time?" I said, "Dailies? We never had dailies." It's true, we never ran the film. The director never saw the film, never, never! If he wanted to come into the cutting room and I didn't have too much to do, I'd run some film for him; that was it. Nobody ever saw dailies. Roger wouldn't pay for a screening room. Are you kidding me? I never saw the film until it was on my bench broken down into little pieces.

In The Driver *there is a great action scene in a parking garage where Ryan O'Neal gives the guys who were trying to set him up an idea of his driving skills. How was it put together in the cutting room?*

Originally, it was storyboarded as a realistic scene, and it was shot as a linear scene. When we ran the dailies the director, Walter Hill, said to me, "Forget reality, I want you to do something crazy." I was stumped. I sat there and I ran the footage, I ran it, and I ran it. I just kept looking at it. Then I assembled selected sections. At the end of the select roll, there was a bunch of cuts of the car slamming into the support poles and smashing lights. I suddenly had crash, crash, crash and I said, "This feels right, this is what it should feel like." I kept running that little section over and over again to get the rhythm inside me. Then I went back to the beginning and I started doing the same kind of jump cuts in that section. Then I ran that series of cuts over and over again. I had to get into a groove until I got up enough speed to go on to the next cut. I have never looked at a section of film so much in my life. Once I had a series of five or six cuts, it became easy. The problem was solved, but I didn't have a clue, until I saw that little hunk of film at the end of the roll.

What technical problems did you come up against in cutting the creature sequences in Gremlins?

The creatures were lifeless, expressionless. Cutting puppets is not like cutting a dog. A dog has expressions. You can get a dog to appear intelligent. All you have to do is hold something in front of him and he gets a quizzical look in his eyes. With the puppets, I'd run the footage and wait for a little glimmer in the eye, something that showed any expression. I would mark up those pieces and put them into a select roll. I had all this MOS footage and nothing to listen to. It drove me crazy. I would turn on National Public Radio and listen all day long to the shrinks, psychics, and wizards so I wouldn't fall asleep. Kathy Kennedy came up with the idea that the Gremlins should breakdance in the bar scene. The picture was cut, finished, the crew's wrapped, everyone's gone. The director, Joe Dante, said he was too busy finishing the film to shoot it. So he sent the producer, Mike Finnell, up to Industrial Light and Magic and Mike got four or five shots: one of the little feet going up and down like in *Flashdance,* one of a Gremlin spinning on its back, and a couple of other shots. When Mike came back we looked at the film and we just sat there in silence. Joe said, "It's terrible." I sent my assistant to transfer a *Flashdance* song to 35mm. I knew I couldn't use it in the finished film, but it would be good beat to cut the picture against. So I sat there with this footage of these dumb little feet going up and down. I thought, "You call yourself an editor. You can't even come up with something interesting to do with this footage. You're a wimp." I called myself every name in the book. I thought of the garage scene in *The Driver* and I said, "Look, you did that, you came up with something there." Then I thought, "I wonder how many frames it takes for a foot to go up and down?" It was seven frames. I chopped the foot shot into little seven frame pieces. I put one in right side up, one flopped, one upside down, and then, upside down and flopped. The rhythm was right in sync with the music. It really got you into it. Once again I kept running it over and over, trying other pieces that maintained the rhythm. I found all the footage of them "walking" that we had taken out of the bar scene and tried it against the music. Now they looked like they were dancing. Suddenly, this unusable footage was appropriate with music behind it.

The scene where the Gremlins attack the mother in the kitchen is very nicely cut.

Yes, that was pretty easy except for the plates.

You had to match cut the plates?

Yes, that was rough. There were two people creating each throw: one person moving the Gremlin arm, and another throwing the plates. The arm and the plate had to sync up. It's not easy to do. They could never do two in a row. You had to keep cutting away, to give the illusion that the plates were being hurled one after the other.

How would you describe your work routine? Organized? Disciplined?

Both. I know there are editors who are very sloppy. They run the film on the floor, throw their film into the bin without hanging it on the hooks, and they don't write down the code numbers on short pieces. Their results may be good, but I could never work that way. How can you waste your assistants' time, having them clean up after your disaster? Being sloppy costs you time and money.

How do you work with your assistants and your apprentices? What do you expect out of them?

As far as I'm concerned, the first assistant runs the room. I go in my cutting room, shut the door, and do my work. He comes in and says to me, "It's time for dailies." I leave it up to the assistant to hire an apprentice. I've worked with assistants who do amazing things. They come to me at the end of the day and say, "We almost had the rug pulled from under us, but it's all taken care of." They protect me.

Many editors today complain about the pressure put on them to get films out faster and faster. How do you feel about this?

You've got big films out there with directors playing with three and four cameras. They're printing 600,000 feet for a 90-minute film and they just expect the editors to put the film together on a six-month schedule. That's why there are so many films that have multiple editors. That's why people aren't able to do as good a job as they might, why they have to work all those weekends. Almost everyone I know works seven days a week for an extended period of time, and I think it's criminal because the human body can't function well working that way. The studios that think they're saving money or time are probably only getting the equivalent of five days a week, because people just generally slow down after a while. When I've had to work seven days a week, I have the assistant and the apprentice switch off Saturday and Sunday, so they only have to work six days. More and more, studios are giving chances to people to direct first or second films when they really don't know what they're doing. Their solution is to shoot more film, print more takes, hire more editors. Let the editors make the movie. And I think the editors are undervalued. For the last two movies I did, they produced a fan magazine that had chapters on each of the producers, the DP, the special effects supervisor, the writer—everybody but the editor. If you didn't have a good special effects person you wouldn't have good puppets or good opticals, but I really think of the editor as being up there in that group of the people who make the movie.

When you are watching other people's work, are you aware of problems that were confronting the editor?

I was looking at something the other night and there were two very loose over-the-shoulder shots. The actress's reactions on one side were completely different than the other. What do you do? She's smiling in one shot and you cut around to the other side and suddenly she's very serious. I felt sorry for the poor editor.

In the future, do you think that editors will get more recognition for their contributions to films?

I certainly hope so. The fault lies mostly with the directors. They have really been unwilling to give editors credit. How many times do you hear a director say, "I'm editing my film now," as if he's doing the job? I think it's more ignorance than maliciousness. Many of them really don't understand most of what we do.

What personality traits do you think are necessary to be a good editor?

You have to be a team player. You have to be very supportive of the director. In many ways it helps to be a positive person as opposed to a negative one. It's all very well to see what's wrong with something, but you also have to be able to see what's right with it, and how to make it better. It takes a lot of patience. Film editors are the finest people I know. I don't think I've ever met an editor I didn't like. They're the most wonderful, dedicated, hard-working people I know. They work for the satisfaction it gives them and never expect a thank you, because they rarely get it—rarely.

18

Craig McKay

After working at a New York commercial house with Richard Marks and Barry Malkin, Craig McKay moved into feature films as an assistant to both Alan Heim and Evan Lottman. His own editing career began in 1976 when he cut *Thieves*.

In 1980 McKay edited *Melvin and Howard* for director Jonathan Demme. Since then, McKay and Demme have joined forces on *Swing Shift, Something Wild, Married to the Mob*, and *Silence of the Lambs*.

In 1981 Craig McKay and Dede Allen headed one of the largest editorial departments in American film history while editing *Reds* for Warren Beatty. The film broke ground with its inventive use of documentary interviews intercut with fictional scenes and created a unique editorial challenge that resulted in an Academy Award nomination.

1977	*Thieves*
1980	*Melvin and Howard*
1981	*Reds* (with Dede Allen)*
1984	*Swing Shift*
1986	*Something Wild*
1988	*Married to the Mob*
	Crack in the Mirror (with Alan Miller)
1989	*She Devil*
1990	*Miami Blues*

1991   *Silence of the Lambs*
                              Shining Through

*Academy Award nomination for best achievement in film editing.

What is the job of the film editor?
The film editor is responsible for what you see, and how long you see it, for what you hear, and how long you hear it. We are orchestrators of picture and sound. That's pretty overwhelming, but in fact that is what we do and it starts to give you some idea of the significance of the contribution.

When did you first realize you wanted to be a filmmaker?
When I was five my grandmother took me to see *Bambi*. From the first moment I saw movies I wanted to be involved with them. I used to make puppets and put on shows, and by eight or nine years old I had a darkroom. The combination of puppets and photography got me interested in animation. When I was ten, I started making little 8mm science fiction films around the neighborhood. I'd use all of the kids. We had a barn in the back of our house and the top floor was converted into a little studio.

When did you get your first job in the film business?
In 1964 I got a job as a can carrier for Cinemetrics, a commercial house. I started there with Richie Marks and Barry Malkin. We would screen hundreds of prints and ship them out to TV stations all over the country. I would go out and shoot low-budget commercials, bring them back, and then cut them. I wanted to be a cameraman. Then I got more interested in storytelling and performance, in what happens when you put two images together. I was at a crossroads. It was the content that made me jump to editing. I decided to go with editing.

Do you think that your early experience with cinematography has helped you as an editor?
When you're shooting you have to visualize how angles are going to cut together. When I look at dailies, I can visualize what the scene is going to look like together. That's a result of my familiarity with the camera.

How did you get into feature films?
Feature work was just starting in New York at the time. *Midnight Cowboy* was being done, it was starting to really accelerate. I met some freelance people, made a lot of contacts, and began to freelance as an assistant. I went to work for Alan Heim as his assistant on a Sidney Lumet film. Then I worked with Evan Lottman as his assistant on *Puzzle of a Downfall Child* and *The Exorcist*. I became an associate editor on *Scarecrow*.

How did you get the opportunity to cut scenes on Scarecrow?

I was originally hired as an assistant. I went on location because Evan Lottman was finishing *The Effect of Gamma Rays on Man in the Moon Marigolds* that we had both worked on. While we were caravaning across the country shooting, I said to the director, Jerry Schatzberg, "When we get back to New York, I'd like to cut a few scenes." He said, "Well, if it's all right with Evan, it's all right with me." When I got back to New York I said to Evan, "I'd like to cut a few scenes." He said, "If it's all right with Jerry, it's all right with me." A week later I was in a cutting room with an assistant.

What sequences did you cut?

I worked on the scene when Gene Hackman does a striptease in a bar and the scene at the fountain when Al Pacino freaks out.

What was this initial cutting experience like?

The striptease was a cutting nightmare. It was a difficult scene to try and keep the energy up. The final shot was a tag shot of Pacino; it zooms into him and he's holding a package for his little kid. I picked up the shot later, so you never saw the package. Schatzberg came in to look at it and he turned to me and said, "That's a good scene, but you forgot the package." Schatzberg was very gracious about it. I went back and put it in, but I can remember the embarrassment of it. I'd been so involved in the mechanics of putting the scene together, I forgot the content. When you're starting out as an editor there are oversights. It's interesting because I've gone totally 180 degrees from that. The last thing I think about now is a splicer or a Moviola.

What was your main objective in cutting the striptease scene?

In my original cut, the strip took forever because I was playing it so literally in real time. I began compressing it with temporal cuts and it took a while to weave my way through. The scene tells you what it needs. That's what it said to me: You've got to get this thing happening faster. I played with compression for the first time by getting him to strip fast.

What is interesting is that you used compression to make it look like it was happening in real time.

Right, that's the trick. Although we compressed it, it seems to be the normal continuity. Most movies are very long. You get a 120-page script, but you get a 2-hour-and-40-minute movie. So you're continually trying to bring it down to two hours. That's generally the way you approach it, with the utmost in brevity.

How did you become a full editor?

I worked for Barry Malkin as his assistant on *Who Is Harry Kellerman?* with Dustin Hoffman. From Barry I learned high organization. I came to him at a point when I was really starting to move out as an assistant. On that film I met Herb Gardner. We had a good relationship so he introduced me to Marlo Thomas, who he was with at that time. She was doing a kids show called *Free to Be You and Me*. Herb recommended me and I went over and did it. In 1976 Herb called me and said that Marlo was doing a TV movie and would I be interested. I had just read that he was starting a feature, *Thieves*, which Marlo was going to do. I said "I understand you're doing a movie. How could you do a movie without me?" There was a pause and he said, "You're right." So *Thieves* was my first feature. I learned a lesson very early: If you want something you have to ask for it.

You have had a continuing relationship with Jonathan Demme. What is he like to work with as a director?

We're kindred spirits. When you work for Demme he gives you a lot to run with; he's not sitting on you all the time. He knows what he wants. He likes you to fully contribute to the film and everybody gets an opportunity to do that. He has an infectious spirit, and in working on *Melvin and Howard* that was infused in the film. The way it came together for me is one of my best experiences.

Was there a lot of reaction material for the opening scene of Melvin and Howard *when Jason Robards and Paul LeMat ride in the truck? How was that scene put together?*

Yes, many thousands of feet. It's a reactive scene. That's the way it was cut for the most part. The footage was very dark. I had to lock myself in the room and close everything. I was in the dark for three weeks doing it. There were A and B cameras. One camera would be front and one would be camera right. Jonathan shot it mostly in pick-ups. He'd take it so far, then somebody would blow a line and he would shoot a pick-up. Paul LeMat had his script right on the seat, which was a problem that I had to cut around. I would say that 50 percent of the reactions are in real time and the other 50 are from other places close by. It was difficult to do. I had all the pieces, but I had a tremendous amount of material to go through. Fortunately, most of it is played off of Jason's reactions; he was absolutely brilliant. It was a pretty bold move to start a movie with a ten-minute scene in a truck in the dark. I always find that Jonathan's extending himself, trying to do things that are more interesting. That's why I like working with him.

How do you work with Jonathan Demme in the editing room?

He has a very strong sensitivity to the editing. I usually do a first cut, which I call my European cut, because the shots play long. I pick the most beautiful parts of the shots to play, the slow, quiet rhythms, and then Jon comes in and we discuss it. We may get into arguments—there have been a couple of beauts—then we get closer. Jon has a real movie sensibility and a real American sensibility. It's in the collision of those two that what we do together happens.

Do you have any theories on how to cut comedy?

I don't treat it like a comedy, I treat it like a real-life situation. Comedy comes from truth in a situation and that's really funny. There are scenes in *Melvin and Howard* where it would have been easy to spoof those characters, but we didn't. It was decided up front that we should respect these people as human beings and always treat them seriously, as ridiculous as they got. My other priority is to find the timing that's correct for the scene. Comedy is the most difficult material to do. It's all timing. It's how and when you deliver a line, when you show something.

Reds had one of the largest editorial teams ever assembled for a motion picture. How did you and Dede Allen co-edit the film?

It was the largest editorial undertaking ever, no question. There were 64 people in postproduction. It was a real collaboration. Dede and I did the big scenes and together we supervised the associate editors, Richard Hiscott, Angelo Corrao, Brian Peachy, and David Ray, who were doing the other scenes. Kathy Wenning was in charge of the witnesses; she was a whole department. Dickie Martin was hired in London and put one scene together. Jerry Greenberg came in and helped out with a couple of scenes because he was free and we had an incredible schedule. Paramount was on our ass to get the movie out.

How was this large staff utilized?

We had a tremendous amount of film. The need to have people do specific kinds of work came out of trying to get it done on time. So in essence, a mini-studio was created. Departments were set up. There was a video department, there was coding, there was an optical department, and the witnesses department.

What was your working relationship like with Dede Allen?

It was really wonderful. We did the first cut of the movie and we were really tuned into each other. It was as if we knew what a scene needed. It was almost unspoken. Sentences wouldn't get completed and we each knew what the other meant by it. Part of the job was being a general and I learned how to be a general from Dede. She knew where everything was and how it worked. That was the lesson I learned on the film: the dynamic of handling people, getting things done and problem solving. Dede is one of the most remarkable editors I've ever witnessed. I've seen her put stuff together and was just dumbstruck by how brilliantly it was done.

What was the most difficult aspect of cutting the film?

We had a picture that had a narrative line. Concurrently, we're popping in the witnesses in a sort of documentary fashion and having them tell about a real-life experience. That's very difficult because you think it's going to put the brakes on the narrative line. So the editorial challenge was to develop the narrative story and have the witnesses come in and support the narrative line. We did a version without the witnesses to see if it would work as a movie and the movie didn't work, so we put them back in. Finding the right place for the witnesses was a challenge. You just couldn't plop them in anywhere.

You use just about every technique with them. They are on screen, used as voice-overs; they talk about exactly what is going on, about something related. They even talk to each other. Did you ever try anything conceptually that just didn't work?

A lot of the time. What ended up in the final version is the result of trying them all over the place. As we were cutting the film, these people were constantly floating all over the place. You think of a combination, we'd tried it. When they really worked, they told us that they worked. That was the element that got played with the most.

How were you able to keep that massive amount of material organized?

We had a video set-up that we bought from Stanley Kubrick that his editor, Ray Lovejoy, had jury-rigged. We used it to shoot dailies from a Moviola. It was rigged in such a way that you would look at the tape and there would be a running code number on it. If we didn't have access to pick performances and takes, we'd probably still be cutting that movie. So tape was a real boon in getting that movie together and out on time.

Did you and Dede work together in the same room?

No, she had her room, I had mine. We were constantly running in and out of each other's rooms. There were daily meetings on logistics, meetings with Warren for scenes to be shot, meetings just to coordinate when things would get done, on top of both of us in our own room, each cutting the picture. It was quite an exercise in concentration because we were continually interrupted, and we were working six and seven very long days a week for 19 months.

Did all the editors have input into every scene?

Yes, somebody would put a scene together and we'd all sit down and look at it and make suggestions. Everybody looked at everything. On top of all the meetings, if an editor finished a scene, Dede and I would show it to Warren along with the associate editor. We would oversee every change.

Of the scenes that you cut, which is your favorite?

The storming of the socialist convention. I had a tremendous amount of footage on it, over 90,000 feet, and it's a four-and-a-half-minute scene. I got it to work. When you have that kind of footage the problem is, what do you keep? Beatty would shoot a tremendous amount of coverage, and as his editor, I could always see in the dailies that the scene was in there. I had to go in and find it. He tried a lot of alternate versions and variations. He always delivered the scene; you just had to find it.

How did Warren Beatty use the editing process?

When we were putting the movie together, he decided, based on what we had cut, that new scenes needed to be shot for the story to work.

Do you feel Warren Beatty was directing the movie through the editing process?

This was very much Warren Beatty's vision. It was his idea for the scene. He shot it. Dede and I would cut a scene together and we'd get it to a point where it played, and we were satisfied with it. Then we'd bring Warren in and he'd tell us what he thought. We'd make changes and show it to him again. We were able to help him execute it and I feel that it was a major contribution, but it was still his vision.

Do you feel that the only reason to be an assistant editor is to become an editor?

No, some people may want to learn what happens in a cutting room and use it elsewhere. As an assistant you get a sense of overview, organization, and dynamic. You may want to be a director or a producer. I think that everyone should have some cutting room experience.

Do you feel a responsibility to teach your assistants the craft of film editing?

Yes, absolutely. I feel that responsibility to every one of my assistants. The reality is that's how people learn to do it and there is no other way. A lot of editors work with their doors locked and the assistant in the other room. I always have somebody next to me and I'm saying virtually on every cut, "What do you think?" How else are you going to train them? You keep them in the other room, they're not going to know anything. It does a lot for their morale, too, because they're involved creatively. They give you feelings. That's what it's all about.

Do you consider yourself fast as an editor?

I can be. I'll tell you what I am, I'm thorough—which means I try a lot of stuff. You can pick three takes and use them to put a scene together, and I know a lot of guys who do that, but if there is a better line-reading in take seven and there is a better reading of the next line in take four, I try it.

Do you find it necessary to talk about what you are doing while you are cutting?

There are a couple of editors who talk you through everything. Mine is more weighted with comments about character, and, "Is this the right behavior for this beat? Does that work or doesn't that work?" It's limited to that focus.

What technical procedure do you use to cut a scene?

I look at the dailies. Then I decide where I want to be for specific lines of dialogue: I want to be in the wide shot on this dialogue, I want to be on this two-shot for this line, and I'm going to cut to a reaction on this line. I assemble a first cut on a synchronizer. Then I do a second cut on a Moviola and refine it. I may tighten, shorten, generate an overlap, and do pacing things. After that, it's on the shelf and I'm on to the next scene.

What are your objectives on those two cuts of a scene?

The first one is the right time and place, the second is for the rhythms. I'm very careful about the story line aspect of editing, being at the right place at the right time with my shots, so the audience gets the right information. There are a lot of people who play information off of a character; I like to be right there getting direct eye contact.

Do you ever lose perspective on a project, and how do you resolve it?

It's only happened once with me. I had a scene that I just couldn't get. I knew what it was supposed to be, but I just couldn't get it for some reason. I solved it by putting it on the shelf for a week and just continuing on with the movie and then coming back to it. I needed that perspective. When you're in the heat of battle working scene by scene, a beat at a time, it's impossible to have an overview. You have a lot of things there to help you. You've got the script and actors conveying emotion. You fight this battle from beat to beat until you get it all together. It's not until you look at your first cut that you start to get any overview. That's the next step in the process.

Is audience feedback important to you?

I've had several movies previewed. You can really tell from an audience when something is working and when something is not. Movie audiences are very helpful; they give you a tremendous amount of information. You also discover laughs that you never knew you had.

Why do you think that film critics so rarely discuss editing in their reviews?

I think intellectually they have some idea of what we do, but I don't think they have a real idea of the contribution. They get caught up in the emotional sweep of a film. The cinematographer's contribution is obvious; ours is not supposed to be. Pauline Kael will mention why scenes work and don't work. That comes close, but she never gets specifically into editing. They don't know what putting two shots together means; they don't understand the dialectic of editing.

That putting two shots together can make three.

Yes, or two becomes something else and that's the real craft.

Do you think you have a style as an editor?

I don't really have a sense of myself having a style. Some people impose a style on the material. It's limiting; then you've got to meet the requirements of that style. I work just the other way. I let the material tell me what it needs and that's how I approach it. It will always tell you, all you have to do is listen to it.

What personality traits do you think are necessary to be a film editor?

An editor has to be pretty even-tempered and has to be able to get along with a lot of people very well, especially a crew. You spend a lot of time in very close proximity and it better work. In most instances, an editor is the grounding force. I think that directors have come to expect that. Most editors are generals who can get a director through a movie. You have to know how to do that. I'm not talking about an act of will,

I'm talking about an act of intelligence. More than anything else you have to be a very good problem solver. That's the priority. A lot of it is compromise, but in many instances, the real difficulty is finding the best compromise.

How have you changed as an editor over the years?

As an assistant I had a notorious reputation for being highly organized. Everything was handwritten with a ruler, it was perfect. The minute I started cutting, all that went out the window. I think less about the mechanics of making films. I'm not thinking about the Moviola, or the synchronizer, or the track. To me, it's an intellectual, emotional experience.

In the future, what medium do you think editors will be working in?

I think down the line that digitized images are certainly the future of this business. Maybe six years from now videotape will be out the window; everything will be stored on laser disc, digitized and random-accessed. I'm glad it's moving in that direction. That's definitely where it has to go.

Do you ever turn down projects?

I'm very selective about what I decide to do. I always read a script and wouldn't think of taking something without finding out about the director. I think you have to. I mean, you put so much of your life into one film. I know I do. If you like something about a project, that means it's significant to you.

19

Susan E. Morse

Susan E. Morse attended the New York University Graduate Film School and simultaneously launched her editing career as Ralph Rosenblum's apprentice.

After assisting Rosenblum on Woody Allen's *Annie Hall* and *Interiors*, Morse became the director's editor on his next film, *Manhattan*. Their relationship has spanned 14 years and 15 films.

Woody Allen and Susan E. Morse have developed a unique working method. A first assembly is constructed during or immediately after shooting. The director and editor then spend marathon sessions discussing the film. Out of these sessions new scenes are planned, shot, and integrated into the final cut of the film.

Since 1980, beginning with *Stardust Memories*, Morse has cut all of Woody Allen's films at the director's postproduction facility, the Manhattan Film Center. The center is equipped with two Steenbecks, a Moviola, a coding machine, a turntable, a dual cassette player, a CD player, microphones, a Nagra and transfer facilities for mag track, a scratch-mixing console and dubbers, 35mm and 16mm projectors, and video transfer equipment. This complete working environment has given the editor and director the resources and control necessary to produce such challenging films as *Zelig*, *The Purple Rose of Cairo*, and *Hannah and Her Sisters*, which was nominated for an Academy Award for best film editing in 1986.

| 1979 | *Manhattan* |
| 1980 | *Stardust Memories* |

1981	*Arthur*
1982	*A Midsummer Night's Sex Comedy*
1983	*Zelig*
1984	*Broadway Danny Rose*
1985	*The Purple Rose of Cairo*
1986	*Hannah and Her Sisters**
1987	*Radio Days*
	September
	Another Woman
1989	*New York Stories* (Woody Allen segment, "Oedipus Wrecks")
	Crimes and Misdemeanors
1990	*Alice*

*Academy Award nomination for best achievement in film editing.

Have you had any life experiences other than artistic ones that influenced your desire to become a film editor?

It would be a mistake to say I ever actually decided to become a film editor or even that I wanted to become a film editor per se. I think I'm temperamentally suited to it because I've always enjoyed problem solving—math was one of my great strengths in school—and I've always enjoyed team sports. I guess the analogy I'm stretching for is that filmmaking is fundamentally a matter of team work, and editing is an opportunity—the last chance, in fact—to highlight each team member's strengths and downplay each person's weaknesses, all in hopes of making the entire team look good.

How have you applied those experiences to film?

A film has the greatest chance of succeeding if everyone is working for the good of the film rather than for his own glory. On Woody's films we have been lucky enough to hold together essentially the same team for years. We know each other's strengths and weaknesses and help each other so the end result hopefully shows everyone off well. Woody is the key in that his perfectionism inspires everyone to try his hardest, but Bobby Greenhut as Woody's producer also deserves a lot of credit for giving each department enough autonomy to allow for creativity. He gives honest and incisive feedback and gives us each a pat on the back when it is deserved.

How did you get your first job in editing?

A month after arriving at the NYU Film School a friend and I discovered a notice on the lobby notice board announcing a job opening in the cutting room of a film that Roberta Hodes, one of our teachers, had directed. We both made a beeline for her office and were told that we were the first candidates for the job and that the only requirement was that we could splice. Well, we both had that down so it was simply up to Roberta to choose between us. She chose me.

How did you become Ralph Rosenblum's assistant?

I was a quick study on Roberta's film, so Jack Sholder, Roberta's editor, recommended me to Ralph Rosenblum as an apprentice. I'm very grateful that I was in film school at the same time I was working in professional cutting rooms. By day, I'd watch an experienced editor grapple with and solve cutting problems, and by night, I'd face similar problems in my own films and attempt similar solutions. Each experience enriched the other.

On which films did you assist Ralph Rosenblum?

The first one was called *Remember Those Poker-Playing Monkeys*, which didn't even open in New York until three years later under the name *The Great Georgia Bank Hoax* and lasted perhaps one weekend. The next film was *Annie Hall*, a job I elected to take in lieu of returning to NYU for my second year of graduate school. I preferred to be paid while learning, rather than to go more deeply into debt. I gambled that Ralph and Woody would give me an education, which they certainly did.

What was that experience on Annie Hall *like?*

I was flattered by the degree to which Ralph and Woody asked my opinion and seemed to take what I said under serious consideration. I was certainly busy at the time with standard assistant's tasks—pulling select takes, putting away trims, filling out room tone, and double splicing—but I was always keeping one ear cocked to the conversation between Ralph and Woody. It was always interesting to hear why certain takes were preferred over others, where they felt they had left too much slack, how the pacing affected the humor, and how the jokes sometimes obfuscated the story line and undercut the emotional impact of the film.

My most vivid memory was the day that Ralph suggested a memory montage of moments that Annie and Alvy had shared for the end of the picture. While Woody and Ralph chatted about the pros and cons of such a notion, I envisioned such a sequence in my mind and began flipping through the log book in search of likely candidates. By the time they had decided to go ahead with it, I had pulled out virtually all of the cuts you see in the final version. When Ralph turned around to ask me to look for the raw material they would need, I could simply hand it to him. It was a terrific moment for me because I felt very much a part of the process. I'm sure it was a great moment for them because they didn't have to break stride between the decision to try something and the chance to execute that decision.

I think the greatest lesson I learned from Ralph was to think of the

film I was working on as raw documentary footage crying out for co-
herence, rather than strictly as a linear script. It's a very liberating approach to let the footage lead you, even if it means deviating from the
emphasis implicit in the script. *Annie Hall* found itself in the cutting
room, which is neither to say that the dailies weren't terrific—which
they were—nor to give all the credit to Ralph. Ralph deserves a lot of
the credit for the success of that film, but what I witnessed in that cutting
room was not one man's handiwork. It was the teamwork, the collaboration between Ralph and Woody, that made the reworking of the film
a success and that, tangentially, inspired me to stick with editing, at
least for a while.

*Manhattan is the first Woody Allen film you edited. How did the spectacular
montage of New York City, which opens the film, develop as a sequence?*

The daytime material was cut in a regular rhythm and carried by the
"Chapter One" voice-over, which united the images, introduced you to
Isaac, the central character of the film, and let you know you were about
to see a comedy. Equally importantly, it focused attention on the style
as well as the content of the photography. Only in the nighttime footage
did the cutting rhythm become more energetic as "Rhapsody In Blue"
did, still striving not to distract from the photography. The point was
to convey Isaac's idealized view of the city and to introduce Manhattan
itself as a character in the film. Making the cutting itself more flashy
would have distracted from both of these intentions. Woody had originally conceived of that montage as a sort of overture to the picture. We
were always a little bit wary of how it would play, so for months,
whenever we discussed the running time of the film, we made a point
of qualifying it as the running time with the montage, so we could
subtract in our minds and find out what the real running time was.

How did the editing help to create the illusion of documentary reality in Zelig?

The whole point was to disguise the seams between the old and new
footage. People always compliment us on the scenes when Fanny Brice
serenades Zelig on the rooftop of the Westbury Hotel and the Nazi rally
being disrupted by Zelig waving frantically behind the podium where
Hitler was speaking. In neither case had we done anything extraordinary
in the editing. When people tell you they loved or hated a sequence, it
is important to look to the preceding material for the reason. We got
credit for miracle making because of the way we introduce Zelig. The
opening glimpses of him in the tickertape parade are convincing throw-
aways. We matched the production footage to the stock footage con-
vincingly in lighting, contrast, flicker, and grain, but it was obvious that
the stock shot was extremely wide while our footage was much closer
and shot from a distinctly different camera angle. However, after a grainy
still photo, we next show Zelig live with Babe Ruth. Woody is in the
background of the shot, his feet are in frame and his shadow follows

his actions. Ruth's bat dissects Zelig's body when he swings at a pitch and nothing looks fake! We convince the audience that we can do anything. This is unmistakably Woody and unmistakably Babe Ruth. That shot, for me, is the key to the success of the documentary style of the film as a whole. We established what we could do and thereafter could get away with a little bit more. That "we" is not exclusively editorial. It includes Woody; Gordon Willis, the director of photography; Mel Bourne, the production designer; and Santo Loquasto, the costume designer; with a strong assist from Joel Hynek and Stuart Robertson of the optical house, R/Greenberg Associates. The masterpiece was the Babe Ruth optical, and leading with it established a level of expectation in the audience, which their expectations fulfilled for us as much as we fulfilled it for them.

How did the nightclub montage in The Purple Rose of Cairo *develop during the editing process?*

Woody had wanted to create a 1930s-style nightclubbing montage with multiple superimpositions. He shot a dozen or so set-ups, but once you start layering them you find that's not much to work with. I found a couple of Times Square shots from our *Zelig* stock footage to use as background in the beginning of the montage. With the help of friend and film buff extraordinaire Jim Davis, I located a half-dozen such montages in 1930s films and came up with a short list of key shots that said "1930s": a rotating prism shot of swirling champagne glasses, a piano keyboard, neon signs, hands chilling a bottle of champagne in an ice bucket, and an extreme close-up of champagne bubbles. I put together a rough version of the montage on video in a couple of hours, to demonstrate to Woody the need for more material. It was a pleasure to be able to show Woody what I wanted rather than have to describe it in arduous detail. Once I had Woody's feedback on that preliminary version, he asked Gordon Willis to pick up whatever I needed. The original dozen or so shots became the narrative line of the montage, and the additional shots we picked up provided the layering that enabled me to mimic the thirties' style. Of course, in trying to evoke a recognizable style, you exaggerate to make your point, but that's the fun of it. I went back to the video house to put together a final version and then turned that over to the optical house, R/Greenberg Associates, along with a chart of the five interwoven strands, and told them to give me the equivalent on film.

What other responsibilities have you handled on Woody Allen's films?

On *Radio Days* I was responsible for hiring the musicians, coordinating the recording sessions, negotiating with the music publishers and record companies, and even putting together a model shot—the U-boat Joe sights from the beach. On several of Woody's films I've recorded voiceovers and done a great deal of scratch mixing. I guess I learned in film school or team sports or more likely, from my parents, that you simply do whatever needs to be done without worrying about whether it falls under your job description.

How much impact can editing have on the style of a film?

Godard has always been given enormous credit for his audacity in using jump cuts in *Breathless*. I would be very surprised to hear that he began shooting the film with that thought in mind. I would much more readily believe that he and his editor threw caution to the winds in the cutting room in an effort to solve pacing problems, because it made emotional and philosophical sense in that picture to break the traditional rules of filmmaking. I don't know this for a fact, but I do know that such stylistic elements often evolve in the cutting room rather than spring full-grown from an auteur's mind. By the same token, if editing solutions work to the point of being truly seamless, it is entirely possible that no one will see through them and therefore no credit will be given for them.

Woody and I had a good chuckle over a comment someone made in a recent screening to the effect that the film looked as though it had been shot that way, that nothing had been discarded and reshot or in any way reworked—this on a film where the reshoots ultimately comprised 40 percent of the final film and where the climactic scene had not even been a part of the original script. As is the case with most of Woody's films, the editing solutions overlap to such a degree with rewrites and reshoots that it would be more correct simply to call them postproduction solutions and not attempt to pigeonhole them more exactly. The point remains, if they work, they feel organic to the film and therefore invisible.

Do you think an editor can have a style?

An editing style is intrinsic to the style of a given picture, as in *Breathless* or *Zelig*. One could point to certain signature devices that given editors use repeatedly. A friend of mine always seems to find an excuse for using a lyrical pair of slow dissolves to link three establishing shots together in his films. It's simply a recognizable fillip, like a handwriting flourish that tells you who wrote a line. I'm not sure I can give you an example in my own work. Maybe my style is to be invisible.

20

Arthur Schmidt

Arthur Schmidt's first exposure to editing occurred in his father's cutting room, where the elder Schmidt edited *Sunset Boulevard* and *Some Like It Hot*.

Schmidt initiated his career as an apprentice at Paramount and continued to build his credentials as an assistant on *Little Big Man* and *Sounder*. His assignment as standby editor on *Marathon Man* proved pivotal when he became Jim Clark's assistant, gained Clark's confidence and ultimately garnered an associate editor credit.

As editor, Arthur Schmidt has collaborated with Michael Apted on *Coal Miner's Daughter*, for which he received an Academy Award nomination, and *Firstborn*. He worked on Caleb Deschanel's *The Escape Artist* for Francis Ford Coppola's Zoetrope Studios and edited *Ruthless People* for the trio of Zucker, Zucker, and Abrahams.

Schmidt has had a long relationship with director Robert Zemeckis, editing *Back to the Future* and its two sequels. Zemeckis offered him the challenge of his editing career, *Who Framed Roger Rabbit?*, which achieved near perfection in combining animation and live action with an attention to detail never before accomplished. The complex technical requirements stretched Schmidt's role as an editor with countless demands on his time and talent. His enormous contribution to the film was rewarded with the 1988 Oscar for best editing.

1976	*Marathon Man* (with Jim Clark)
1977	*The Last Remake of Beau Geste* (with Jim Clark)

1978	*Jaws II* (with Neil Travis)
1979	*The Fish that Saved Pittsburgh*
1980	*The Idolmaker* (with Steve Potter and Neil Travis)
	Coal Miner's Daughter*
1982	*The Escape Artist*
1984	*The Buddy System*
	Firstborn
1985	*Fandango*
	Back to the Future (with Harry Keramidas)
1986	*Ruthless People*
1988	*Who Framed Roger Rabbit?***
1989	*Back to the Future II* (with Harry Keramidas)
1990	*Back to the Future III* (with Harry Keramidas)
1991	*The Rocketeer*

*Academy Award nomination for best achievement in film editing.

**Academy Award for best achievement in film editing.

Who Framed Roger Rabbit? *is a landmark film editorially in the way it combines live-action photography with animation. How did you prepare for this complex project?*

They did a test that convinced everybody we could make the movie. It wasn't more than a minute. It was just Roger in about four shots. I put it together. Animation is time-consuming and expensive, so they ended up animating only two of the cuts. I had my first taste of what this madness was going to be like. I thought, "What am I doing working on a movie that has animation?" I had no background in it. I looked at a lot of cartoons: the old Bugs Bunny Looney Tunes, the old Disney cartoons, and animated features like *Song of the South*. I had to find out what the animators' needs were and how we would all be working together because I knew I had to pass my edited footage to them. Industrial Light and Magic was doing the special effects. We had to work out a coordinating system because the animation was going to be done in London, we were going to be cutting in Los Angeles, and ILM is up in northern California. So initially, the logistics of the film gave us a lot of headaches. There was always a lot of communicating going on and we evolved a system. We wrote a little book, *The Roger Rabbit Postpro-duction Booklet*, on what to do.

What was in the booklet?

We all wrote a simplified version, very brief and succinct, of what we did in our respective areas. ILM wrote up what they did, I wrote up what editorial did, and Don Hahn, the producer of animation, wrote up what animation did. He also got the animators to illustrate various pages. We had a glossary explaining all the animation and ILM terms because they are so unique. We did it so we didn't have to keep ex-plaining why we did things to everybody on the postproduction end of the film. We thought the booklet would be there for anybody who'd be crazy enough to make another movie like *Roger Rabbit*.

What was the very first material you received on the film?

The very first material I received was the voice tracks for the opening cartoon. One night, about five o'clock, while I was working on a tele-vision movie at Disney waiting for *Roger Rabbit* to start, the director, Bob Zemeckis, called me up and said, "Hey, Artie, we're going over to record the voices for the opening cartoon at seven o'clock at Todd-AO. Do you think you should come along?" We went over there and it wasn't or-ganized at all. There weren't any proper ADR sheets made out or any-thing, it was just a script. So I got a yellow legal pad and started making notes because I was the one who was going to have to cut all these tracks together and turn them over to the animators. The animators always have to have the dialogue and effects tracks before they can start animating. I started cutting all these dialogue tracks together with no picture at all. I had a storyboard to refer to, but I just had to imagine the basic timing of it. I called up our sound effects editor and asked for lots of pots and pans crashing to the floor, an ironing board flipping up, and all the things that were indicated in the storyboard.

At that time I thought I was going to go out of my mind. I sat there at the KEM with the sound tracks and kept looking up at the picture but there was nothing there on the screen. So I cut together the sound track. Finally, they got around to doing the animatics so I could cut them in with the dialogue and the sound effects to show the animators what was happening in this amount of time. We turned that over to the animators in England and got them started. They had to start working right away because animation takes so long. The very last scene they were going to shoot for the movie was the first live-action scene, where Roger steps out of the refrigerator and the live-action director steps into the scene. In order to build that set on the soundstage they had to have the animators animate the kitchen and refrigerator right away, so the art director would know how to build the set to match the animation and still have everything on the set look like it's the opening cartoon now with live people walking into it.

Did the animators have to adhere strictly to the guideline of your cut sound track?

We told the animators they could open up the sound track if they had to in order to make their animation work. If they saw Roger spinning around the kitchen for a much longer time than we allowed on the sound track, they had the freedom to do that. First the animators sent us black and white pencil tests so we could say, "Yes, that's what Bob Zemeckis had in mind, go ahead, ink it, paint it, and send it on." When we finally got all of the color elements of the cartoon back and it was all together, we would tighten it up in the editing.

What was the first live-action material that was shot?

They shot all the Los Angeles exteriors in three weeks, before we went to England to shoot the interiors on sound stages. Most of it was the chase material. They shot the Weasel's car and Bob Hoskins or his double in Benny The Cab running down an alley or busy street in downtown Los Angeles. A lot of it was quite mysterious because they were just background plates for the animation. That's basically all I had to work with besides the sound track. Charlie Fleischer, the voice of Roger Rabbit, was there all during the shooting, playing off-stage to Bob Hoskins. That's one of the reasons why Bob was as good as he was. Charlie was always giving his performance and doing a marvelous job. Charlie was off-camera but on-mike so that I could use those sound tracks when I was cutting. I always had the dialogue for the animated characters; having the dialogue is really what determined my timing for the editing.

What was your schedule like during the live-action shooting in England?

When the company is shooting, you've got to be around for the number of hours that they're around and they're usually on a 12-hour work day. I would get to work at 9 o'clock in the morning and get home sometime between eight or nine.

How long were you in England?

I was in England all during the shooting for four and a half months. I stayed another two weeks after the shooting just to get the picture into a rough cut and then came back here to Los Angeles to do all of the editing. Because of our schedule we could never treat the film the way you would a normal film. We had to keep feeding the animation monster so we could meet our summer release date.

When you were working with the live-action material before the animation was complete, how were you able to know where Roger and the other animated characters were in the frame?

Before every set-up that involved an animated character, they did what was called the reference test. They would take a model of Roger Rabbit and move it through the scene with Bob Hoskins so I always had a very rough idea of how he was supposed to move and where Roger was meant to be in the scene. When we turned the scenes over to the animators we would show them the reference tests because they always had to draw in the shadows. Looking at the reference test, they knew where the light fell.

Were there any restrictions on what the camera could do during the live-action scenes that were to have animation added to them?

They did everything you would normally do on a live-action film. They moved the camera a lot, they panned and dollied, they changed focus in the middle of scenes. They did a lot of very adventurous things where there was going to be animation.

Did you use a different kind of coding system than you normally would use?

Not initially. It was the same kind of coding that we do for a normal film. Once we had the film edited and we knew that X number of cuts within the scene needed to have animation, we took the scene number, say, scene 36, and numbered the first cut that required animation 36–1. The next ones were 36–2, 36–3. Then everybody knew which shot we were referring to, instead of saying the third one in the scene with the rabbit doing such and such. Everybody just started talking about 36–3 when we would call animation or when ILM would call us. We could just talk numbers and know where we were.

What are the principles of cutting animation?

My approach to cutting *Roger Rabbit* was to cut it the way I would cut a live-action movie. It was always in the back of my mind that sometimes cartoons go very fast, but I didn't feel that I was really making any concessions to animation. I always tried to cut it as if it were a live-action movie and all the characters were there from the very beginning.

How did you coordinate the editing of the film in Los Angeles with the London animation team?

We had to record all of the ADR for all the animated voices. I would have to cut that; your normal ADR or looping editor couldn't cut it because it was really a picture editor's job. I had to decide where this person's voice went. The fact that we had to do all of the dialogue tracks before the animators could start their work prolonged the picture editing time of the movie. Sometimes the ADR would vary in length and I'd end up recutting the picture to make everything fit. Then we'd hop on a plane, fly to London and spend three or four days there going over all of the scenes with the animators. We would run them on a KEM and Zemeckis would describe to the animators what he saw Roger doing in each particular cut. The animators didn't make it up; Bob was very specific. Richard Williams and the animators would sit there and do a quick pencil sketch of what Bob was telling them to put into the scene. That would become the animators' reference because there were 300 people working in the animation department in London. Richard couldn't draw every frame, but if it were a long cut he would do three drawings: Roger at the beginning of the cut, half-way through, and

Roger at the end of the cut. Richard was very fast at sketching something out, but you'd have to wait for him to do that as you were discussing the scene. That's why it would take days to do these animation turnovers. We did that on top of jet lag and exhaustion, then we'd come right back and continue editing for the next turnover session in London. We made five trips to London from June until November.

How did the animators work with your cut of the live-action material?

They always had a black and white dupe of the cut. Once a scene was locked, a photostat was made of every single frame within that cut. The photostat was like an 8 × 10 blowup of each frame. The animator would put it on his animation bench and put a cell over that so he could draw the animated character in the right position and proportion. It was such an expensive process that I never had an extra frame. Film editors are always used to having extra footage if you want to extend the cut, but they said it was too expensive. If I asked them to do a few more frames of Roger doing something, it had to be in the picture so they had an indication of what they were meant to do. They only did exactly what was indicated in the cut. I would cross my fingers and hope that it was right. I always said to them, "If you can't do what you want animation-wise within the number of frames we have given you, let us know and we will examine the film and open it up or make it shorter."

At what stage did you start to receive composite material, completed animation with the live action?

Oh, not until about a year after the start of shooting.

Then what material was in your work print?

We would cut the black and white pencil tests into the movie. There are about 1,030 shots involving animation. After a while it was just like a mosaic. It was very difficult for anybody to come in cold and look at it because we had scenes that were 35mm color reductions from the VistaVision. Anything that involved animation or special effects was always shot in VistaVision. VistaVision is eight perfs as opposed to four so all of that material had to be reduced for me to edit because there is no editing machine that will cut VistaVision. That was always an expensive process just to begin cutting. The dailies always had to be done twice because VistaVision is twice as long as a normal 35mm picture. We had to have special sync machines built to accommodate a picture that was twice as long as your sound track. We had to put the film through an optical printer just for me to get a rough color print for the work print. Once the VistaVision was reduced to 35mm, they had to do the dailies again so that I would have the film to cut with.

Bob would quite often print four, five, or six takes of a VistaVision shot. In order to save money, we would try to narrow it down and reduce two of those. A film editor always likes to have access to as many takes as have been shot, but we tried to make many decisions viewing the dailies in terms of the best takes of a certain shot. If I got into an editing problem, we would take a VistaVision of that particular scene, run it in the projection room, and reduce another take. We would have temporary composite prints from ILM of their first pass through and then we went on to final composites, but for a long time the movie was just this incredible mosaic constantly changing because we'd get new pencil tests, new composites in every day. Every single shot went through four or five different phases. The assistants must have cut in 6,000 to 8,000 different pieces of film.

How large was your editorial staff?

I had four assistants in London and when I was here in Los Angeles. They were all overworked; they worked harder than they ever worked in their lives. I have no idea what I would have done without them. They were absolutely terrific.

How were their assignments organized?

One assistant would be in charge of ordering all of the photostats for the animators and keeping track of the dialogue tracks. We always had to make sure that everything sent to the animators was in the same sync as we had here in our cutting print. Nothing could slip; everything had to be exactly precise. There was always an apprentice organizing the KEM rolls and putting away trims. Everybody else did everything. They all came in to do battle everyday. They came in earlier than I did. By the time I got here between 9:00 and 9:30 in the morning, they would be exhausted because it was the end of the day in England and the phones were already ringing off the hook. The organization and logistics the assistants had to deal with were really complicated and were an enormous burden.

Did you ever think that this whole project was going to fall apart and not come together?

Oh, yes. That was part of the excitement because you never knew if it was going to work.

How long did it take to make Who Framed Roger Rabbit?

A year and a half. We started shooting in December of 1986 and the film was released a year and a half later in June of 1988.

Was it especially rewarding to win the Academy Award for film editing on this picture because of the tremendous editorial challenges it presented?

I thought it was the most challenging thing I would ever do in my film editing career. It was very satisfying to get that kind of recognition, but when I was doing it, I don't think I ever thought there was an Academy Award possibility at the other end. I didn't think anybody would ever realize how complicated it was. I thought people would look at it and think that the animation came first and that I had a full frame to work with; that the editing was all done after the animation was complete. I didn't know whether people would appreciate all the difficulties and the technicalities that went into trying to pull it all off.

I had never quite had an experience like *Roger Rabbit*. I couldn't wait to get to work everyday. I would go and turn on the KEM and it would just energize me, and that happened every day. The film had an energy that came off the screen. It just kept saying, "I'm really special."

Do you feel you are a better editor now than in the earlier days of your career?

Yes, I hope so, just because I've got that many more films behind me. I feel that I am learning on every film. Every film is a new experience and sometimes you just get the feeling that you haven't been there before. I don't want to say that you are faking it every time out, but I know by the third day on a new film, Verna Fields used to say, "Well, they're going to catch up with me on this one." It happens to everybody because every movie is different and presents different challenges. I think there are moments when you feel terribly insecure and wonder if you can still do it, but that's just part of the whole insecurity of the business. There was a moment half-way through *Roger Rabbit*, when for the first time I consciously said to myself, "I think you finally know what you are doing."

21

Carol Littleton

Oklahoma-born Carol Littleton studied French literature and music and was a Fulbright Scholar before making a transition to film editing in the early 1970s.

Littleton is married to cinematographer John Bailey, with whom she has worked on numerous films including *The Big Chill*, *Silverado*, and *The Accidental Tourist*. Those projects are part of Littleton's long-term collaboration with director Lawrence Kasdan.

In 1982 Carol was nominated for an Academy Award for editing one of the most popular films of all time, *E.T.: The Extra-Terrestrial*, directed by Steven Spielberg.

In addition to the demands of her busy editing career, Littleton is working to improve the status of editors as president of the West Coast Film Editors' Guild.

1975	*Legacy*
1978	*The Mafu Cage*
1979	*French Postcards*
1980	*Roadie* (with Tom Walls)
1981	*Body Heat*
1982	*E.T.: The Extra-Terrestrial**
1983	*The Big Chill*
1984	*Places in the Heart*
1985	*Silverado*
1986	*Brighton Beach Memoirs*

1987	*Swimming to Cambodia*
1988	*Vibes*
	The Accidental Tourist
1990	*White Palace*
1991	*China Moon* (with Jill Savitt)
	Grand Canyon

*Academy Award nomination for best achievement in film editing.

What kind of research have you done for the films you have edited?

Before I did *Body Heat* I saw and read a lot about film noir. I read a lot of Anne Tyler before starting *The Accidental Tourist*. I read anything I feel is remotely related. I realized when I was cutting TV commercials that ideas come from everywhere; you simply bring yourself to the work in so many ways. If I can delve consciously into the subject matter and deal with material which is emotionally related, I find that I'm better prepared. When Larry Kasdan and I were talking about *Silverado*, he was very specific about the emotional feeling of the picture. He had said it was very important that *Silverado* represent the optimism of the opening of the American West. Larry really wanted to capture the feeling of John Ford and Howard Hawks, rather than the realism of the end-of-the-era Westerns. So I looked at a lot of early era pictures, but I also read a lot of the Big Sky books of Alfred Guthrie and a number of books by William H. Goetzmann, including *New Lands, New Men*, which was an historical account of the discovery of the West. They gave me a sense of the grandeur of the canvas on which we were going to be working. I felt I wanted to get back into the optimistic state of mind of discovery and exploration. Looking at other films and reading source material and fiction of the same era allows you to know more than what is in the confines of the script.

What other methods besides research do you use to prepare to cut a film?

When I work on films, I ask the director if I can attend rehearsal, because it gives me an extraordinary advantage to see the script performed all in one take. I'm only going to be seeing the film one scene at a time while I'm working on it. If I have a fix in my mind of how the film is going to unfold emotionally, then essentially I can plug myself into that arc from the very beginning of my work. I find exploring performances in the editing to be the most interesting. If you work with a director who really delves deeply into the characters when the film is being shot, then you really have a lot to work with. Larry Kasdan has been extremely generous in letting both John and me attend the last week of rehearsal. A rehearsal helps me find the emotional tone of a film earlier than I would through the material a day at a time. When Larry has a rehearsal, it's a safe time for the actors to explore the life represented on the pages of the script and the life that is outside of the script—the complex emotional relationships between the characters that existed before the script or extend beyond the end of the script. So my being privy to that helps me in innumerable ways. Like music, it becomes part of the overall emotional life of the piece, so I am more apt to recognize it looking at dailies and deciding to use one take over another. It becomes very practical at a certain point. It filters through me in ways that I'm not even able to articulate; it enrichens my perception of the film even before I start.

Before I start on a movie I'm always terribly nervous, I really don't think I can do it. It's a very anxiety-provoking state of mind. Every film is very different, and I'm always a little frightened before I start. I say to myself, "This is going to be difficult, can I really do this?" Preparing myself by reading and learning about the subject matter helps me.

What happens to that anxious state when you are sitting at the KEM after you have prepared yourself and the material starts to come in?

It kind of disappears once I start doing the work. Once I'm sitting there in front of a scene, I realize it's like every large task; it's simply one day at a time. I don't have to do all of this at once. I do have the luxury of quiet reflection, which people on the set don't have.

Many editors say that they drop the script after the material begins to come in. Do you?

No. I refer to the script all the way through the cutting. A lot of times when a film starts to get off track, the best thing to do is go back and read the original version.

How important is it for a film to have a good script?

If you have a bad script, there's no place to go. The film is rarely ever going to rise above the level of the script. We've gotten to the point where a lot of movies only give you style. You've sat there for two hours and you're hungry. You walk away like you haven't been fed; nothing was there. That's why I really consider my choices very carefully. You want to make sure the script is something you can relate to in one way or another, emotionally or artistically. You want the script to be as good as it can be.

How do you work with material as it comes in while the film is being shot?

A scene may be shot out of sequence, so I usually keep scenes just as individual cut scenes. And when I get several I can hook up, I put them together and then revise that section. Many times I'll revise it completely because I wasn't working with enough information when I cut the individual scene. Essentially, what I do is to block it out in a very rudimentary way. If it's a case of multiple characters when person A is speaking, I'm on person A; when person B is speaking, I'm on person B. No overlaps, nothing. I'm literally blocking it out to just see how it flows. Usually, it looks like hell, it's terrible. It's clearly just an assembly. Then I start going through again. When the performer is best, he stays on camera; when it starts to fall apart, I go away. That's the second level, to get the best out of each person's performance. Then I go for the rhythm and the presentation of the scene, what is most pleasing to the eye and ear. Then I look at it again and again and refine it in a lot of different ways. Sometimes I've been so careful and so neat and so precise that what it really needs is a shocker, so then I just do something in the scene that seems sort of outrageous.

I understand you were originally a music student. How has your musical training helped you as an editor?

I'm aware of a certain musicality in my editing. I'm respectful of the inner rhythms and the cadences in the material, whether it be the speech or the images, but it's not enough just to hit the notes. Playing a passage with feeling is the important thing. What I really hope to achieve in a scene is to heighten its emotional life.

While the crew is shooting, how long are your days?

Those are long days because the crew looks at dailies at the end of the day. We've been working since eight o'clock in the morning and it may be eight or ten o'clock at night by the time we're through. By the time I've looked at dailies, talked to the director, and gone back and dealt with the film that has to be shipped out, it's probably a minimum 12-hour day. More than likely, it's a 14-hour day, six days a week. For the first stages of editing, when the shooting is over until it's turned over to sound, we average a ten-hour day. That's kind of comfortable. My mind starts to flag after ten hours. I don't do very good work.

What kinds of scenes do you feel are the most difficult to cut?

I think the most difficult scenes to cut are those with large numbers of people. When you get four, six, eight, ten people who are actively involved in a set piece, those are really difficult. One-to-one dialogue scenes are also difficult, because it's literally about the very thin connection between two people and that connection can't be violated. You have to be aware of it all the time. They may be connecting or not connecting emotionally, but you have to be aware of what's happening between them the whole time.

You have edited many films on which your husband, John Bailey, was the director of photography. Do you feel you know more about cinematography than other editors because of your relationship with him?

I've learned a great deal from John because we've been lucky enough to work on a lot of movies together and we're both involved and excited by film. We talk about film a lot, even about films we have seen rather than ones that we have worked on. Obviously, notions of photography and editing come up in our conversations. I have had a kind of insider's education. I have a familiarity with the problems as well as the dramatic devices of cinematography and I use them in the editing because I recognize them very readily. I can very much tell the thinking behind the camera placement, the camera moves, angles, and sizes, of how both Larry Kasdan and John were thinking about a scene when it was conceived on set. Usually my first cut is very faithful to their thinking.

All editors have had to delete shots that are beautiful pieces of cinematography because they didn't work in the context of the film. Is it harder for you because you know what labor has gone into it?

If a pretty shot ends up on the floor, it's because it simply didn't work dramatically for the film. When you're rewriting a film in the editing you have to take many things into consideration. Sometimes that means you have to eliminate shots that are perfectly gorgeous but simply do not work for the streamlined narration. That's what we are after when we are editing—the most economical way of telling the story.

Are you aware of a cinematographer's style when you are cutting?

I'm very sensitive to the personalities that have preceded me in the filmmaking process. I'm very aware of the person behind the lens when I'm working, as I am very aware of how different directors deal with material. A good editor needs to be aware of the other contributions and heighten them, to bring out their best qualities in performance, art direction, cinematography, or the direction of a film. It's really my job to be the interpreter of other people's work and ultimately to rewrite the film using image and sound.

What limitations does the editor have in this rewriting process?

I'm using materials that are defined. I can't just use every word that is in the dictionary. My dictionary is restricted. I once had a sweet child about eight or nine years old who loved E.T. say to me, "Oh, you edited the movie, that's wonderful. Can I ask you a question? Where do you put the orchestra when you are shooting?" I thought, of course, in a child's mind everything's done at once.

What was it like to work with Steven Spielberg on E.T.: The Extra-Terrestrial?

Steven is a consummate filmmaker who knows every person's job in every aspect of filmmaking, whether it be cinematography, editing, or art design. He knows everything about his film more intimately than anyone ever possibly could. He has an extraordinary mind not only for detail but for the grand scheme. I worked with him pretty early on in my editing career and, literally, it was like taking a course in post-postgraduate work in editing. I learned a lot from him.

How were E.T.'s sequences cut so he appeared to be really alive?

Anytime E.T. did anything complex, a whole roll of film was shot. Steven and I combed through the material to get the best possible moments for E.T., and the scenes were essentially constructed around E.T.'s best moments. We cut around that.

It's like what a friend of mine, Suzanne Baron, a very fine French editor who has cut most of Louis Malle's films, did on *The Fire Within*. At the very end, Maurice Ronet is walking around in a room and it's a series of jump cuts. It's extraordinary because it represents his state of mind. I asked Suzanne how she happened to do that and she said it was by mistake. They had a lot of coverage of Maurice Ronet doing all of these things in the room as he contemplated suicide: looking at the photograph, handling the gun he was going to be using to commit suicide, items of clothing, different memorabilia. When she cut it straight, it didn't work. She said, "I'll just go back and cut out the best of every scene and put it together, and we'll see how it will work." She showed that to Louis and he said, "This is it. This is a sequence that does everything that I wanted to have happen. Just forget everything else."

It's that sort of serendipitous thing that sometimes happens in cutting. In a way that's what happened with E.T. We put the best of him together and then we discovered how the scene needed to be constructed. It was sort of a backwards way of thinking, but in many respects it gave us the freshest results.

How was E.T. made to speak? Was that done in postproduction?

Every time Steven shot E.T. doing any movement, it was in pantomime. The people who were manipulating the puppet made him say his limited vocabulary, but other than that, E.T. didn't speak until we put the words in his mouth. We always had a scratch track of him saying the words. Either Steven or his friends would come in and record sounds that we could use. It was not the final recording. The scratch track was all replaced by sound designer Ben Burtt's personalized E.T. creation.

In the bicycle chase at the end of the film, just before they fly off, there are two jump cuts on Elliot reacting to the road block. How did this come about?

Steven and I had chosen a piece of music, the Romantic Symphony No. 4 by Howard Hanson, for the temp track. There was a climactic portion in the last movement where the fiddles in the orchestra are sawing away, there's an accelerando that stops abruptly, and there is a hold for a bar in 4/4 time. Then there is a very quick reprise, a coda which we used when they take off, and the bicycle is in the sky. In the very pronounced retard in the last couple of bars before the hold, it just seemed like it cried out for something to punctuate it pictorially. We were looking back and forth at all the footage on the other picture head on the KEM. Steven said, "We have to find something to punctuate it and I don't want to go to the guy with the shotgun."

In retrospect, Steven wished that he had not used guns because he realized this was a children's film and he did not want them to associate feelings of being lost and running away from home with being punished with guns. The only cutaways we had were of men taking out guns and aiming them. So I said, "Why don't we just jump cut it?" It came from working with Howard Hanson's music and doing something musical to match what was happening in that particular moment in our temp track.

What were the challenges in cutting Swimming to Cambodia, *which is a filmic record of Spalding Gray's one-man show?*

I was very aware that the editing was being controlled by the actor in *Swimming to Cambodia.* That was the most difficult film I have ever worked on. Imagine an editor not having any of the devices we use when we're in trouble, no cutaways. What do you do when you have one actor sitting in one position, where the only variables are the performances from night to night? We used three different performances, and a lot of pick-up shots and material we knew was going to be integrated in certain areas of the film. The only variables were his performance, his position, the lighting, and the camera moves—nothing else. You can't hide anywhere.

The director, Jonathan Demme, and I tried a lot of things because we wanted to use the best of Spalding. We were really aware that without the storytelling art, the film wouldn't hold up at all, so we had to keep his narrative alive and respect Spalding's performance as much as possible. Many of the things that we tried just didn't work, so we cut them out. I was extremely aware of Spalding Gray's cadence and his idiosyncratic way of speaking and telling a story. If I tried to force anything upon him in any way, it simply didn't work. I had to be totally respectful of his style. So I had to find an editing pattern and a style that worked with his idiosyncracies. If I tried to do something fancy or became editor and used the art of montage to get around something, it just simply didn't work. I had to restrict myself and get back to the basics.

You have had a long relationship with director Lawrence Kasdan. What is the process of choosing the selected takes when you work with him?

Since we have done so many pictures together, Larry says less and less because he knows that I instinctively know what he likes and dislikes. When he really is working to get something and says, "That's it," I do make a note and I put that in the first cut, but he might look at five or six takes and say nothing at all. When he says something, I know that it's very important; otherwise he doesn't clutter up my mind. He hopes that I will have more time to go over it when I'm cutting and make a lot of the choices myself. I am sensitive to what his needs are and what he wants out of a scene.

In the group scenes for The Big Chill, *where you were dealing with the majority of characters in one scene, what was the coverage like?*

I could be anywhere I wanted to be at any time. For instance, the big climactic scene, where they have an argument about who really loved and appreciated Alex the most, was shot from head to toe in each camera position that you see in the film now. We called that the Big Chill scene, because all of the themes are in that scene. There were about 20 shots and each was shot from the beginning to the end of the scene, so I had the choice of being anywhere I wanted at any time. It's a largely static scene; people are seated. What do you do? A scene like that could be an absolute killer. Larry Kasdan, John, and I went through the script and talked about the key moments in the dialogue, because Larry really wanted to heighten certain moments either with a slow push-in or a two-shot.

There were a number of things that were conceived in the direction itself. When Meg Tilly says something like, "I don't know, I haven't been around too many happy people," there were plenty of static shots of her, but there was one that had a delicate push-in on her. Obviously, that is her whole persona as well as her experience. I knew that was important. When William Hurt gives his long speech about, "You don't really know anything," we had that as a static shot and also with a very slow push. There were a couple of over-shoulders that were from across William to Michael, the Jeff Goldblum character, and also to Sam, the Tom Berenger character. Those three characters represented a kind of triad and those over-shoulders were meant to be used for those exchanges. So there were a lot of clues to the scene.

When I put it together the first time, I literally followed the blueprint of the shooting. It didn't say, "Cut here, cut there," but it was obvious from the coverage and the direction. With the exception of a couple of additional reaction shots, that scene did not change from the first time I put it together. I don't take any credit for that. I say that is a scene that is beautifully conceived photographically, well photographed, and well directed. I had very little to do with that scene; all I had to do was to be sensitive to the way it was done and it never changed.

Was the scene shot with multiple cameras?

No, it was all single camera.

That's the real art of filmmaking.

Oh, that's tough. It's difficult doing ensemble work that way, but I think it's the most successful because you're able to devote total attention to one thing at a time. With multiple cameras, you don't. Something suffers along the way somewhere; the lighting and angles are compromised, your attention is split, the director can't be on two people at once. You are only able to get attention to detail when you shoot with a single camera. I'm talking about acting, I'm not talking about getting a car crash from all different angles because you're only going to do it once; that's a different set of circumstances.

Were there any scenes deleted from The Big Chill *because it became apparent during the editing process that they were not necessary?*

There was a controversial scene at the end of *The Big Chill* which was a flashback of what these characters were doing on Thanksgiving Day in 1969, 15 years before the actual events of the film. It had the whole notion that the seeds of who we are appear when we are very young, and that we simply play out the script of our lives in one way or another. Both writers, Barbara Benedek and Lawrence Kasdan, felt it needed to be in the film because it wrapped up all of the themes and clarified part of the story about Alex. What did he really look like? What was he like? All of the questions you might ask about him. It was a good scene. When I first read the script I felt it was a scene that the writers needed to be able to write in the script, but the themes and concerns of the film were so clear throughout the film that this very final sequence was simply not necessary. We screened the film any number of times while we were working on it, and we tried all different versions of this flashback. When we started previewing the film, a lot of the audience really felt that the flashback made it too specific. The Alex in the mind's eye of our imagination was far stronger than the Alex who was dramatized on camera. The tragedy of Alex's life was very real within the body of the script, we didn't need to see it dramatized at the end. It weakened the drama. So for one preview screening we put on an alternate ending and decided not to show the film with the flashback. It was far more successful.

I understand that Kevin Costner played Alex in that scene. This was to be his first role in a film.

Yes, I suppose I derailed his career for a number of years. . . . I think he's doing pretty well.

One of the things that editors often do is make the decision not to cut. Can you think of an example when you made the decision not to cut and to let something play?

Certainly for the last shot of *Places in the Heart*. We had all kinds of different footage. It could have been done any number of ways. Clearly, the most transcendental moment in the film is that single, long, tracking shot and its most powerful presentation was the single shot.

That shot shows all of the characters together in church, including those who had died. I understand the director, Robert Benton, was concerned as to whether this concept would work.

Yes, I remember the day they were shooting that. He called me out on the set and said, "Carol, I really don't know if this is going to work at all, what should I do?" I had faith in the fact that this was something he had talked about from the very beginning. The notion of the brotherhood of man and forgiveness was the whole reason he made the movie. Not to have the film transcend at that moment and to be literal would have been the worst thing possible. If we had used cuts, it simply wouldn't have had the power; it would not have been unusual.

You have cut several comedies. What is your philosophy in working with comedic material?

You don't want to do what they do in situational comedies on TV where you open up a space so you can get a big laugh. You don't want to cut so the scene is just about a gag. You want the scene to be about something, some conflict. One person's agenda is not the same as another's. Comedy is usually based on the conflict of agenda. You want to cut the scene for its meaning and then deal with the comedic aspects. One of the more valuable things in cutting comedy is to realize that everything is a brick and you're building bricks in the comedy. It's not just one gag and one gag and one gag. Once the audience gets the gag, they're going to want another one and another one and another one. All you are doing is accelerating the tempo and you're not dealing with the real comedy, which is born out of character and incident. I just hate a lot of American comedies these days because they are so cheap. They don't respect the drama behind the comedy. When you look at a Charlie Chaplin film, you've got to agree that the man knew comedy. He knew all about gags, but he knew that comedy was about an underlying pathos and he was very careful to preserve the story.

Jerry Greenberg told me that films are details and details within details. Do you agree, and how does this affect the film editor?

Yes, and it's exponential. It grows and grows. As you narrow the film down, the detail becomes more and more dense. I think editors absolutely have to be detail-oriented. You have to realize that each solitary detail counts. There are so many things that can go wrong. There are a lot of technical considerations that take very careful attention to detail and you just don't want to forget those. Many times I will go through a credit sequence again and again, making sure that everything is fading out and coming up again at a certain moment in the music. Should it pop on or should it fade in? Should it fade on in two feet and pop off? I dare say there are very few people looking at a credit sequence who could ever tell you whether a credit popped on or faded on, but because I'm very aware of the musicality of the images working with the music, I try to get all those things to coordinate. It's sort of an obsessive personality trait.

Do you think that women make better editors?

I think the qualities of good editing have very little to do with gender. We may be a little more patient because we've grown up dealing with a lot of dirty work, so we may have a little more tolerance for it. A lot of the details are kind of messy.

Nowadays all feature film editors work freelance, as opposed to the days when most editors worked on staff for the studios. What are some of the problems of working freelance?

The main thing is you are always fearful you'll never work again, so you put yourself in the horrible position of working all the time. I made myself take three months off at the end of *The Accidental Tourist* because I had done four pictures back to back and I was starting to go crazy. I was getting very, very tired and I was starting to feel claustrophobic about entering the cutting room. I knew if I started to hate entering into that world, I'd better stop for a while. I've given myself a good period of rest, I've been reading a lot, and taking care of the kitty.

What films do you think are landmarks in film editing?

Bonnie and Clyde. Breathless. Tom Jones. These are all kind of related because they are akin to the French New Wave films. It's when film editing was finally freed from the literal notions of time and space. I think the films that came along in the middle and late 1960s opened my mind to looking at film in more radical ways. In the language of film editing, those films are truly landmark films because they shook us up.

In addition to all the responsibilities of your work on features, you are also the president of the West Coast local of the Film Editors' Guild. What interested you in getting involved in these activities?

Hollywood has changed so much in the ten years since I have been in the union. The guild system had ossified, editors were working more and more in freelance situations with a lot of nonunion work. The working conditions were getting more and more eroded. It was just clear that we needed to revitalize the guild system and it wasn't going to happen unless we did it from within. I thought maybe I should do something and I ran thinking I wouldn't be elected. I was, so here I am.

Where do you think film editing is going as a craft?

We're always going to have very fine movies and consequently, very fine editing. I don't think you can separate the two. What disturbs me about a lot of the editing I see today, that I would just call grist-for-the-mill editing, is that it's very derivative, repetitious, and boring. By nature, a lot of what we see on television has to be done so quickly that it's formulaic. I can sit and say, "Okay, two-shot, single, long shot." I can anticipate what they are going to do before it even happens. The other side is the whole notion of style versus content. So many young filmmakers spend so much time on style and not actually on what they have to say that a lot of movies simply don't work because they are just style, just acrobatics. I hate to see that happen. I have a feeling that what we're seeing coming into film by way of MTV is largely experimentation; it will find its level. What's good about it we'll keep, and what isn't will be culled out. Editing is like everything else. It's a reflection of how people think about their times and how we react to the medium. You can look at a film made in the 1960s and know if it was made in 1963 or 1969. Editing is a lively art and it changes with the seasons. So we're always going to have something new and something unusual coming up.

Glossary

ADR: Automatic dialogue replacement, a process whereby lines of dialogue are re-recorded. Also called *dubbing* or *looping*.

Animatics: An animation technique whereby a storyboard or drawings are shot to be used as a reference guide in the work print for special effect sequences that are not yet filmed.

answer print: The first print struck off the negative that has been conformed to the final cut of the film.

breaking axis: Any shot taken from the opposite side of the imaginary line running horizontally through a scene. Also called *crossing the line* or *direct reverse*.

butt splicer: Tape splicer that splices the film end to end without losing a frame.

cheat: The altering of real time and space for editorial purposes.

code numbers: Letters and numbers printed at one-foot intervals in yellow or white ink on the top edge of the film. Used to identify picture and track and to keep the film in sync.

combine track: A magnetic track that contains two or more separate sound elements mixed together.

compression: An editing technique that compresses an event into a shorter space of time than it would take in real time. Although the basis of most editing is to compress time, the editor can drastically alter real time when it is dramatically necessary for a scene.

continuity: Shooting scenes in script order; a logical progression that flows from shot to shot.

coverage: Footage that duplicates or complements the master shot from a different angle or size, thus allowing the editor to make a match or move the film editorially.

cutaway: Shot inserted in between two related shots. Can be used to shorten action, show additional details or reactions, and maintain continuity.

Cutter Moviola: Brand name for upright editing machine without arms. It is gentler on film than a Moviola with arms, and is easier and faster to work with.

cutting in the camera: Technique often linked to Alfred Hitchcock whereby the director shoots only what he needs for the cut with little or no coverage.

dailies: Uncut film, direct from the lab, that contains all the material the director selected for printing from a day's shooting. Dailies are synchronized to the *mag track* transferred from the original 1/4-inch tape recorded on set. Usually screened on a daily basis; also called *rushes*.

dissolve: Optical process whereby one shot fades out as the next shot fades in.

dupe: A copy of a film processed in either black or white or color; also called a *slop print*.

editor: Person responsible for the editing of a film.

supervising editor: Supervises the postproduction process and the work of other editors.

co-editor: Shares equal responsibility for the editing of a film.

associate editor: Cuts scenes and functions in a subordinate capacity to the editor.

additional editor: Usually hired later in the editing process to help keep the film on schedule.

first assistant editor: In charge of running the editing room, syncing dailies, and coordinating postproduction activities. Also supervises the other assistants and apprentices.

assistant editor: Performs many of the same tasks of the first assistant editor but in a subordinate capacity.

apprentice editor: Responsible for filing trims, labeling, shipping, and various related errands and tasks.

sound editor: Responsible for cutting sound effects and the final dialogue tracks.

music editor: Responsible for cutting the music tracks.

ADR editor: Responsible for cutting dialogue tracks which are recorded in looping sessions.

Foley editor: Responsible for cutting in footsteps, sound effects, and various body sounds recorded in the Foley sessions.

fade in: Optical effect in which an image appears from black.

fade out: Optical effect in which an image disappears into black.

fine cut: The final stage of picture editing.

first cut: Version of the film put together by the editor as the film is being shot.

flash cut: A short cut used to shock the viewer or accelerate the pace of the film.

flashback: A scene that takes place earlier in time than the one that precedes it.

flashforward: A scene that jumps ahead out of relation to the time frame that has been established.

flatbed: An editing table that runs picture and track horizontally in sync or independent of each other.

Foleys: Sounds such as footsteps, sound effects, and body sounds which are recorded in sync to the picture in a Foley studio.

grease pencil: A China marker used to write on film and track.

hot splicer: Splicer that uses heat and liquid cement to splice film.

insert: A short shot, usually filmed separately and cut into a scene. An insert can be a shot of a clock, a newspaper headline, or a detail that helps to explain the action or meaning of a scene.

intercutting: Editing technique whereby shots or scenes are cut together in alternate sequence to create a dramatic relationship. Also called *cross-cutting*.

jump cut: A jump in action caused by removing part of a continuous shot or by the joining of two shots that do not match in action or continuity.

KEM: Brand name for a flatbed editing machine.

lift: A cut section removed from the work print and filed away in its entirety.

log book: Book containing information concerning scene numbers, scene descriptions, and code numbers used to locate specific pieces of film.

looping: Process whereby lines of dialogue are re-recorded. Also called *ADR* or *dubbing*.

magnetic track: Film stock used for sound tracks; also called *mag*.

marks: Lines drawn on the film with a grease pencil to indicate where an edit point or optical effect should take place.

master shot: Continuous shot that includes the entire action of a scene.

match cut: Two shots that link or match a related action.

mix: Process of re-recording and combining all the sound tracks to create the final composite sound track.

montage: A series of shots that establishes the passage of time or compresses an action or event.

MOS: Film shot without synchronized sound.

Moviola: Brand name for the upright editing machine widely used by feature film editors. Sound and picture can be operated in sync or independent of each other. Picture and track run vertically off reels through a viewer. The company also makes a flatbed machine.

narration: Words spoken by an off-screen voice, either an unidentified speaker or one of the characters in a film. Also called *voice-over*.

negative cutting: Process whereby the negative is matched frame for frame with the editor's final cut.

offscreen: Action that takes place outside camera range.

onscreen: Action that takes place within camera range.

opticals: Special effects added to a shot by means of an optical printer. Opticals can include titles, dissolves, fades, wipes, and other effects.

outs: Shots not used in the work print.

overlap: The sound of an outgoing shot extended into the incoming shot.

over-the-shoulder shot: A shot in which the camera shoots past the back of the head and shoulder of a character on the left or right side of the frame to the person the character is seeing.

pick-up shot: A shot that picks up a portion of the action of a longer take. Used to supplement material that has already been shot.

playback: A previously recorded track of a musical number that is played on the set as the performers are filmed; also called a *set track*.

postproduction: Process that begins when shooting is completed, including picture editing, optical effects, sound editing, music scoring, mixing, and print production.

pre-mix: Prior to the mix, large numbers of tracks are mixed down into smaller manageable groups.

production tracks: Sound recorded on set during the shooting of the film.

reconstituting the trims: Process usually performed by the apprentice editor in which the trims are spliced back into the material not being used in the work print, in code number order.

release print: A composite print used for theatrical distribution.

rewind bench: A table, used to splice and assemble film, that has hand rewinds on each end. It allows reels of film to be rewound in both directions and commonly has a lucite light box to examine film and a rack to store rolls of film and supplies.

room tone: The environmental background sound of a location.

scratch track: A temporary piece of sound used for the editing process.

selected takes: Specific takes of scenes chosen by the director and editor, used to create the cut of the film; also called *selects*.

sequence: A group of scenes with a common action or subject.

slate: A clapboard used as a reference point for picture and sound to sync up dailies. Contains information that includes scene, camera roll, and take numbers.

slug: A black piece of film or leader cut into the work print that represents a title or effect shot not yet available to the editor. Also used to replace missing or damaged material.

sound editing: Process of preparing the dialogue, sound effects, ADR, Foley, and music tracks for the mixing process.

split reel: A two-part reel used so that film on a core can be put on or removed without winding or rewinding.

spotting: Process of determining where a particular image or sound will go.

sprocket holes: Perforations on the edge of film and track that allow it to be transported by a projector or editing device.

Steenbeck: Brand name for a flatbed editing machine.

stock footage: Pre-existing film, purchased from a stock footage library.

storyboard: Drawings that depict the action of a scene; used to plan the shooting.

synchronization: The effect of sound and picture running side by side in direct relation to each other; also called *sync*.

synchronizer: Device used to run film and sound tracks in sync while editing; also measures feet and frames.

temp dub: A temporary mix of several sound elements.

temp track: A temporary sound element used for the editing process and replaced during sound editing.

trim: A head, tail, or section of a take not used in the work print.

trim bin: A lined container with a rack of pins used to store and organize trims.

trim book: A book in which small trims are stored and identified in code number order.

wipe: An optical effect in which one image wipes another image off the screen. Wipes can be made in almost any shape or direction.

work print: The cut picture and track used by the editor during the editing process.

Bibliography

PERIODICALS

American Cinemeditor. A publication of the Honorary Professional Society—American Cinema Editors, Inc. C. E. Publications, P. O. Box 16490, Encino, CA 91416–6490.

Editing. Eagle Eye Film Company, 4019 Tujunga Avenue, Studio City, CA 91604. Publishes interviews with film editors of feature films, television, videos, and commercials.

Film Comment. "The Film Editor," Vol. 13, no. 2, March-April 1977. Special issue devoted to the film editor. Contains 75 well-researched filmographies, Robert Wise on editing *Citizen Kane*, and other useful information.

BOOKS

Filmographies

As of this writing, no one volume has been published that includes all film editors and their credits from the beginning of the craft to the present. Each of the following books covers a variety of editors and time periods.

Ash, Rene L. *The Motion Picture Editor*. Metuchen, NJ: Scarecrow Press, 1974.

Bales, Kate. *Cinematographers, Production Designers, Costume Designers and Film Editors Guide*. Beverly Hills, CA: Lone Eagle, 1988. Second annual edition compiled by Susan Avallone, 1990.

Brenner, Debbie, and Gary Hill. *Credits*. Vol. 1 compiled by film title, vol. 2 by production category, vol. 3 by individual. Wallington, NJ: Magpie Press, 1985.

The Film Year Book. New York: St. Martin's Press (published annually).

Monaco, James. *Who's Who in American Film Now*. New York: New York Zoetrope, 1981. Updated edition, 1988.

Editing Theory

Bordwell, David, Janet Staiger, and Kristin Thompson. *The Classical Hollywood Cinema*. New York: Columbia University Press, 1985.

Dmytryk, Edward. *On Film Editing*. London and Boston: Focal Press, 1984.

Eisenstein, Sergei. *Film Form*. Translated and edited by Jay Leyda. New York: Harcourt Brace Jovanovich, 1949.

————. *The Film Sense*. Translated and edited by Jay Leyda. New York: Harcourt Brace Jovanovich, 1942.

Goldstein, Laurence, and Jay Kaufman. *Into Film*. New York: E. P. Dutton, 1976.

Kozloff, Sarah. *Invisible Storytellers: Voice-over Narration in American Fiction Film*. Berkeley: University of California Press, 1988.

Pudovkin, V. I. *Film Technique and Film Acting*. New York: Bonanza Books, 1959.

Turim, Maureen. *Flashbacks in Film*. New York: Routledge, 1989.

Film Sound: Theory and Practice. Weis, Elisabeth, and John Belton, eds. New York: Columbia University Press, 1985.

Reference

Baker, Fred, and Ross Firestone. *Movie People*. New York: Douglas Book Corporation, 1972. Contains interview with editor Aram Avakian.

Brouwer, Alexandra, and Thomas Lee Wright. *Working in Hollywood*. New York: Crown Publishing, 1990. Contains job descriptions of film editor and assistant editor through discussions with editors Freeman Davies and Carmel Davies.

Brownlow, Kevin. *The Parade's Gone By....* New York: Alfred A. Knopf, 1968. Contains chapter on silent era film editing and interviews with editors Margaret Booth and William Hornbeck.

Chell, David. *Moviemakers at Work*. Redmond, WA: Microsoft Press, 1987. Contains interviews with editors Carol Littleton and Thom Noble.

Madsen, Roy Paul. *Working Cinema*. Belmont, CA: Wadsworth, 1990. Contains a section on film editing written in collaboration with editor Peter Zinner.

McClelland, C. Kirk. *On Making a Movie: Brewster McCloud*. New York: New American Library, 1971. Contains a general discussion on the editing process and of the editing of *Brewster McCloud* with editor Lou Lombardo.

Oumano, Ellen. *Film Forum*. New York: St. Martin's Press, 1985. Contains section with film directors discussing editing.

Rosenblum, Ralph, and Robert Karen. *When the Shooting Stops*. New York: Viking Press, 1979.

Sayles, John. *Thinking in Pictures—The Making of the Movie Matewan*. Boston: Houghton Mifflin, 1987. Contains discussion of the editing process in general and the editing of the film *Matewan* by the director.

Sherman, Eric, for the American Film Institute. *Directing the Film*. Boston: Little, Brown and Company, 1976. Los Angeles: Acrobat Books, 1988. Contains section with film directors discussing editing.

Taub, Eric. *Gaffers, Grips, and Best Boys*. New York: St. Martin's Press, 1987. Contains descriptions of the jobs of film editor, assistant editor, apprentice editor, and sound effects editor through discussions with editors Mark Warner and Frank Warner.

Vaughan, Dai. *Portrait of an Invisible Man: The Working Life of Stewart McAllister, Film Editor*. London: BFI Books, 1983.

Wiley, Mason, and Damien Bona. *Inside Oscar*. New York: Ballantine Books, 1986. Contains nominations for and winners of the Academy Award for film editing from 1934 to 1987.

Technical

Balmuth, Bernard. *Introduction to Film Editing*. London: Focal Press, 1989.

Burder, John. *The Technique of Editing 16mm Films*, 5th edn. London: Focal Press, 1988.

Crittenden, Roger. *The Thames and Hudson Manual of Film Editing*. New York: Thames and Hudson, 1981.

Hollyn, Norman. *The Film Editing Room Handbook*. New York: Arco Publishing, 1984. Reprint. Beverly Hills, CA: Lone Eagle Press, 1990.

Kerner, Marvin M. *The Art of the Sound Effects Editor*. London: Focal Press, 1989.

Lipton, Lenny. *Independent Filmmaking*. San Francisco: Straight Arrow Books, 1972.

Pincus, Edward. *Guide to Filmmaking*. New York: New American Library, 1969.

Reisz, Karel, and Gavin Millar. *The Technique of Film Editing*. London: Focal Press, 1953.

Roberts, Kenneth H., and Win Sharples, Jr. *A Primer for Filmmaking*. New York: Bobbs-Merrill, 1971.

Robertson, Joseph F. *The Magic of Film Editing*. Blue Ridge Summit, PA: Tab Books, 1983.

Schmidt, Rick. *Feature Filmmaking at Used-Car Prices*. New York: Penguin Books, 1988. Contains a section on postproduction for extremely low-budget feature films.

Walter, Ernest. *The Technique of the Film Cutting Room*. New York: Hastings House, 1969.

Index

ABOUT THE AUTHOR

Vincent LoBrutto is a New York freelance film editor and writer. He has been a film production coordinator for the ABC television network and has worked on the postproduction of numerous documentaries for Fox television and the HBO cable network. He has a bachelor of fine arts in filmmaking from the School of Visual Arts Film School and is currently writing his second book for Praeger Publishers, *By Design: Interviews with Film Production Designers*.